THE FOUR HEATONS

THE POSTCARD COLLECTION

IAN LITTLECHILDS & PHIL PAGE

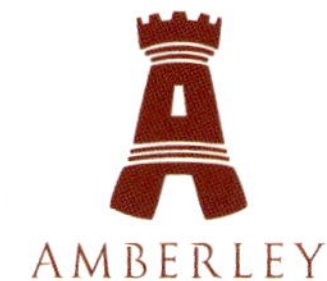

AMBERLEY

First published 2015

Amberley Publishing
The Hill, Stroud, Gloucestershire, GL5 4EP
www.amberley-books.com

Copyright © Ian Littlechilds and Phil Page, 2015

The right of Ian Littlechilds and Phil Page to be
identified as the Authors of this work has been asserted
in accordance with the Copyrights, Designs and Patents
Act 1988.

ISBN 978 1 4456 4577 3 (print)
ISBN 978 1 4456 4581 0 (ebook)

British Library Cataloguing in Publication Data.
A catalogue record for this book is available from the
British Library.

Typesetting by Amberley Publishing.
Printed in Great Britain.

CONTENTS

INTRODUCTION

The area we know as The Four Heatons today was once little more than woodland, heath and poor agricultural ground located between the northern outskirts of Stockport and the southern areas of the city of Manchester. The name 'Heaton' derives from the Anglo Saxon for a farming enclosure on heath or high ground, and there are many points across the Heatons where you can enjoy fine panoramic views across to the Pennines and the Cheshire Plain.

Early records tell us that, in the twelfth century, access to the area was granted to William le Norreys who paid an annual rent of around 10s. for the land. The area eventually became known as Heton Norreys after its owner, and it was some legacy as the name continued to be used over centuries up until the present day. The area continued to be developed and farmed in traditional ways up until the Industrial Revolution when the areas started to develop their own separate identities. Heaton Chapel took its name from the church that was constructed on Manchester Road to alleviate the need for worshippers to travel to churches in Manchester of the south side of Stockport. Heaton Mersey developed its own identity with the coming of Samuel Oldknow's Bleach Works on the banks of the River Mersey. The land around the open green spaces between Didsbury Rad and Wellington road became the fashionable residential district of Heaton Moor and the south-east corner of the land retained its original name of Heaton Norris with the distinction of being the oldest of the Heatons.

The photographs on the postcards capture an age when The Heatons were quiet residential suburbs and life moved at a pace much slower than that of today. Apart from presenting the pictures, we have tried to explore how the messages on the back of the cards gave an insight into the lives of the residents in The Heatons and the thoughts, friendships and interests which were shared with others in the same way as texts, tweets and e mail messages are exchanged today.

SOURCES

The majority of photographs printed on the cards in this book indicate how little the area has changed over the last century. Although a few of the landmarks have disappeared, most of the Heatons has escaped the curse of the developer and retained its special identity through the existence of houses, buildings and public spaces that have survived since Victorian and Edwardian times. Today the Four Heatons contain some of the most popular residential areas to the south of Manchester in which families can still benefit from the preservation of green open spaces and the strong sense of community, which has characterised the area since Victorian times.

Many of the views on the cards will be instantly recognisable to people who live in the Heatons today giving a strong sense of connection with the past and a desire to maintain the character and traditions of these four unique suburbs.

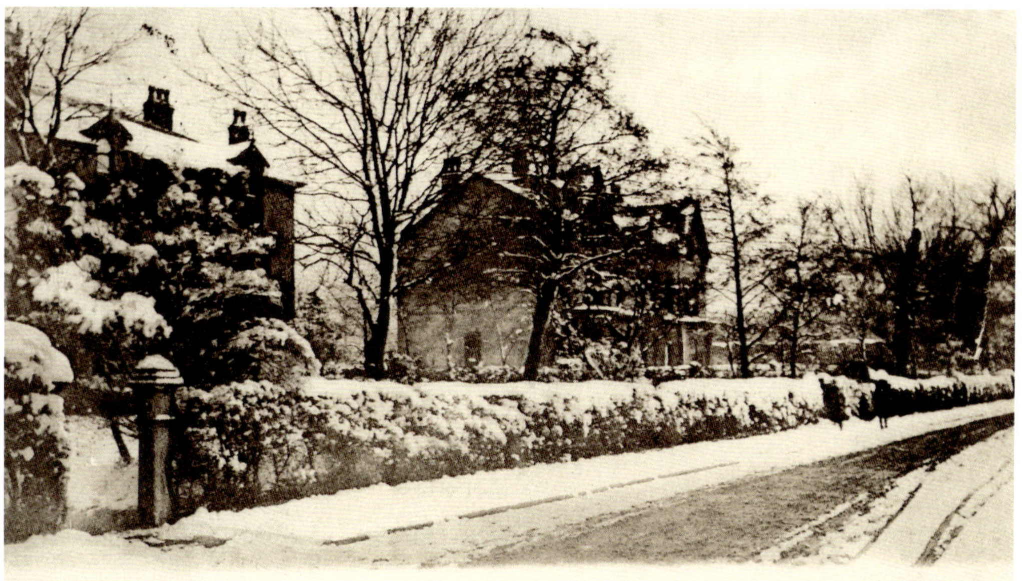

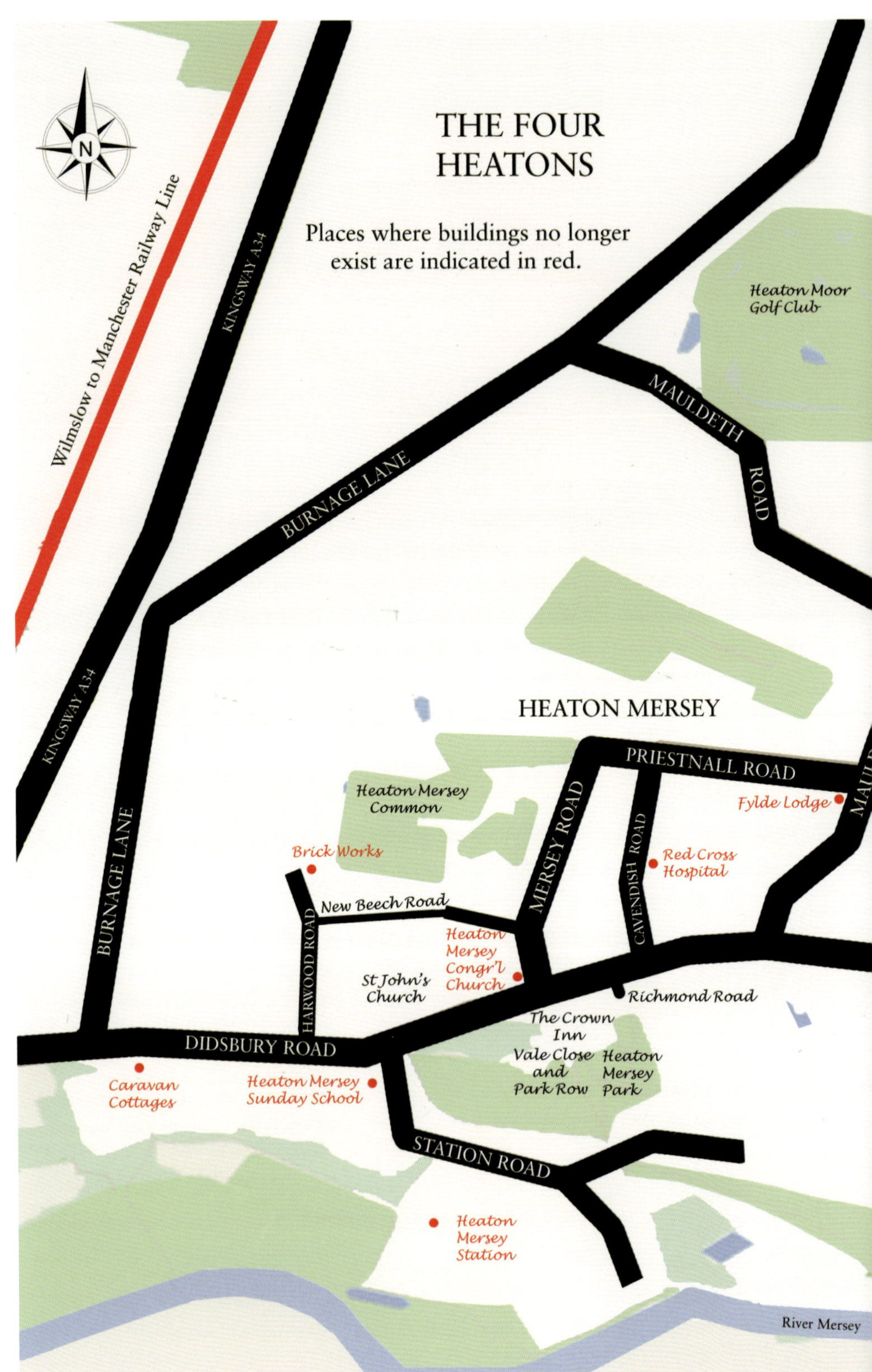

THE FOUR HEATONS
Places where buildings no longer exist are indicated in red.
N
Wilmslow to Manchester Railway Line
KINGSWAY A34
KINGSWAY A34
BURNAGE LANE
BURNAGE LANE
MAULDETH ROAD
Heaton Moor Golf Club
HEATON MERSEY
PRIESTNALL ROAD
MERSEY ROAD
CAVENDISH ROAD
MAUL
Fylde Lodge
Heaton Mersey Common
Brick Works
Red Cross Hospital
New Beech Road
HARWOOD ROAD
Heaton Mersey Congr'l Church
St John's Church
Richmond Road
The Crown Inn
Vale Close and Park Row
Heaton Mersey Park
DIDSBURY ROAD
Caravan Cottages
Heaton Mersey Sunday School
STATION ROAD
Heaton Mersey Station
River Mersey

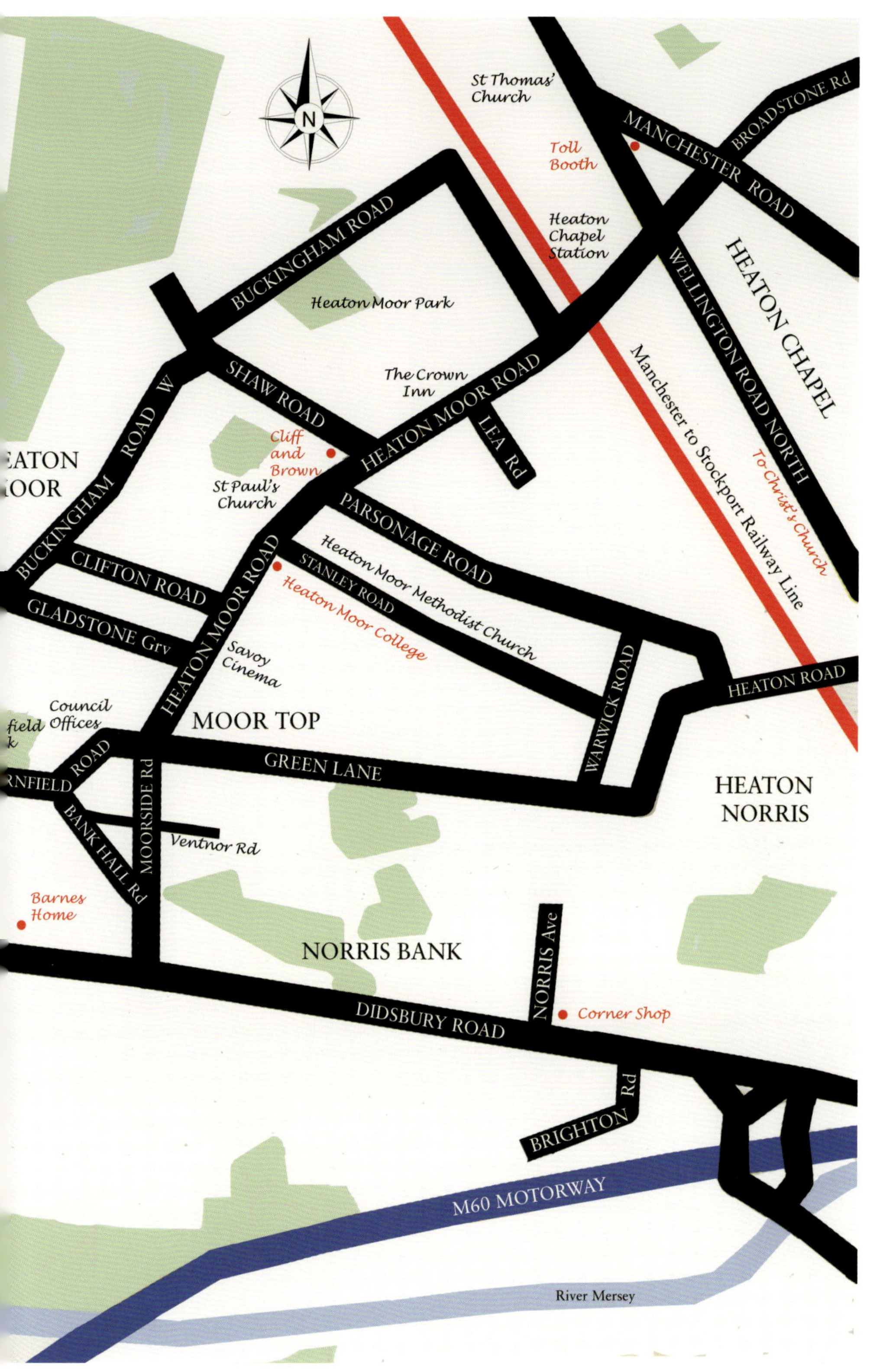

N
St Thomas' Church
Toll Booth
BROADSTONE Rd
MANCHESTER ROAD
Heaton Chapel Station
BUCKINGHAM ROAD
HEATON CHAPEL
Heaton Moor Park
WELLINGTON ROAD NORTH
SHAW ROAD
The Crown Inn
HEATON MOOR ROAD
Manchester to Stockport Railway Line
ROAD W
LEA Rd
To Christ's Church
HEATON MOOR
Cliff and Brown
St Paul's Church
BUCKINGHAM
PARSONAGE ROAD
Heaton Moor Methodist Church
CLIFTON ROAD
HEATON MOOR ROAD
STANLEY ROAD
Heaton Moor College
GLADSTONE Grv
Savoy Cinema
WARWICK ROAD
HEATON ROAD
Council Offices
MOOR TOP
field k
ROAD
GREEN LANE
HEATON NORRIS
RNFIELD
MOORSIDE Rd
BANK HALL Rd
Ventnor Rd
Barnes Home
NORRIS BANK
NORRIS Ave
DIDSBURY ROAD
Corner Shop
BRIGHTON Rd
M60 MOTORWAY
River Mersey

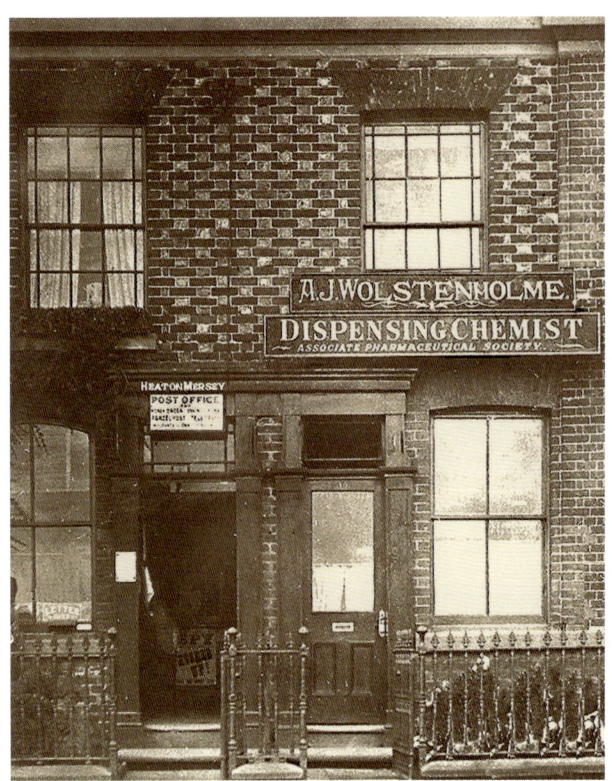

Post Offices in the Heatons

Post offices are often pictured on postcards sent from the Heatons; the main ones represented being on Didsbury Road, Heaton Moor Road and Moorside Road.

Leigh's booksellers and newsagents was established by the Misses Sarah and Martha Leigh in the late 1800s. It was situated next to A. J. Wolstenholme's Chemist's Shop, providing stationery supplies; it also doubled as a post office until the purpose-built post office opened further along Didsbury Road. In 1888, Albert Cooper bought a plot of land from John Padmore for £600 and constructed a large double-fronted shop on the corner of Greenbank Avenue and Didsbury Road, utilising one half for post office business only.

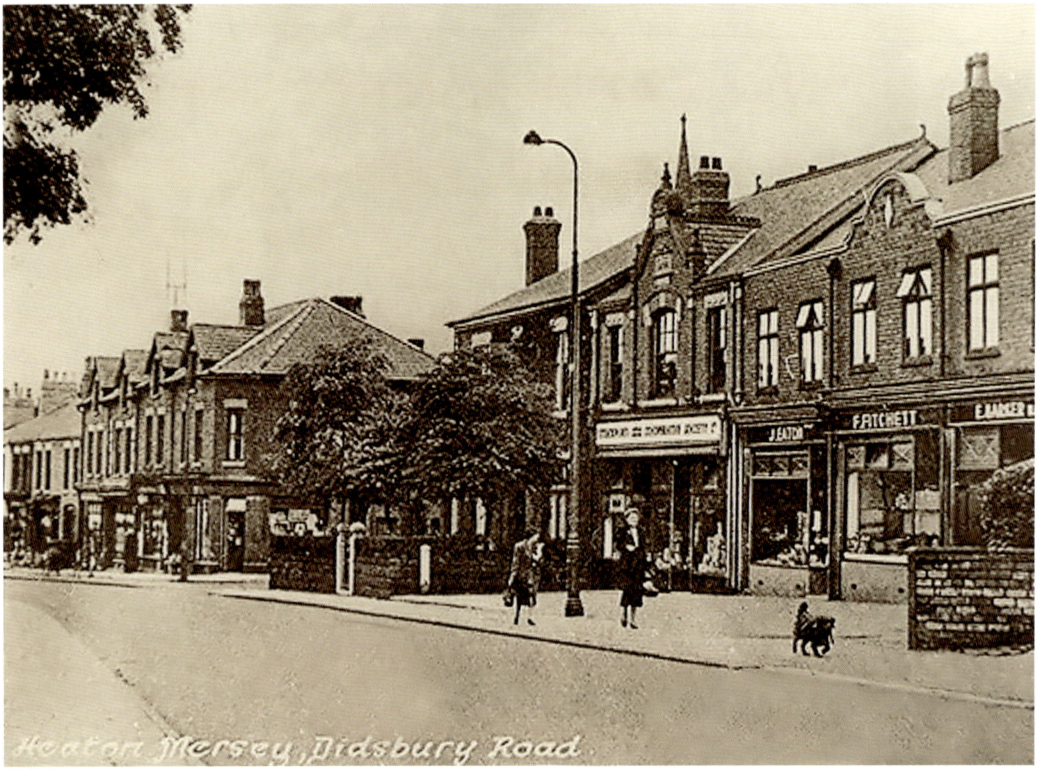

The post office on Heaton Moor Road, *c.* 1930. The post box outside is still there today and dates from Victorian times.

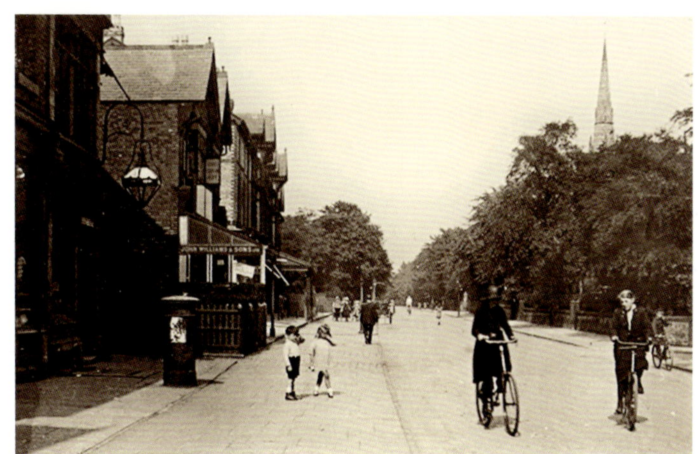

The post office on Moorside Road, *c.* 1968. The post box outside has a directional sign on top which would point customers in the direction of the post office.

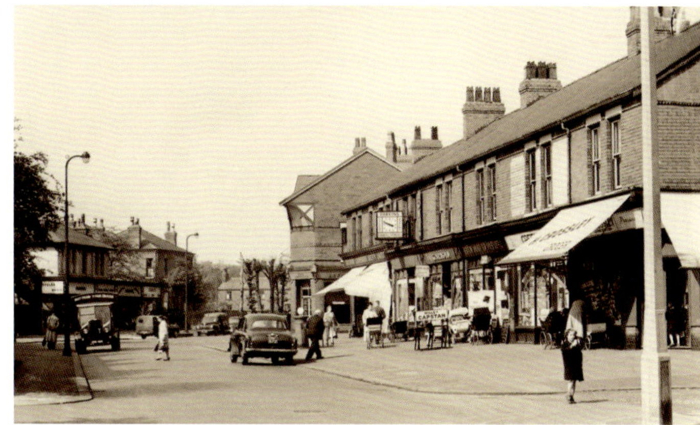

A postman wends his way down Didsbury Road after collecting his deliveries from Heaton Mersey Post Office.

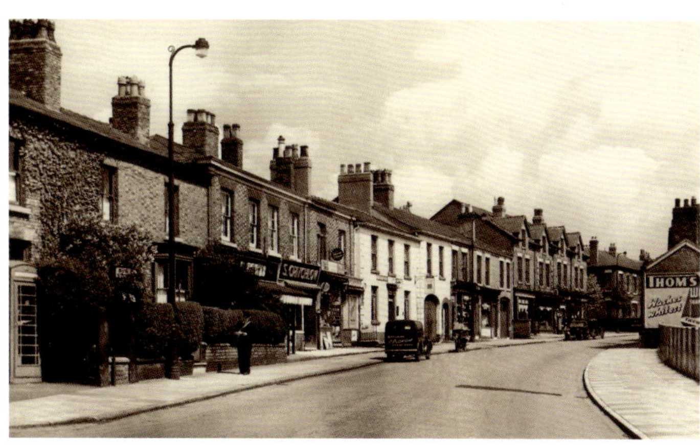

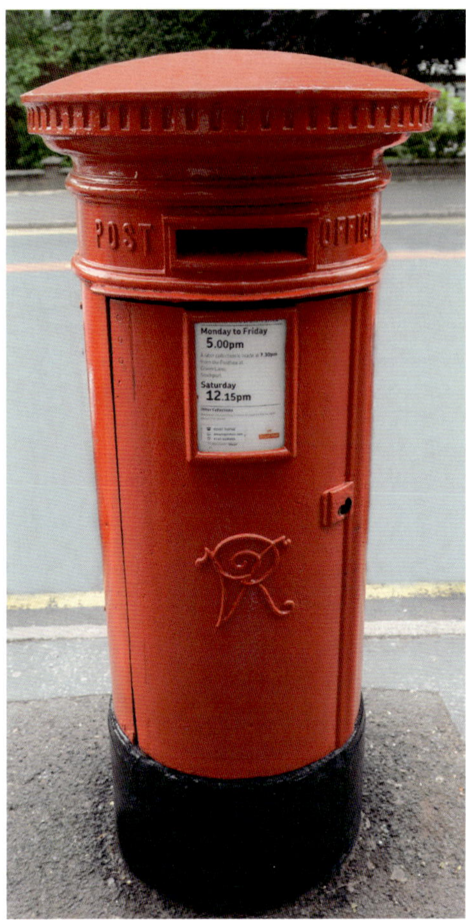

One of Britain's iconic symbols standing proudly outside Heaton Moor Post Office, on Heaton Moor Road. The cylindrical red post box dons the letters VR, which refer to the reign of Queen Victoria.

The Postal Service and Post Boxes

The cylindrical design for post boxes, in the Heatons and across Britain, has become one of our most recognisable symbols. The postal reform took place in 1840 when a Uniform Penny Post was launched by Rowland Hill that opened up the postal system to almost every person in Britain. Rowland Hill, a Postal Administrator and Social Reformer, suggested, at that time, the idea of introducing roadside letter boxes for Britain as they were already being used successfully in France, Belgium and Germany. However, they were not introduced until 1852 when the first letter boxes were erected at St Hellier in Jersey and then, in 1853, on the British mainland. The colour of the early boxes on Jersey was red, but between the 1850s and 1879 the standard design was the hexagonal Penfold, and green was adopted as the standard colour. The colour change to red took place in London in July 1874, but it took another decade before all of the boxes were painted this colour. By the 1870s, cheap-rate postage led to a dramatic increase in the sending of letters and cards at Christmas, so, during the Edwardian era, when the sending of postcards became popular, the posting process was a well-established custom. Post collection from the Penfold posed problems so, in 1879, the cylindrical design became the standard shape and still remains so today.

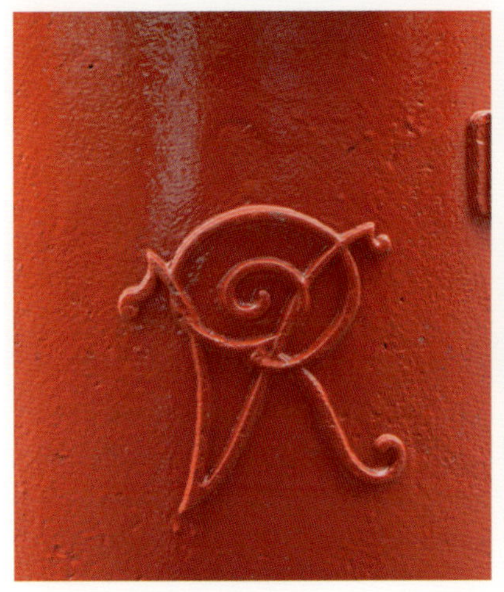 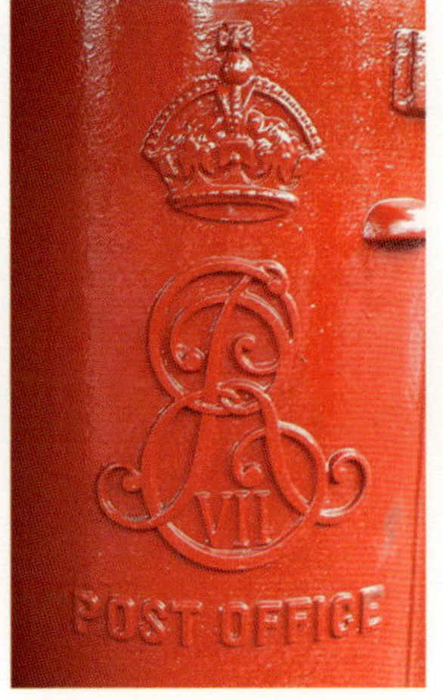 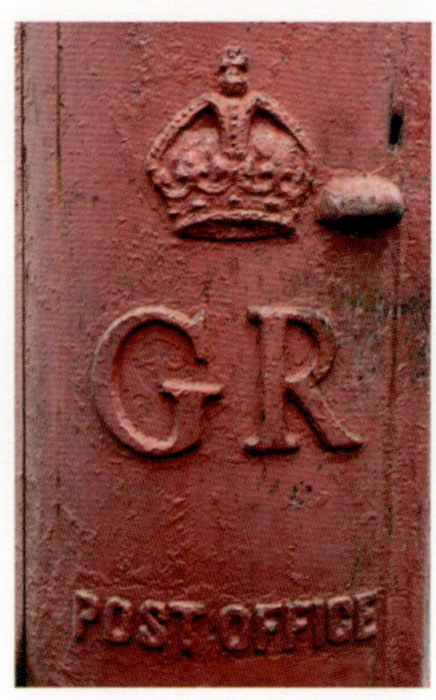

Left: VR post box   Middle: EVIIR post box   Right: GR post box in need of some TLC

The Postal Service and Post Boxes Continued

History is alive in the Heatons, and evidence of this can simply be found on post boxes. Many of the boxes today will have the letters EIIR on them referring to Queen Elizabeth II, our monarch from 1952. However, just take a moment when posting your next letter or postcard as you may see either VR, or EVIIR, or GR (GVR) or GVIR on the post box. The lettering refers to our previous monarchs: Queen Victoria (1837–1901), King Edward VII (1901–10), King George V (1910–36), King George VI (1936–52) and Queen Elizabeth II (1952 to present day).

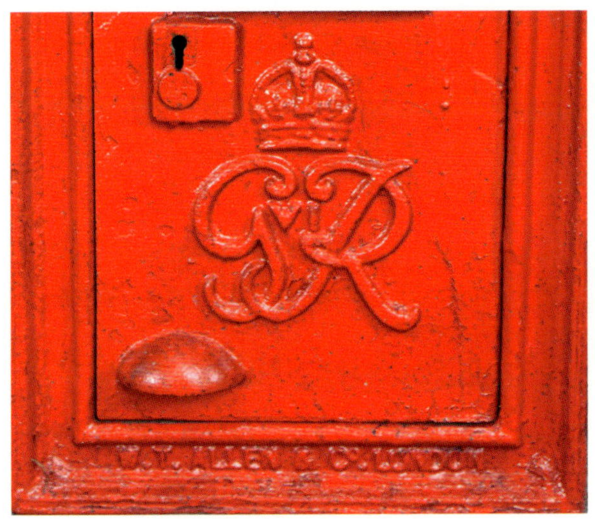 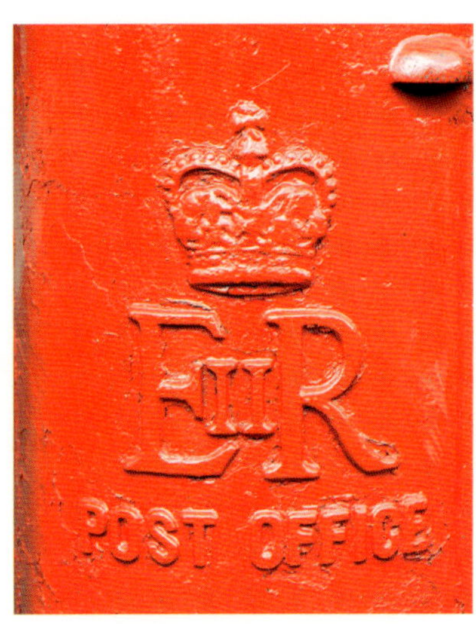

Left: GVIR post box   Right: EIIR post box

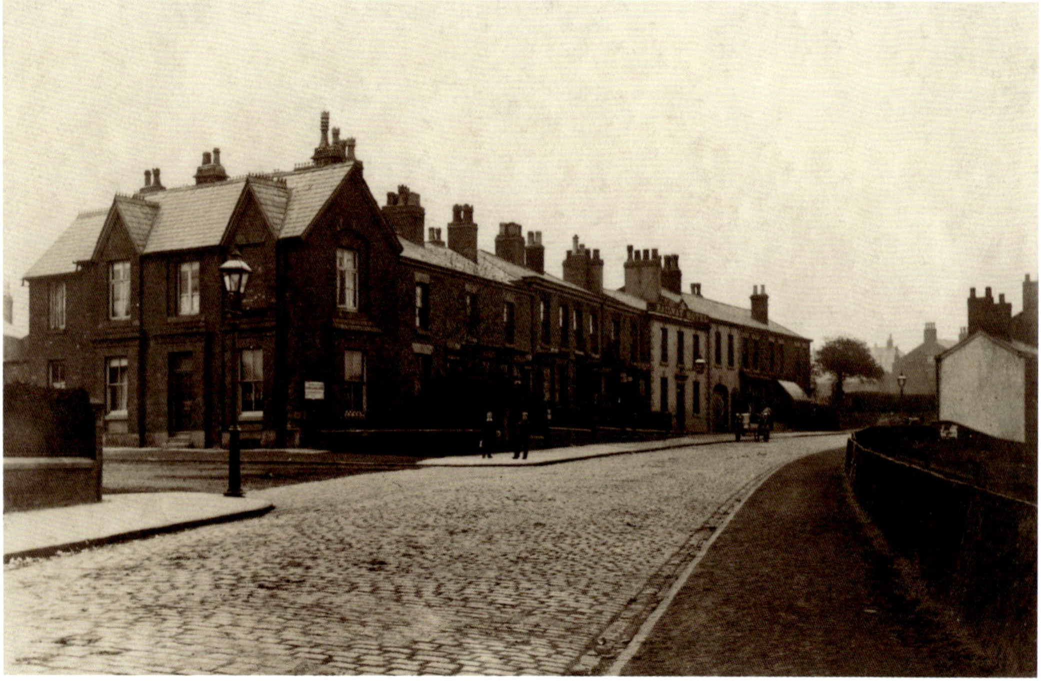

Along Didsbury Road

Didsbury Road is the main traffic route through the southern part of The Four Heatons, running approximately two miles from the boundary between Manchester and Heaton Mersey to Junction 1 of the M60 in Heaton Norris. The first reference to its name occurs in trade directories from the years 1887–88, and it is probable that this was the time when it was adopted. On early maps of the area, it is marked as Heaton Lane that stretched from the t-junction at Burnage Lane right through to Tiviot Dale. Centuries ago, it was an important part of the old saltway running through the area to Northwich. On most old postcards, it is shown as cobbled or covered in mud from agricultural vehicles and droppings from passing farm animals and horses. Although the postcards can often paint an idyllic picture, the smell on hot summer's days must sometimes have been overpowering.

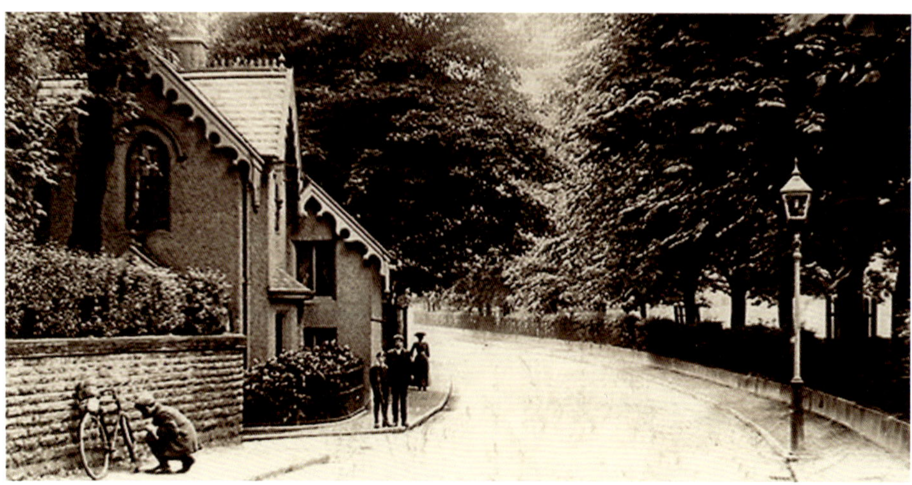

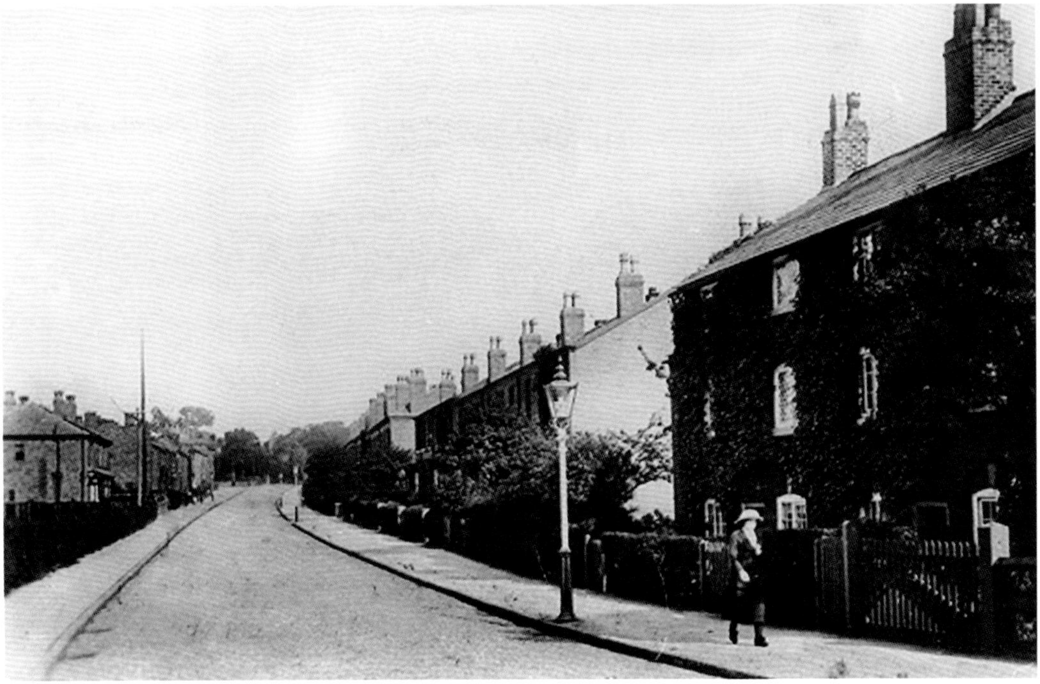

Caravan Cottages, Didsbury Road, 1900s

These cottages were situated at the lower end of Didsbury Road close to where the Dog and Partridge Public House is sited today. The origin of the name, Caravan Cottages, is debatable, but it probably originated from the vehicles that were parked outside and used by the inhabitants. Caravans were originally covered carriages or carts and were often parked up along the side of main roads that afforded enough space to accommodate them. Another possibility derives from the slang word for haricot beans or 'caravanses' that were harvested in the area.

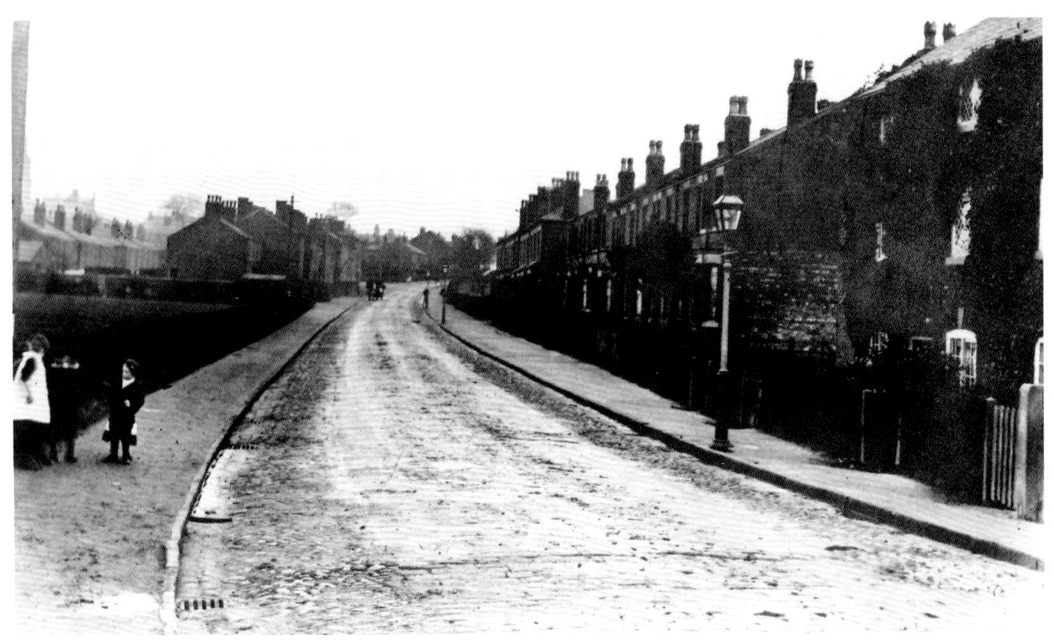

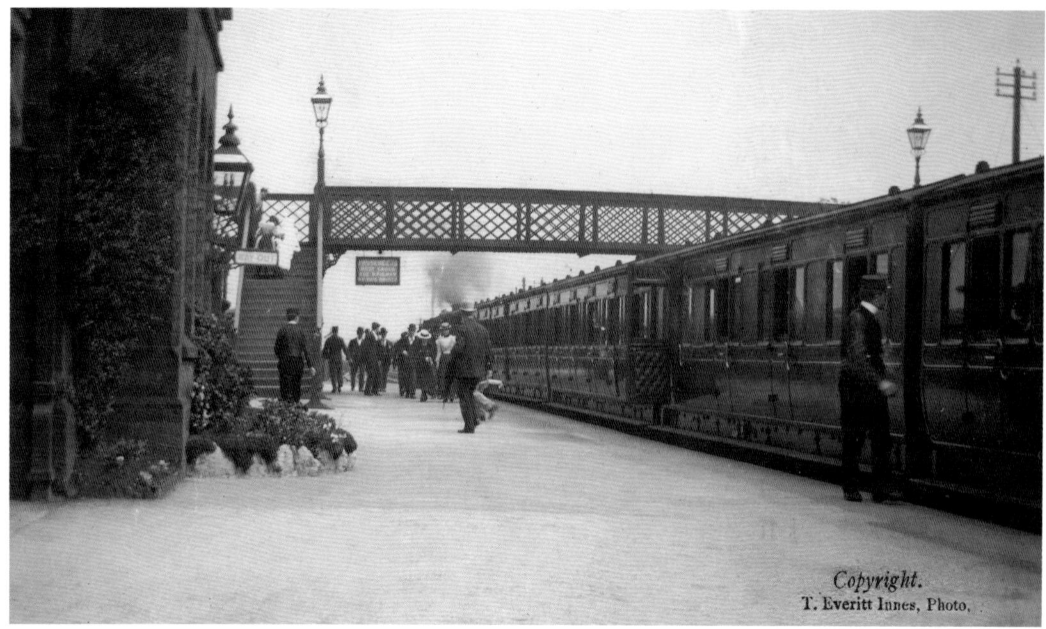

Heaton Mersey Station, 1907

When Heaton Mersey station opened on 1 January 1880, it was served by trains, which ran from Manchester Central, or London Road, to Tiviot Dale station in Stockport. Although Heaton Mersey was one of the quieter stops on the line, fourteen trains in each direction stopped at the station every day. By 1901, a new line had been opened by the Midland Railway that allowed passengers to travel directly from Heaton Mersey as far as New Mills. Here they could change and enjoy travelling deep into the Peak District to those exciting country destinations around Buxton, Millers Dale and Matlock.

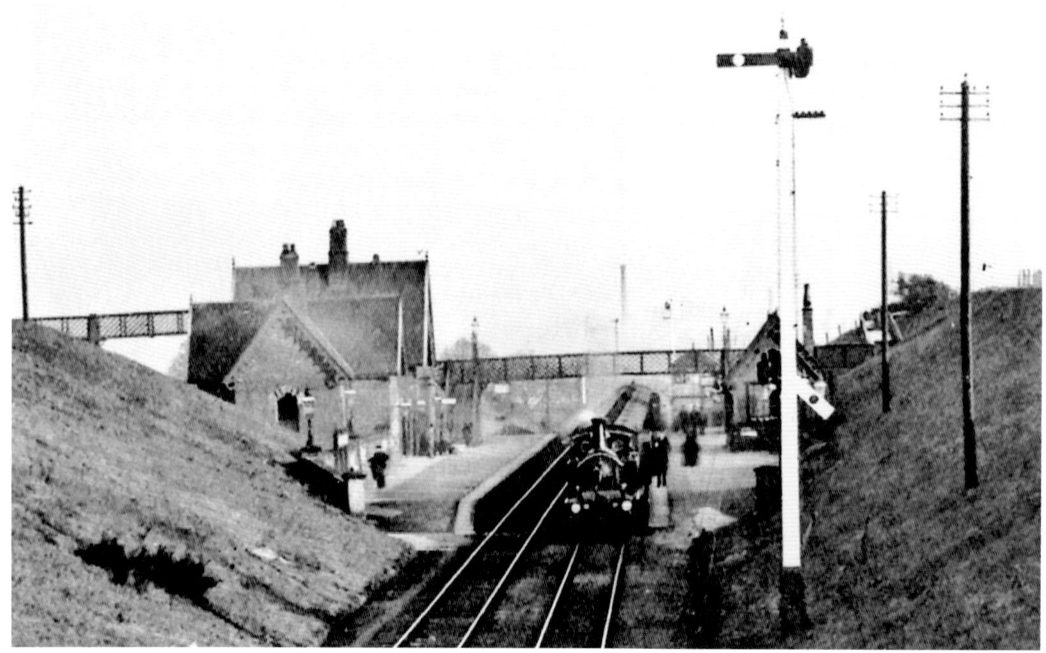

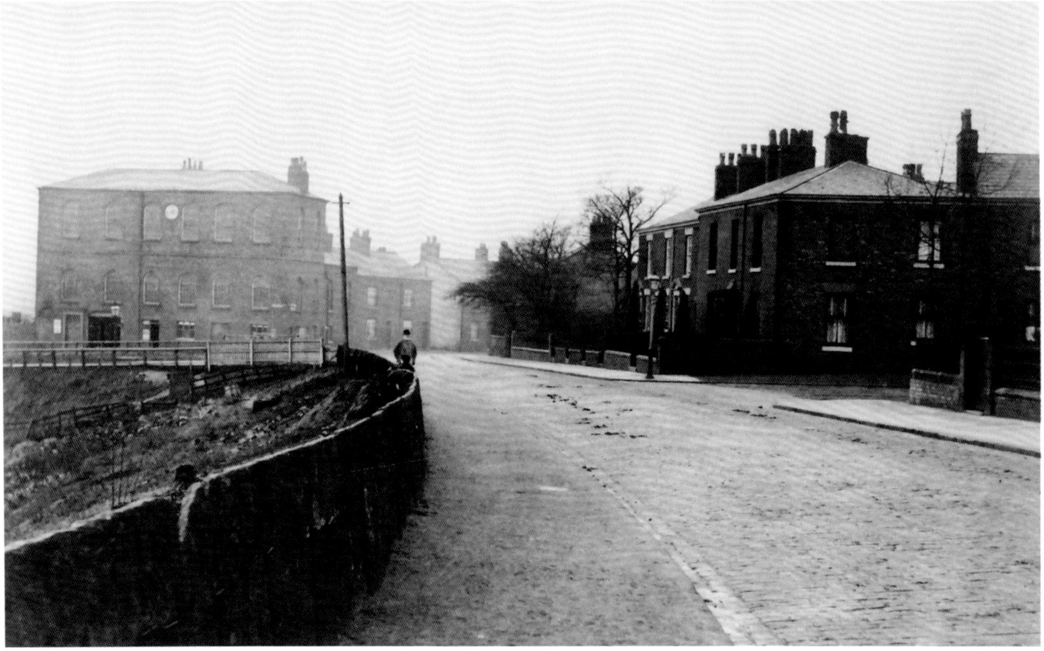

Heaton Mersey Sunday School, 1900s

The Sunday School was located on the corner of Didsbury Road and Station Road. It was opened in 1805 and was an offshoot of the larger Stockport Sunday School. The building was paid for by Robert Parker, who was the owner of the bleachworks at that time, out of a desire to give young children a positive focus on Sundays and prevent them from just 'playing about' in the streets. By 1815, the school was regularly attended by over 200 children.

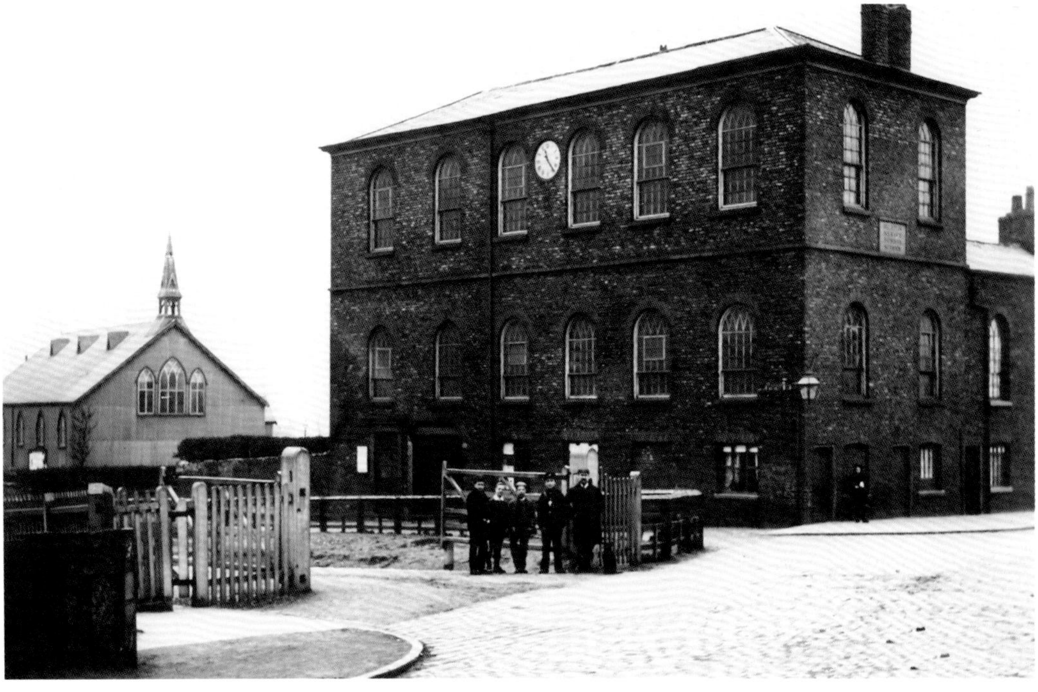

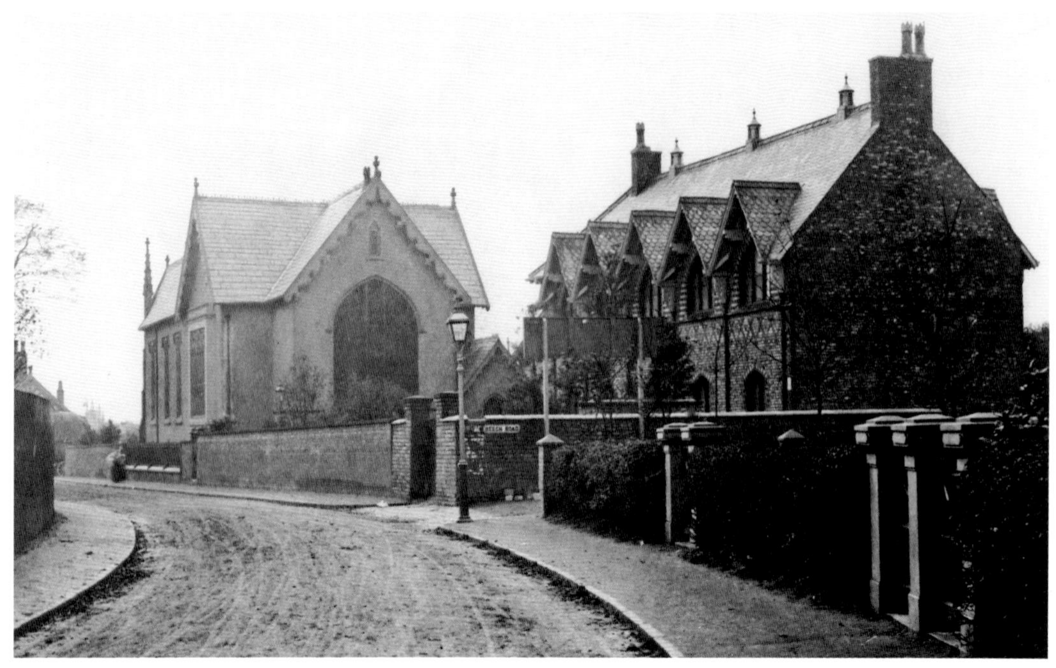

St John's Church, 1930s, and Heaton Mersey Congregational Church, 1920s
The early picture of St John's Church is interesting because its distinctive stone lych-gate has yet to be constructed. This was designed by architects Taylor and Young and was added to the church in 1927. The Congregational Church originally sited at the junction of Didsbury Road and Mersey Road was constructed by 1840 and survived until 1988 when it had to be demolished due to a severe infestation of dry rot.

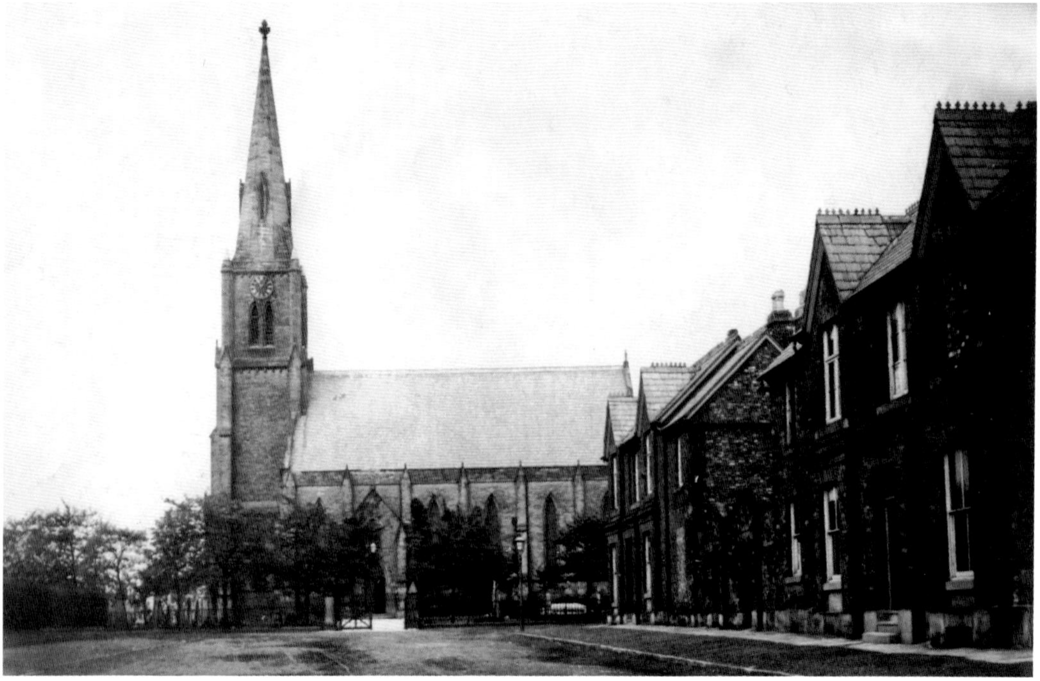

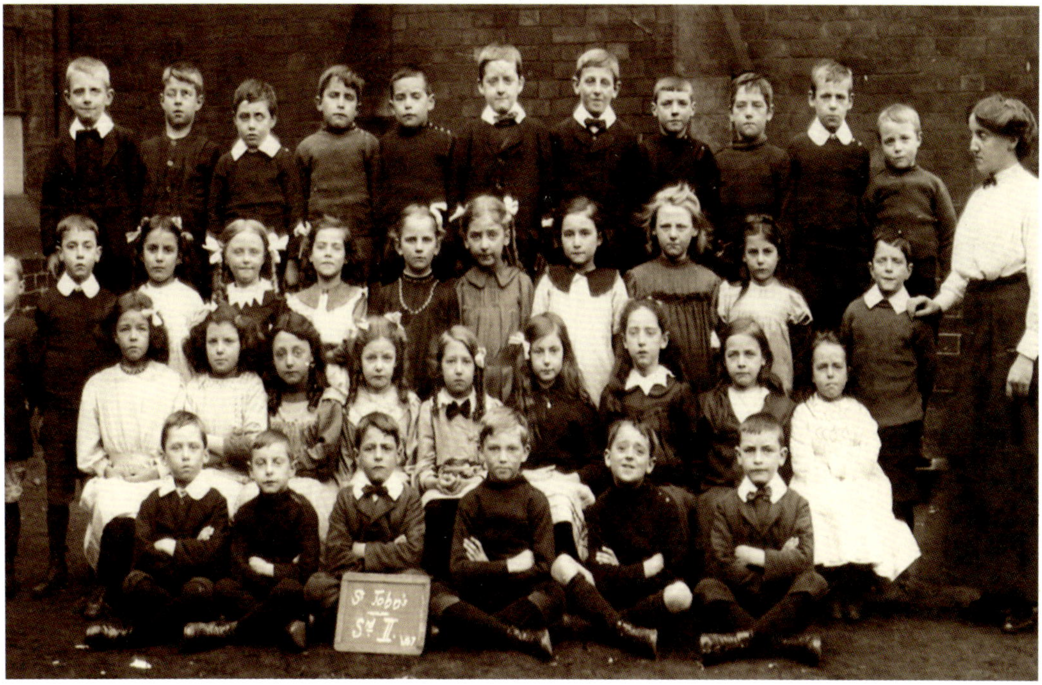

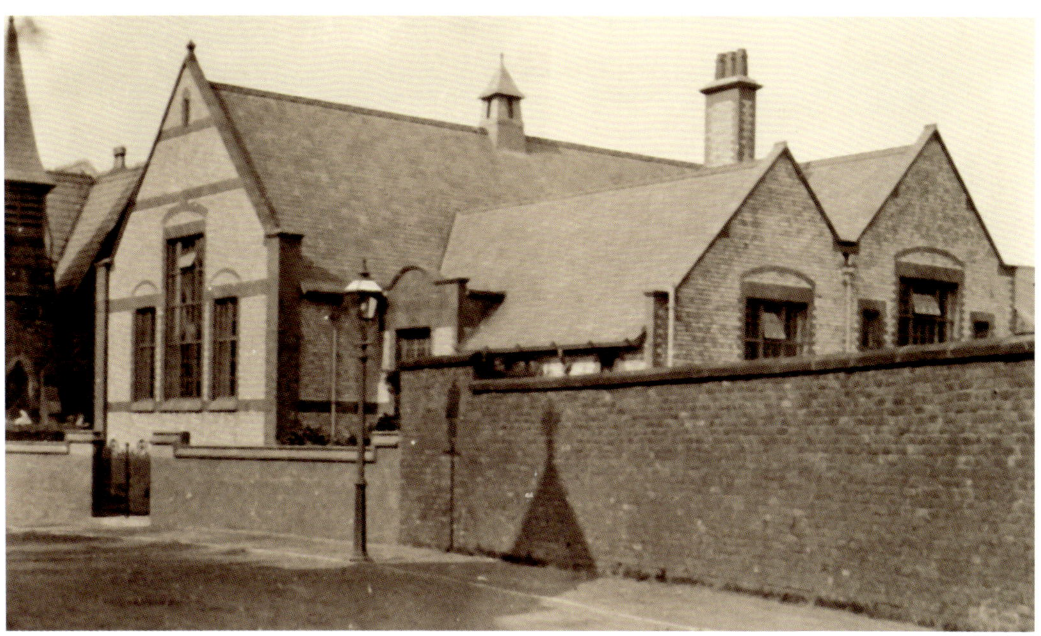

St John's Church and School Pupils, 1905

The construction of St John's Church by the first Bishop of Manchester recognised Heaton Mersey as a growing village whose residents were entitled to their own church to meet their spiritual needs. When work was completed, the church had space for around 536 people but this proved not to be adequate, and further modifications were made to the chancel in 1880 to increase capacity. Several outbuildings were built around the church including the schoolroom, which supported the education of local children.

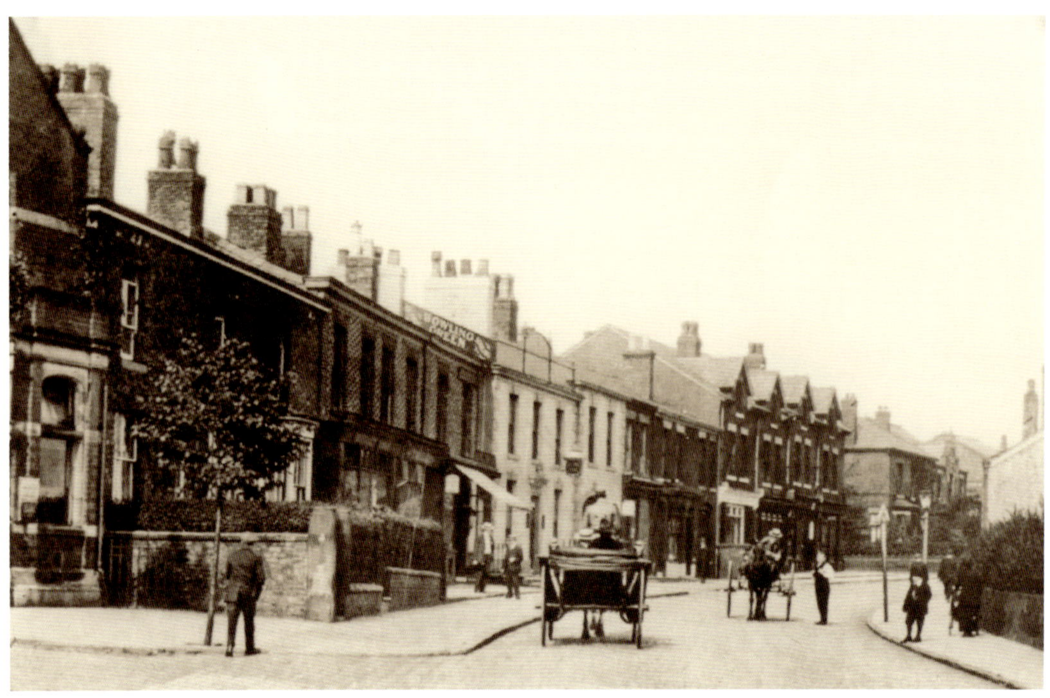

Didsbury Road Shops, 1914

This card from around 1914 shows the range of shops along Didsbury Road. The premises on the corner of St John's Road, covering Nos 484 and 486, are still recognisable as the former bank building. In 1909, it was a branch of The Lancashire and Yorkshire Bank. It passed to Martin's Bank in 1928 and then to Barclays in 1969 until its closure in the mid-1980s.

Moving along the row, the next business was Alfred Mosely's hardware shop (482) and next door was Frederick Mosely's butcher's (480), but there are no records to show the two were related. Next came William J. Sleigh, the bookseller's (478) and Abel Joseph Wolstenholme's chemist's (476).

The Railway Hotel, now The Frog and Railway, was at No. 474, and the licensee at the time was John Williams. The pub had changed its name in the 1880s to mark the opening of Heaton Mersey Station and the coming of the Manchester–Stockport railway line. Previously, it had been known as The Bleachers' Arms in deference to the workers who lived in the cottages opposite and were employed in Robert Parker's and Samuel Oldknow's bleaching and dyeing factories.

Next door to The Railway sat James T. Neild's draper's business (472). Harry Payne's butcher's shop was next (470) followed by Henry Savage's boot and shoe business (468), Charles Schofield's sweet shop (466), with another draper's run by William Kay (464). The last premises on the row were John Watson's post office and grocers (462), a business that had been built and established by Alfred Cooper in the late 1800s. On the corner of Greenbank Avenue sat Hugh James Dickey's surgery (460) in the premises occupied by Heaton Mersey Health Centre today.

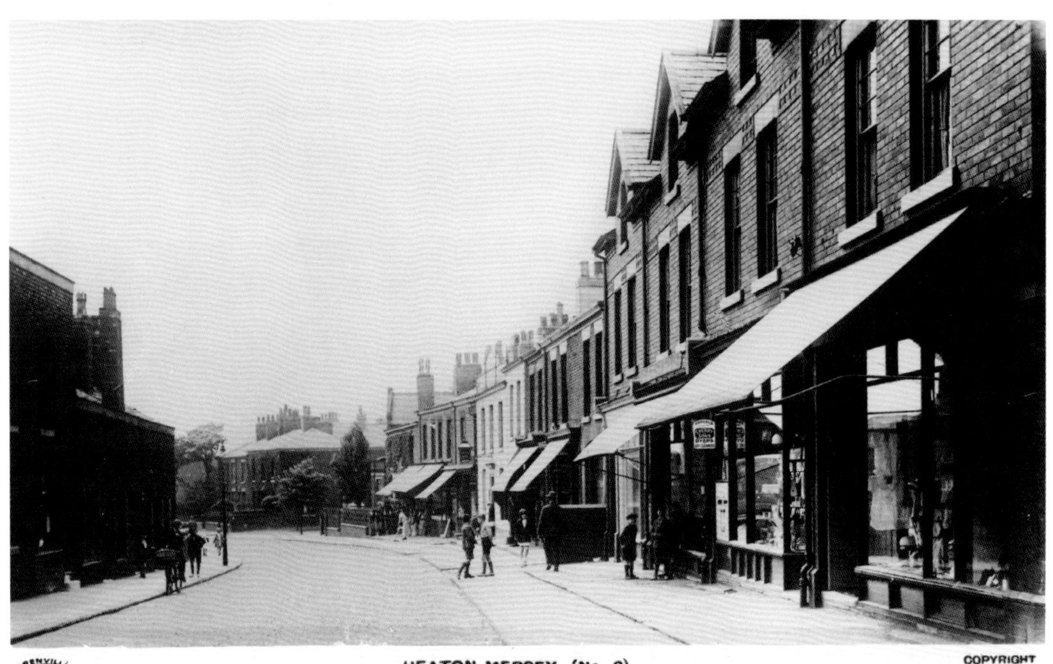

Didsbury Road, 1907

Besides selling local provisions, Albert Cooper's shop on the corner of Greenbank Avenue also doubled as a local post office. His business was promoted as an Italian Warehouse and also incorporated a sorting office and base for local postmen. The sign above the door offers a telegraph service and insurance for parcels. In the early 1900s, around forty businesses were situated in and around this part of Heaton Mersey village.

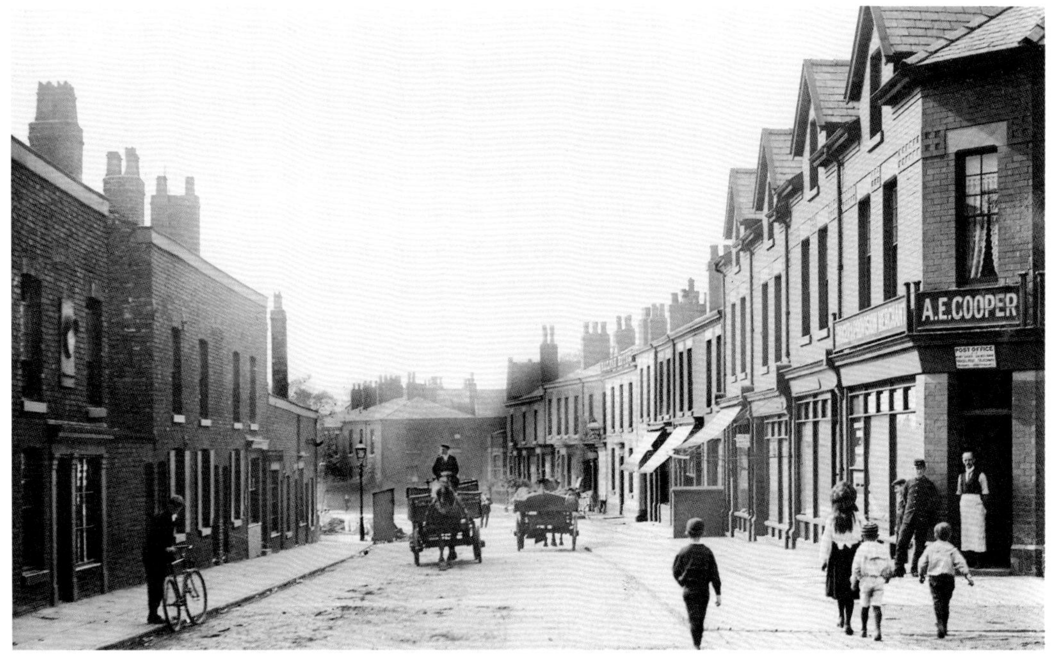

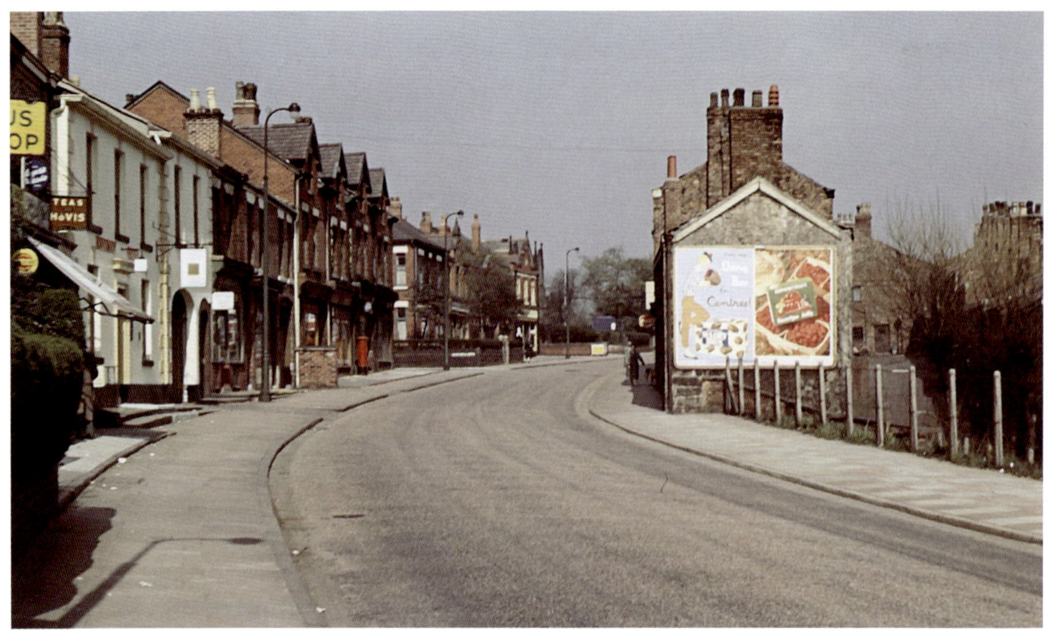

Didsbury Road, 1950s and 1913

This postcard from the 1950s shows a traffic-free Didsbury Road looking towards Stockport. The row of shops on the south side, which no longer exists, can be clearly seen. These shops were less prestigious than their neighbours on the other side of the road, and their original clients would have been residents from the industrial and working classes who relied on a variety of cheaper services to provide them with basic necessities. The row was a mixture of small shops and houses including a fishmonger's, butcher's, dressmaker's and a clogger's essential for the provision of sturdy footwear for those working in the nearby factories. The roofs of the housing in Heaton Place can be seen to the right of the picture.

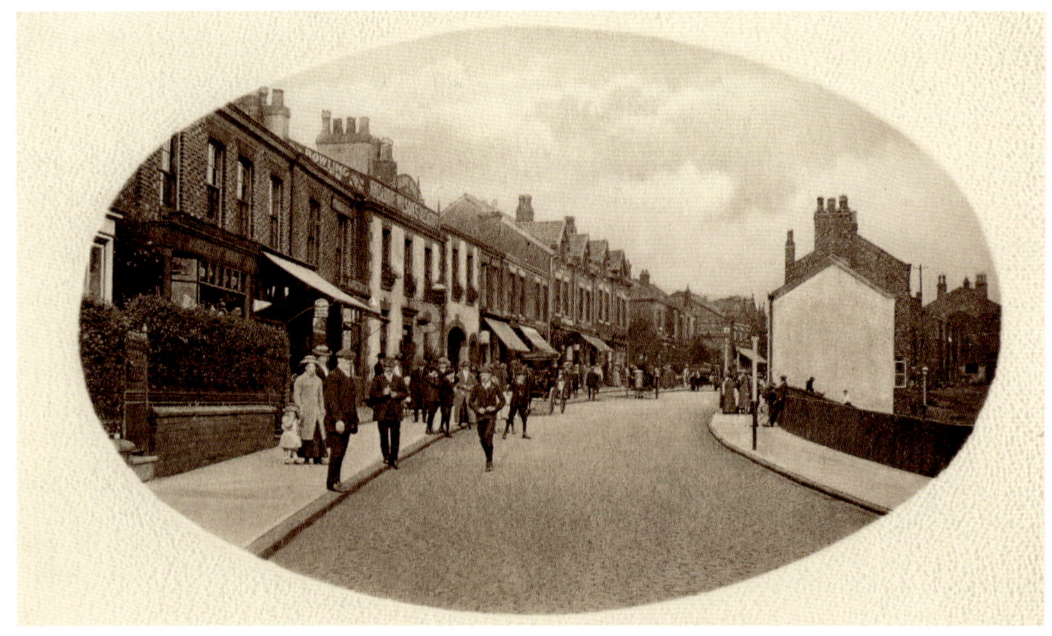

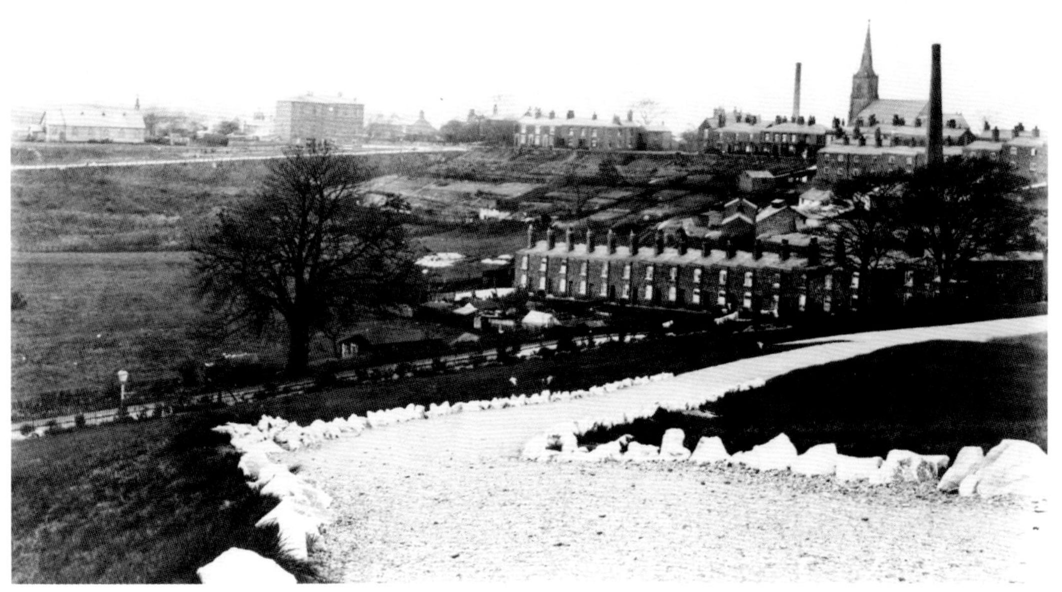

Heaton Mersey Village, 1904

These photographs show two views of Heaton Mersey village from the same year from slightly different angles. The photographs are taken from the ridge at the top of Heaton Mersey Park. The Upper Bleachworks, built by Robert Parker, can be seen nestling on the slope between Park Row and Heaton Place. Station Road can be seen in the upper right of the pictures with Heaton Mersey Sunday School standing at its junction with Didsbury Road. To the left of the Sunday School is the 'Tin Chapel' erected by the Methodist Church and used for worship until they moved to a purpose-built church on Cavendish Road in the mid-1800s.

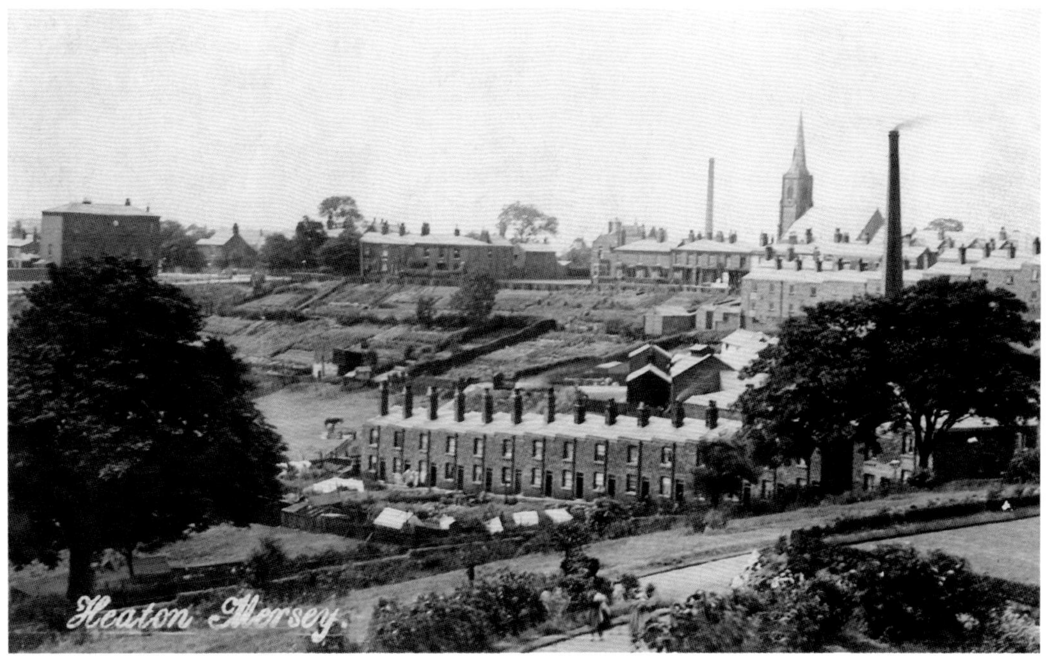

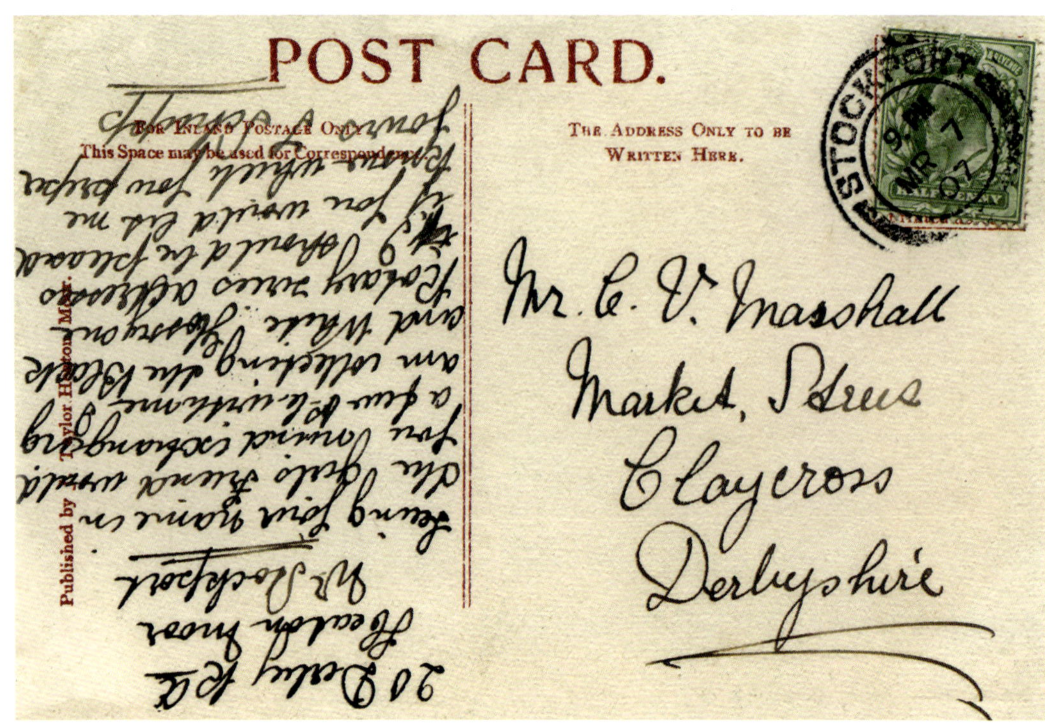

A postcard sent on the 7 March 1907.

Postcard History: Deltiology

The years between 1902 and 1914 (although some historians use 1898–1918) has been called 'The Golden Age' of picture postcards. The telephone was not widely used, so sending a postcard was the most convenient and easiest way of communicating. The postcard soon became a status symbol reflecting a person's position in society. In 1902, the divided back was introduced, which meant that a comment was no longer written around the picture on the front, and as a result, postcard collection became a public obsession. Many of the high-quality postcards were being printed in Europe and imported to Britain during this time. The German printing methods were superior, providing the brightest colours and finest artwork. In fact, many artists moved to Germany to work on postcard production until the supply of imported postcards from Germany came to an end during and after the First World War. The communication on the postcard above was sent on 7 March 1907 and asks 'would you mind exchanging a few P. C.'s with me, am collecting the Black and White glossy ones Rotary series'. The sender is referring to a particular type of postcard that was printed by The Rotary Photo Company who used rotary photo presses to mass-produce photographic postcards. There were two types of postcard at this time, printed cards and photographic cards, both being produced on a large scale. Although the Rotary series used real photographs, they were still classed as printed cards. The 'Real Photo' postcards, or photographic cards, were photographs printed directly onto postcard-sized photographic paper and were introduced in 1900.

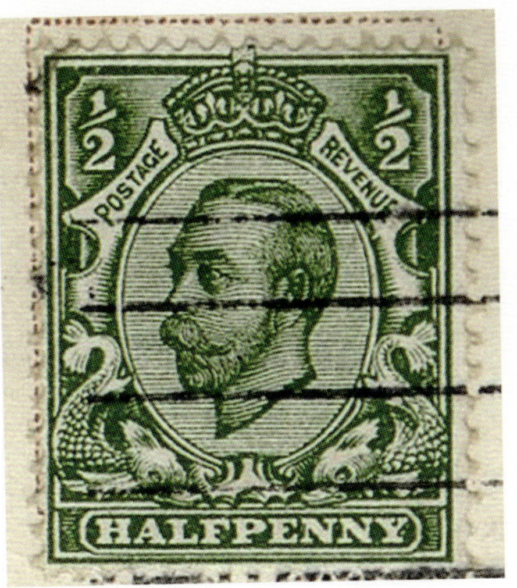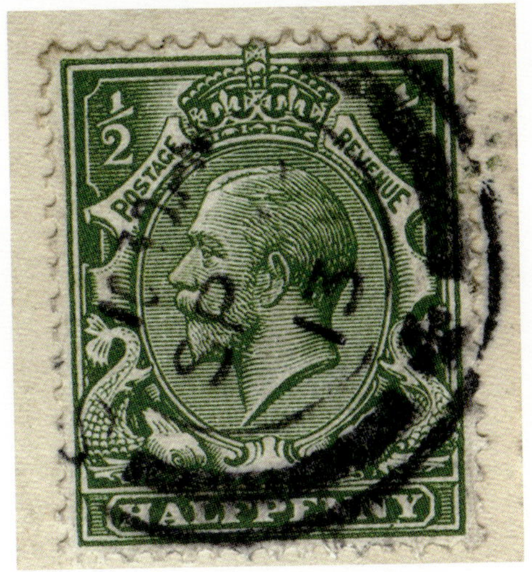

The two King George V, ½*d*, definitive stamps. The stamp on the left shows the 'Downey Head' where the Kings head is three-quarter profile. This stamp was later replaced with the full profile stamp on the right.

Postcard History: British Postage Stamps

British postage stamps were introduced in 1840, and there were three changes in design up to 1936 as there had been three monarchs: Queen Victoria 1837–1901, King Edward VII 1901–10 and King George V 1910–36. The head of the monarch was, at that time, always the dominant feature on the stamp until the reign of King George V when the British postage stamp saw many 'firsts'. The first 'postage due' labels were introduced in 1914, it was the first time that the photogravure method was used, and the first 'commemoratives' were introduced following the British Empire Exhibition in 1924. When King George V acceded to the throne in 1910, new photographs were needed for coin, medal and stamp designs. The definitive stamps were originally based on a three-quarter profile photograph taken by W & D Downey, the Court Photographers. The first ½*d* and 1*d* values received much criticism for their poor quality because new printers were contracted, and the Royal Mail was engaged to create the printing plates and neither had any experience of stamp printing. Other values were prepared, but only the lower values were put on sale as further issues were abandoned in favour of issuing stamps with a full profile head.

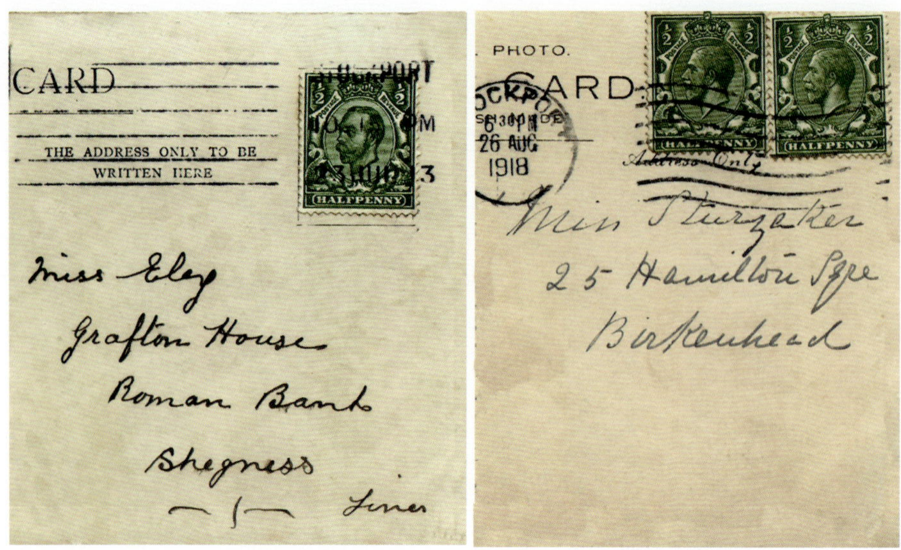

Postcard History: Postage Rates

The sending of postcards in Great Britain was made easy and affordable during the 1800s. There were a number of innovations during this time that helped create a new postal age. In 1837, Rowland Hill proposed that letters be charged by weight, not distance, and the fee be collected in advance from the sender, leading in 1840 to the introduction of uniform penny postage stamps. Between 1918 and 1921, the postage rate for sending a postcard increased twice from ½*d* to 1*d* in June 1918 and then to 1½*d* in January 1921. However, in 1922 the rate was reduced back to 1*d* following a public protest.

The four postcards on this page show the changes to the postage rate. Top left: ½*d* (halfpenny) until 1918, franking date 23 July 1913. Top right: increased to 1*d*, June 1918, franking date 26 August 1918. Bottom left: a further increase to 1½*d* in January 1921, franking date 2 September 1921. Bottom right: rate reduced to 1*d* in 1922, franking date 3 July 1927.

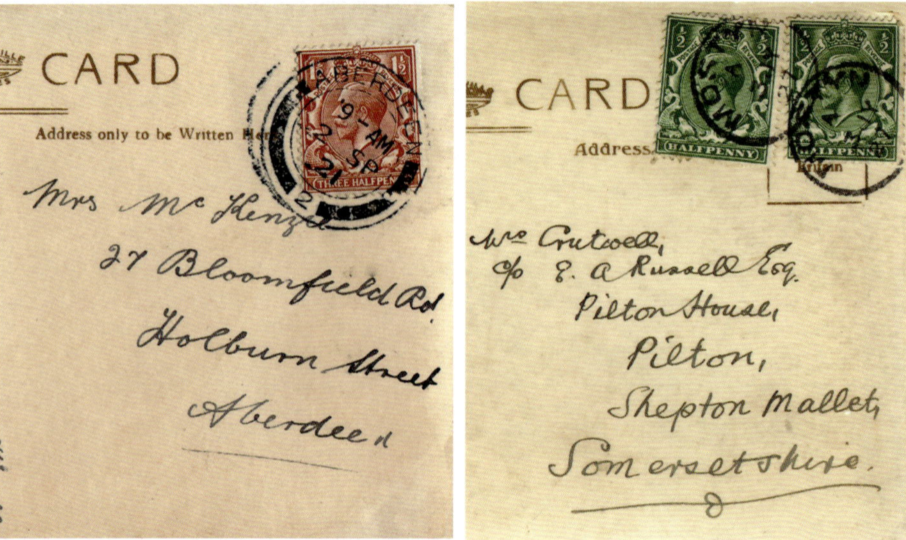

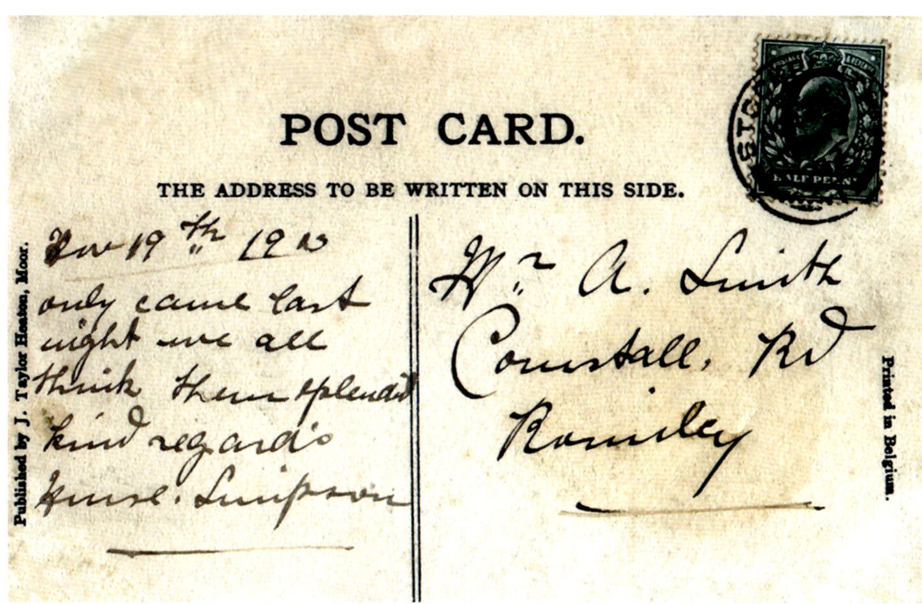

Postcard History: The Divided Back

In 1899, standard size postcards were introduced in Britain to fall in line with other countries. The postcard had a picture on the front and an undivided back on the reverse for the address. A comment would be written on the front in the space around the picture. In 1902, the Divided Back postcard was introduced in Britain that allowed the message and address to be written on the same side of the postcard hence freeing up the whole of the front for a picture. The upper postcard, which was sent on 19 November 1903, shows that the printer was using one of their earlier templates; although it has a divided back, it still says 'THE ADDRESS TO BE WRITTEN ON THIS SIDE'. The lower postcard, sent on 10 December 1903, has a heading for both sections on the back, 'THIS SPACE MAY BE USED FOR COMMUNICATION' and 'THE ADDRESS ONLY TO BE WRITTEN HERE'.

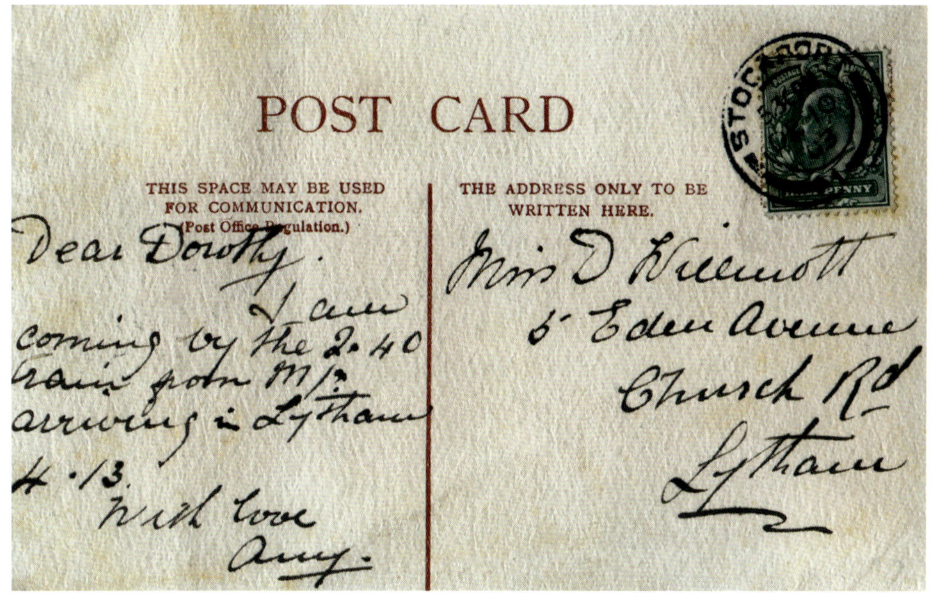

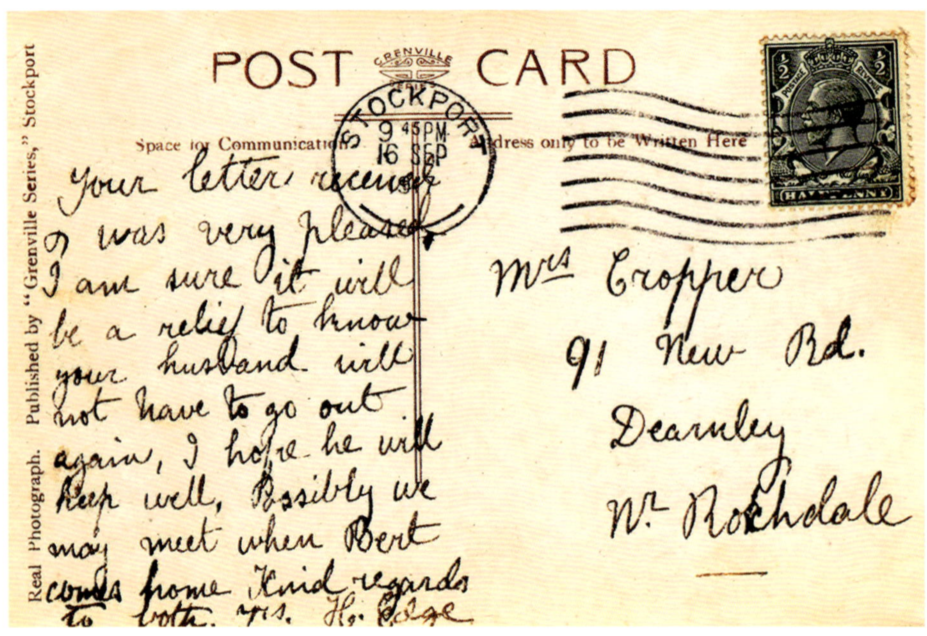

A postcard sent on 16 September 1917 sent from H. Edge to Mrs Cropper.

Postcard History: The First World War

Before the First World War started, postcards were going through 'The Golden Age' with many thousands being sold not only to write messages to family and friends but also to collect and save so when the war broke out a picture postcard was already the perfect form of communication from home to the men on active service. In France and Belgium, local women were embroidering silk postcards and sold them as souvenirs to the soldiers serving on the Western Front. This industry brought a useful source of income for the families in the area.

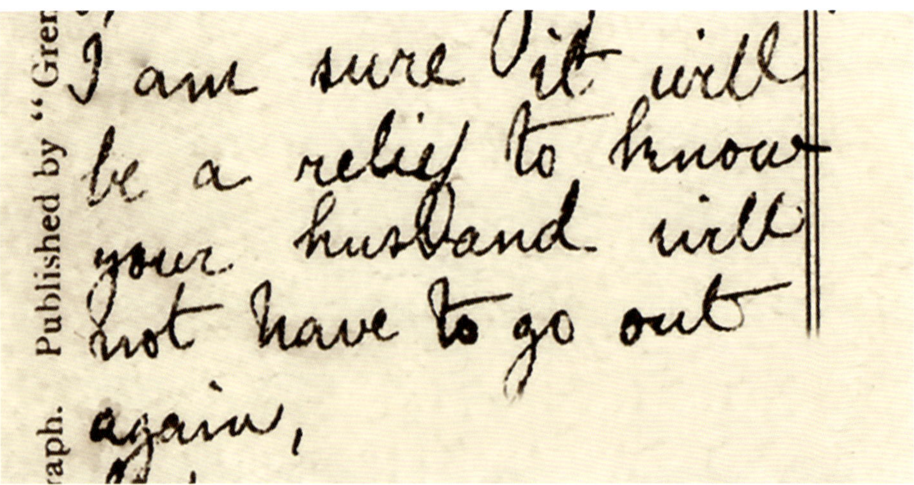

The sender says 'I am sure it will be a relief to know that your husband will not have to go out again'. Reading between the lines, we can assume the husband will not be going out, possibly to the Western Front, to fight again.

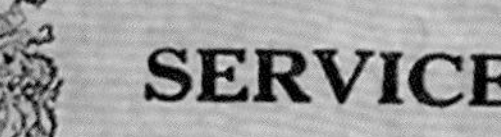

Postcard History: The First World War Continued
The Army Postal Service introduced the Field Service postcard, Army Form AFA 2042, which was an attempt to curb problems of censorship. The buff-coloured postcard had a number of messages printed on them which could be kept or erased as appropriate. On the card, it stated: 'NOTHING is to be written on this side except the date and signature of the sender. Sentences not required may be erased. If anything else is added the postcard will be destroyed'. Examples of the sentences that appeared on the postcard are shown in the photograph right.

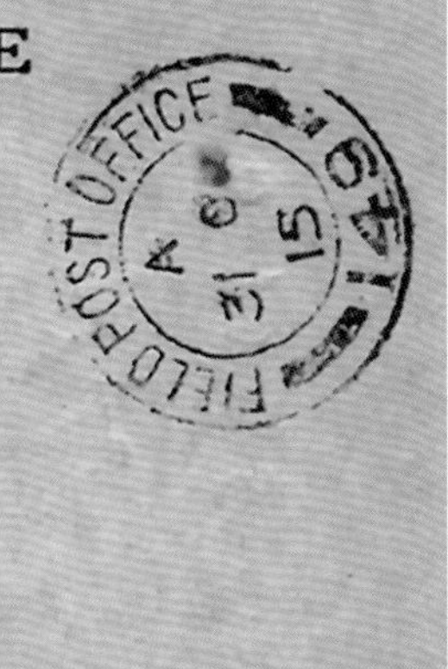

NOTHING is to be written on this side except the date and signature of the sender. Sentences not required may be erased. If anything else is added the post card will be destroyed.

[Postage must be prepaid on any letter or post card addressed to the sender of this card]

I am quite well.

I have been admitted into hospital
{ sick
  ... } and hope to be discharged soon.

{ letter dated ________
I have received your { telegram ________
  { parcel   „   ________

Letter follows at first opportunity.

Signature only } Trevor
Date 27/10/15

Wt.W65—P.P.948.   8000m.   5-18.   C. & Co., Grange Mills, S.W.

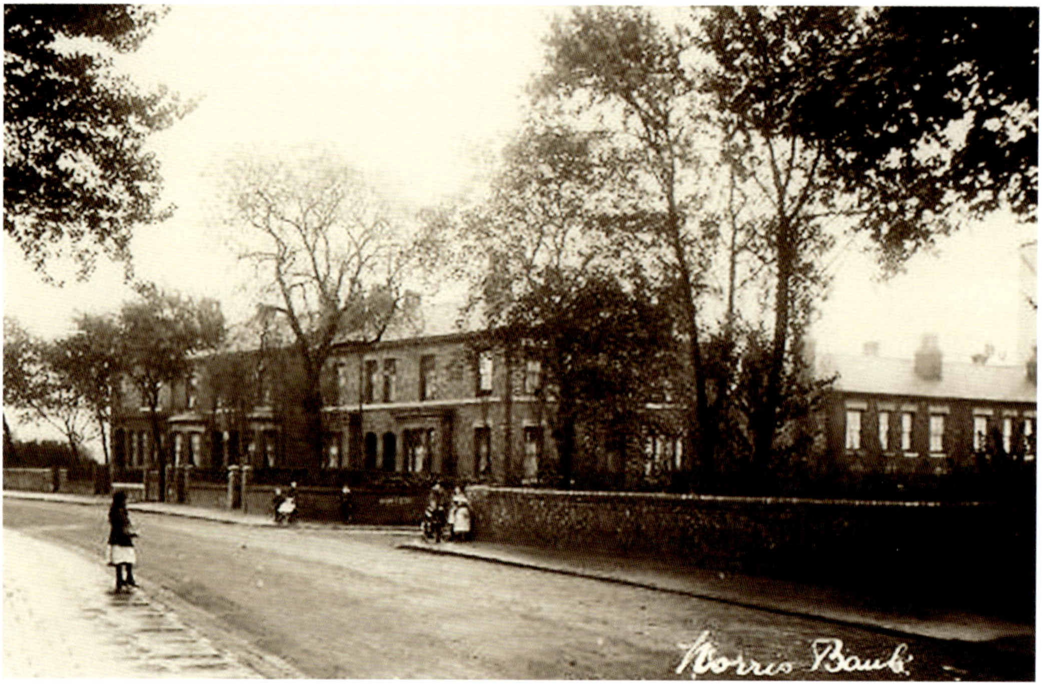

Along Didsbury Road Continued

The views south along Didsbury Road would have afforded wealthy Victorian families some of the finest views in South Manchester across the Cheshire Plain. However, as the road dropped down through Norris Bank and headed for Stockport, there would be sense of leaving the semi-rural village atmosphere behind and entering the industrial world of a large manufacturing town. The area around Brighton Road would have been much less wealthy than its near neighbours at the top of the ridge with many of the residents working tiring and demanding shifts in the nearby factories often in rooms with noisy machinery and no health and safety regulations to protect them.

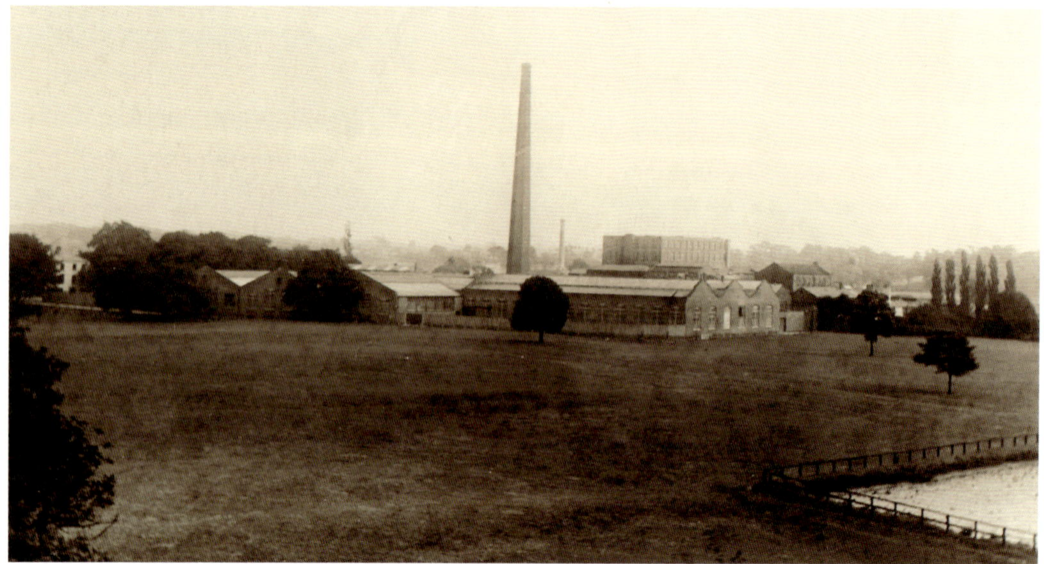

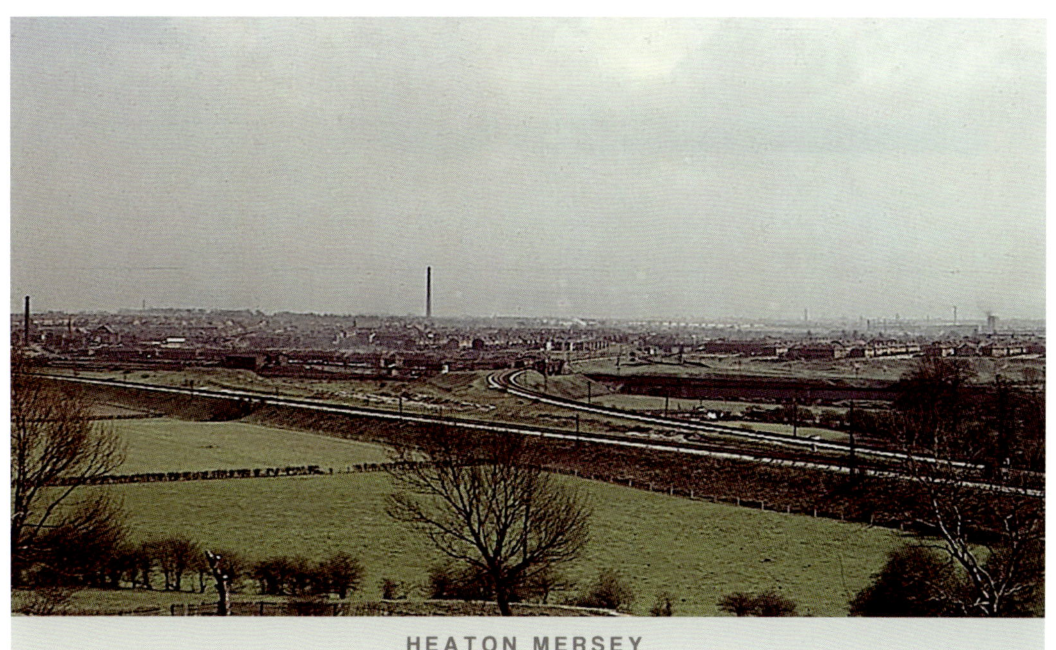

HEATON MERSEY

Vale Road and View from Heaton Mersey Park, 1940s

A stroll down Vale Road up into Heaton Mersey Park would have given residents a fine view across open fields and the railway lines to Stockport and the Cheshire Plain. The entrance to Tait's Buildings can be seen on the right of the lower picture. The original Tait's Buildings were three storeys high and offered grim, almost derelict, accommodation for Mortimer Lavater Tait's apprentices from the Lower Bleach Works. There were known locally by the name Barracks Yard.

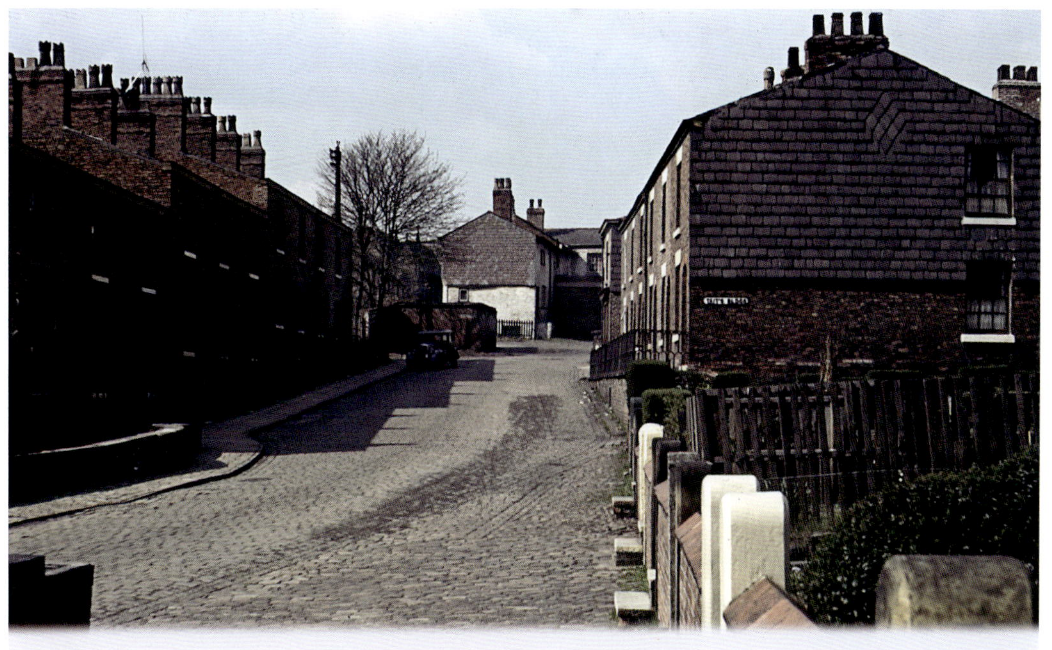

VALE ROAD HEATON MERSEY

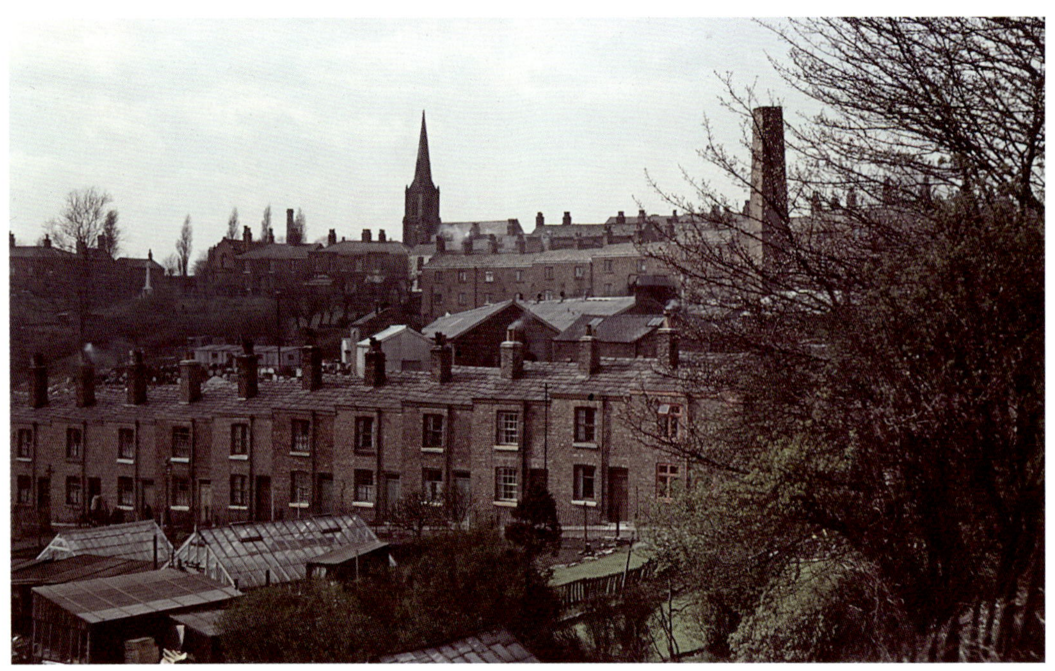

Vale Close, 1940s and 1908

These two views of Vale Close show the important relationship between the development of Heaton Mersey as an industrial village and the need for new industries to provide suitable accommodation for their workforce. The building of the Upper and Lower Bleach Works resulted in the building of a number of rows of small terraced housing. Heaton Place, which can be seen at the top of the colour photograph, was demolished in the 1970s, but Park Row still survives despite attempts in the 1960s to clear it to make away for an access road to the Embankment Industrial Estate.

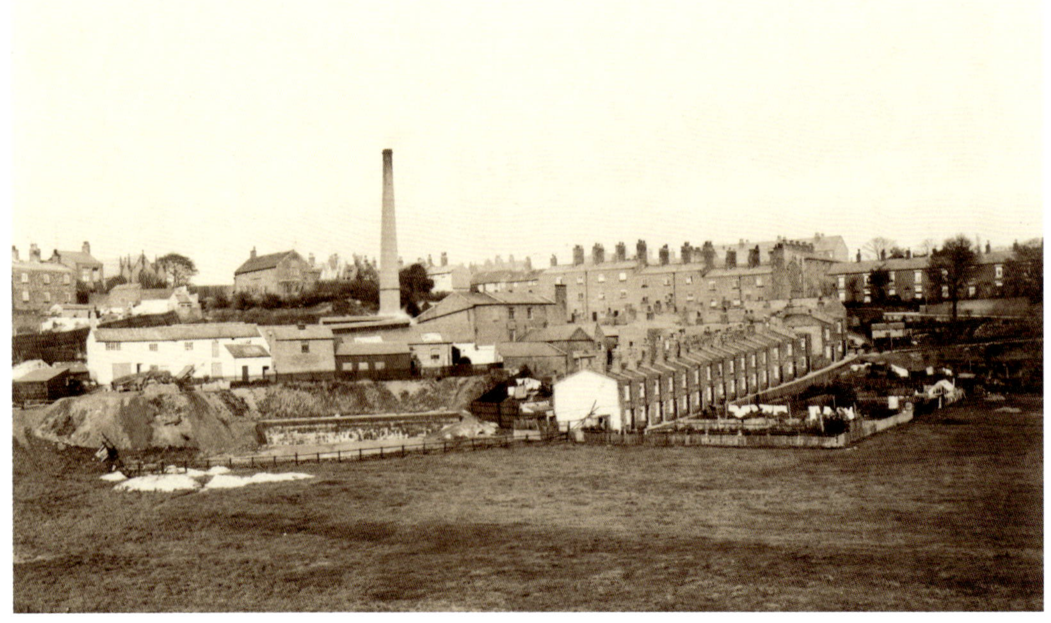

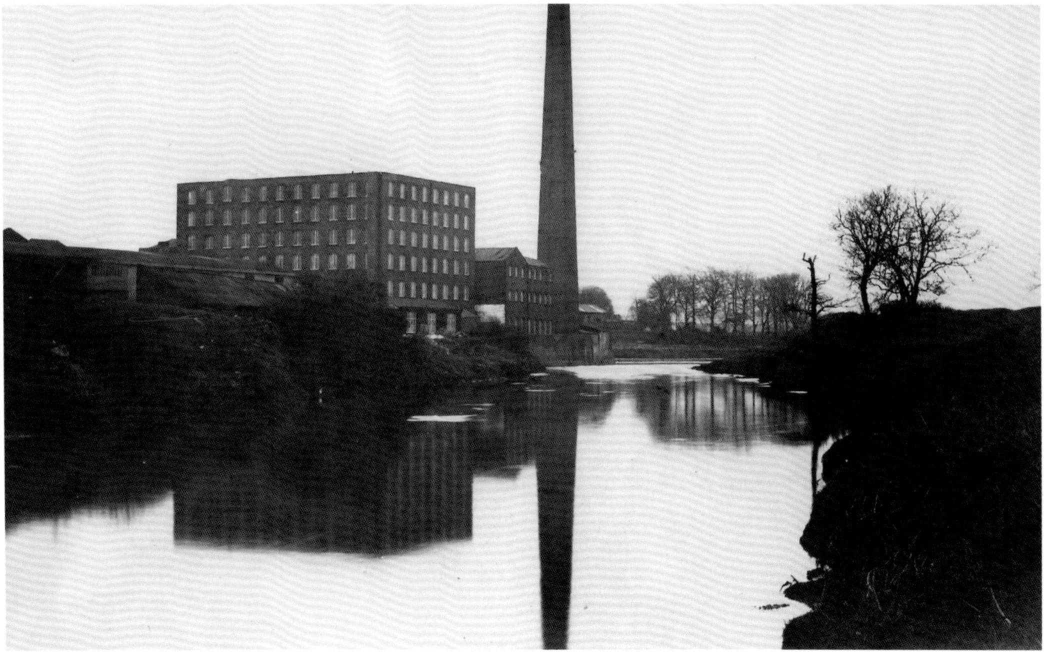

Heaton Mersey Bleach Works, 1920s
The building stood on the river Mersey next to where the Embankment Industrial Estate is situated today. The mill provided finishing processes for which included bleaching, to remove the dingy brown colour from the fabrics, and printing the clean white cotton with a range of attractive designs. The bleaching procedures were heavily dependent on water power, and the weir that fed the water into the mill race is still visible today. The mill continued to operate successfully for many years eventually closing in 1992.

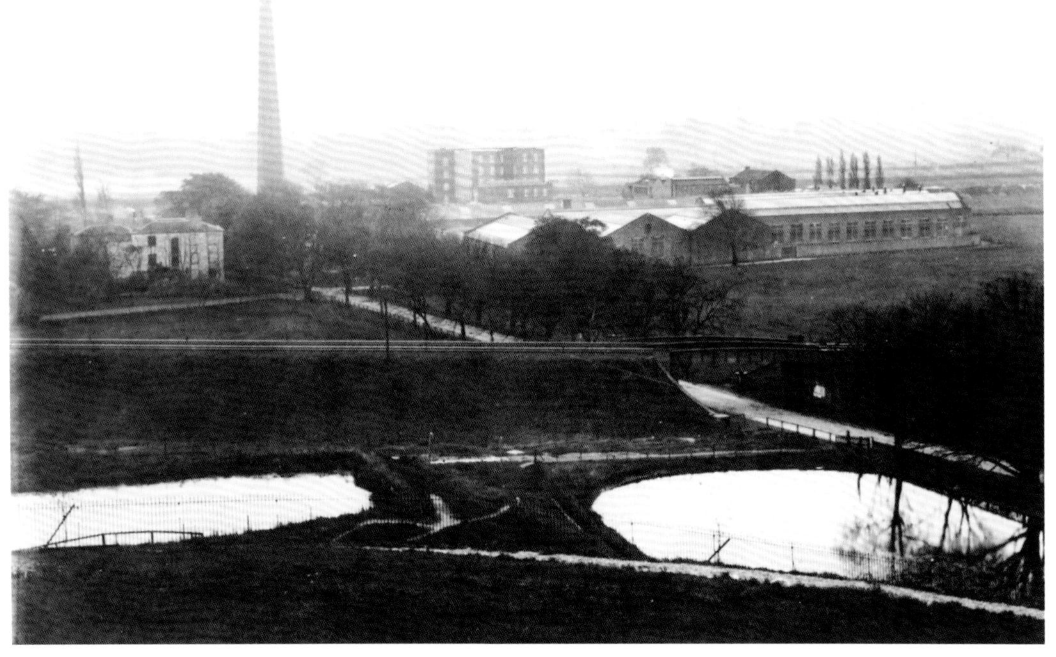

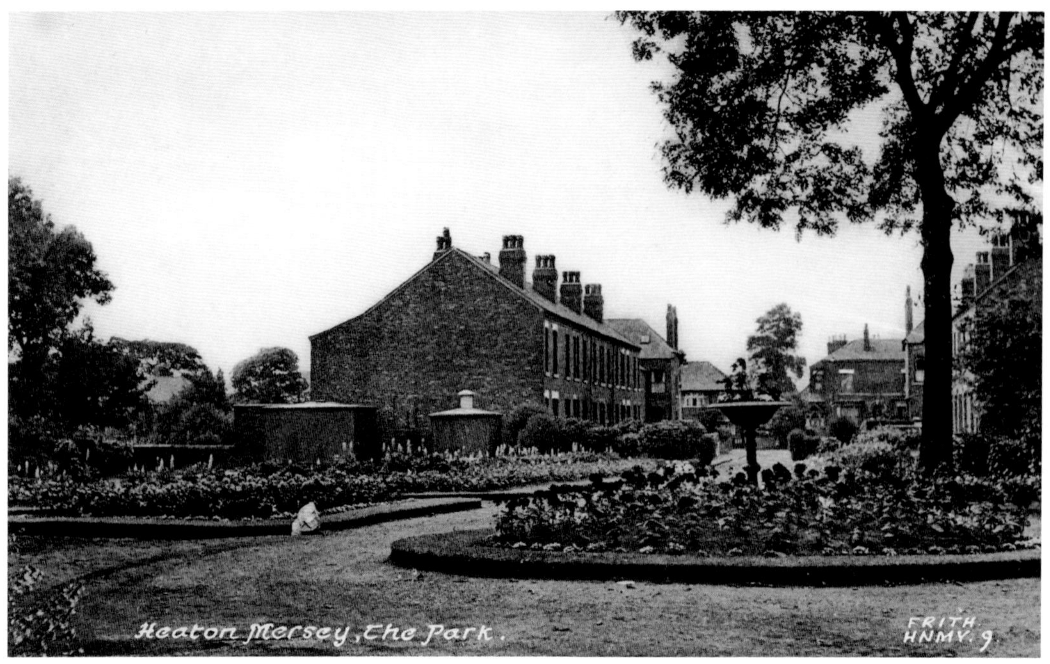

Heaton Mersey Park and Richmond Road, 1920s

A substantial rise in the population of Heaton Mersey took place during the Industrial Revolution as people moved into the area to supply labour for the brickmaking, bleaching and dyeing industries. Residential housing was built to accommodate the workers, and their families, and Heaton Mersey Park was developed in around 1880. The area designated for the park was an open space with panoramic views over the Cheshire Plain and incorporated a bowling green, bandstand and tree-lined walks. It was accessed through a set of fine wrought-iron gates on Richmond Road.

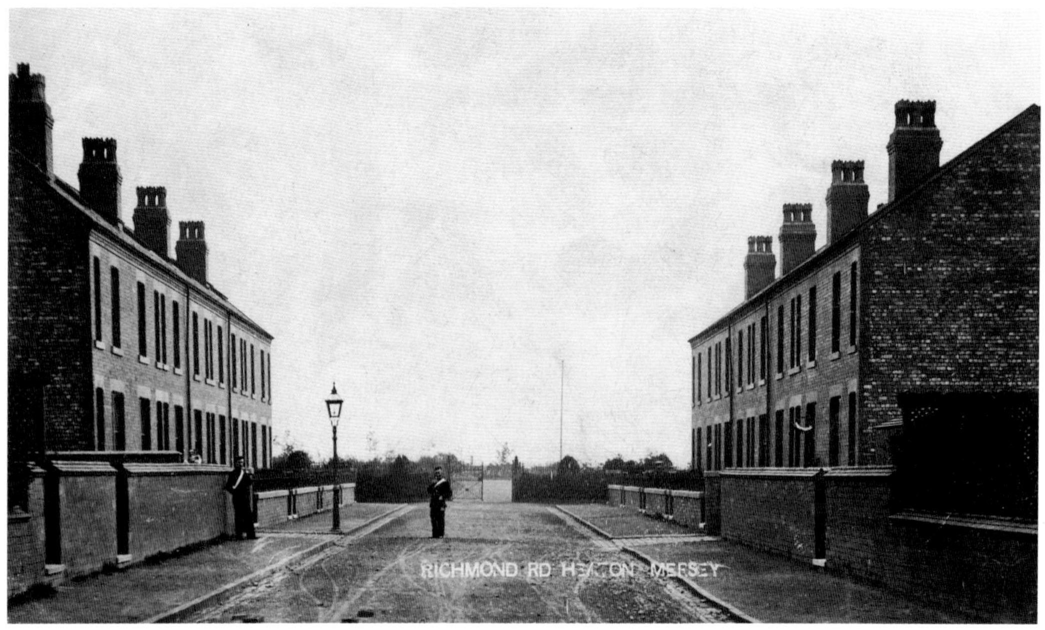

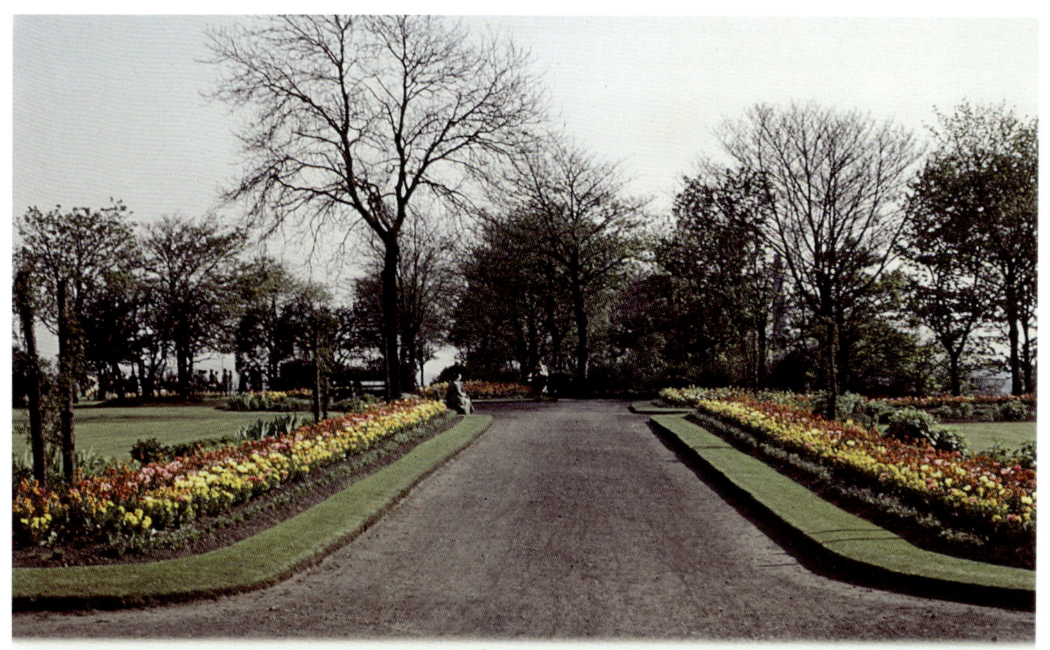

Heaton Mersey Park, 1920s

These two views of the park from the 1950s give a clear indication as to why it was such a popular amenity for local residents. Although both pictures seem to have been taken in early spring, the flower beds are colourful and well-laid-out in readiness for the summer months. The bowling green, set in a hollow below the main park, provides a quiet and sheltered location for bowlers enjoying the relaxation of participating in this popular sport.

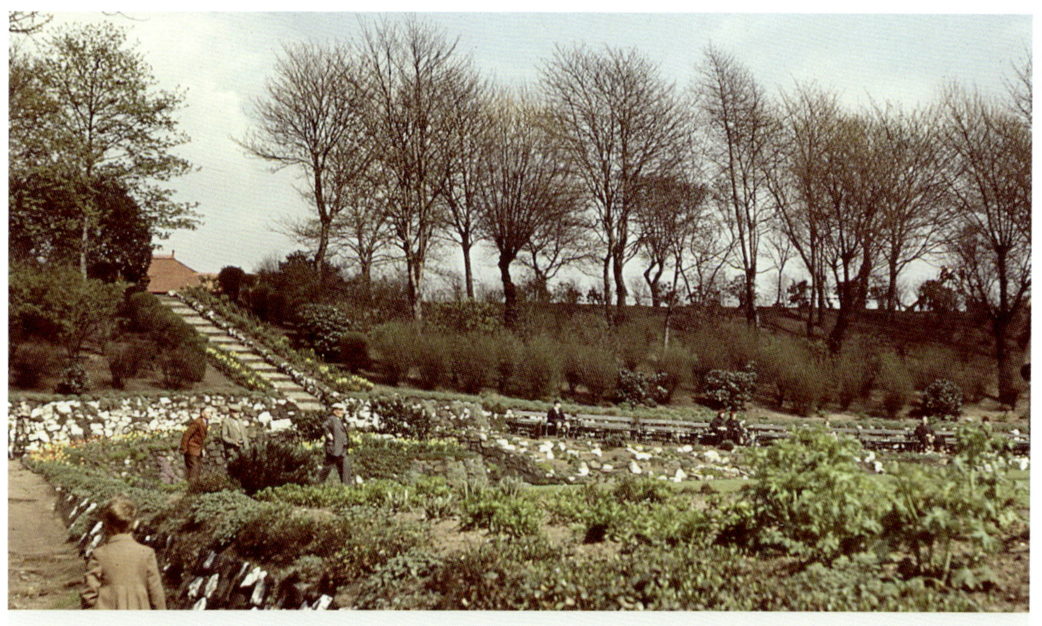

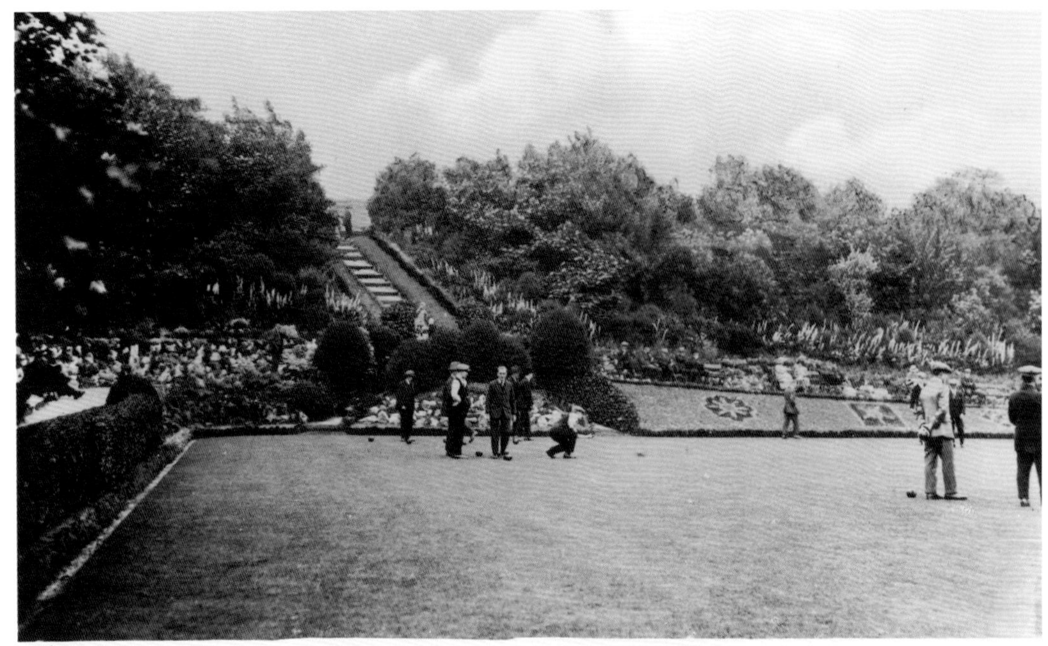

Bowling in the Parks, Early 1900s

These two cards reflect the popularity of bowling at the turn of the nineteenth century. Every park in the Heatons had its own bowling green and, being a popular pastime for local residents, professional bowlers could earn up to £50 for winning local tournaments. In addition to their winnings, the players would also receive a share of the gate money and, sometimes, even earn commission on bets laid on matches in which they were involved.

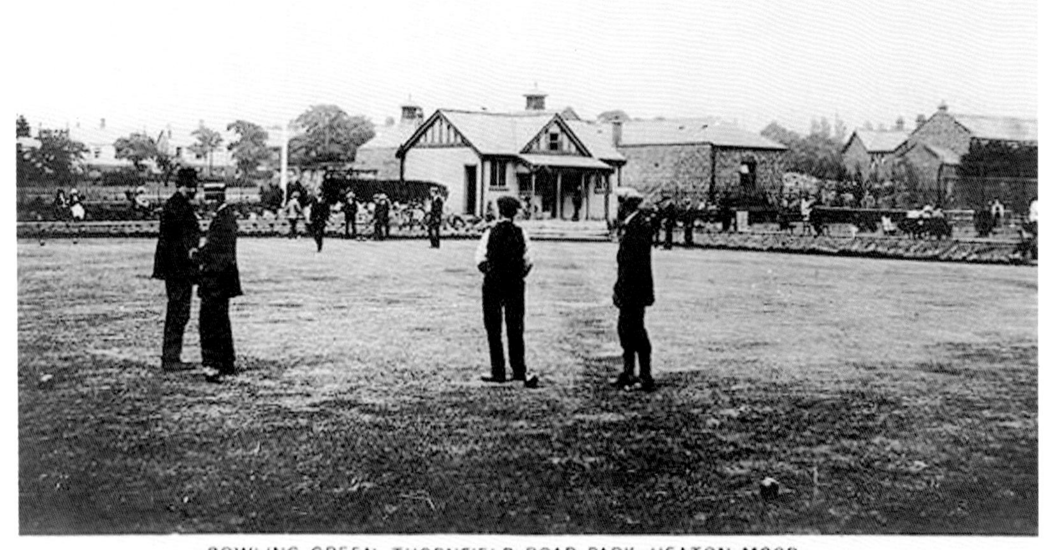

34

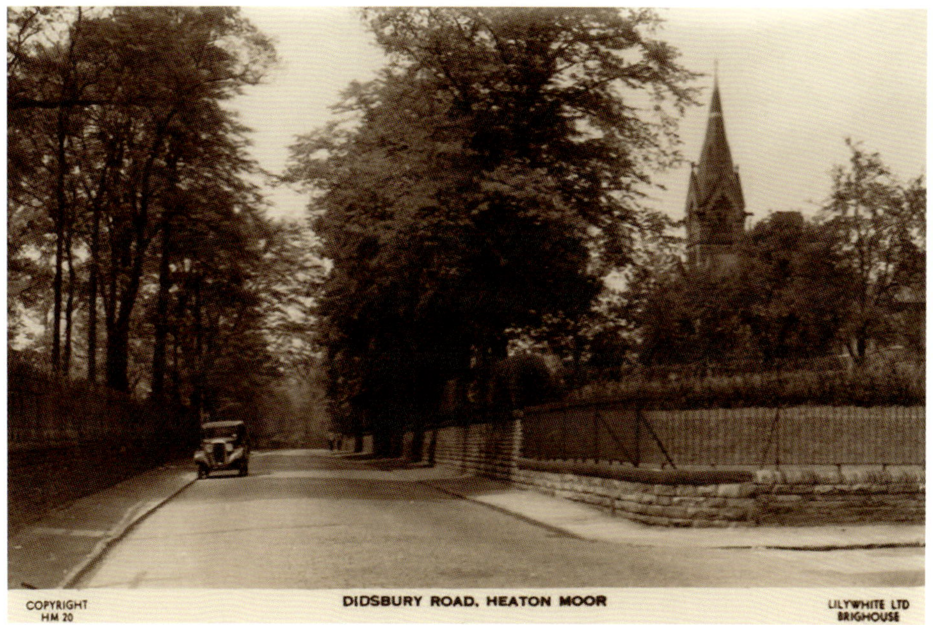

Didsbury Road, 1930s

The picture above is taken from the junction of Didsbury Road and Bank Hall Road. Today houses, sitting in an elevated position, line the road to the right, and the busy junction is controlled by traffic signals. The tower of Barnes Industrial School, which can be seen rising from the trees, was designed by Alfred Waterhouse (of Manchester Town Hall fame) and constructed in 1871. In the late 1800s, it was home to nearly 300 orphaned or neglected boys. It finally closed in 1958 and was demolished to make way for a new housing estate.

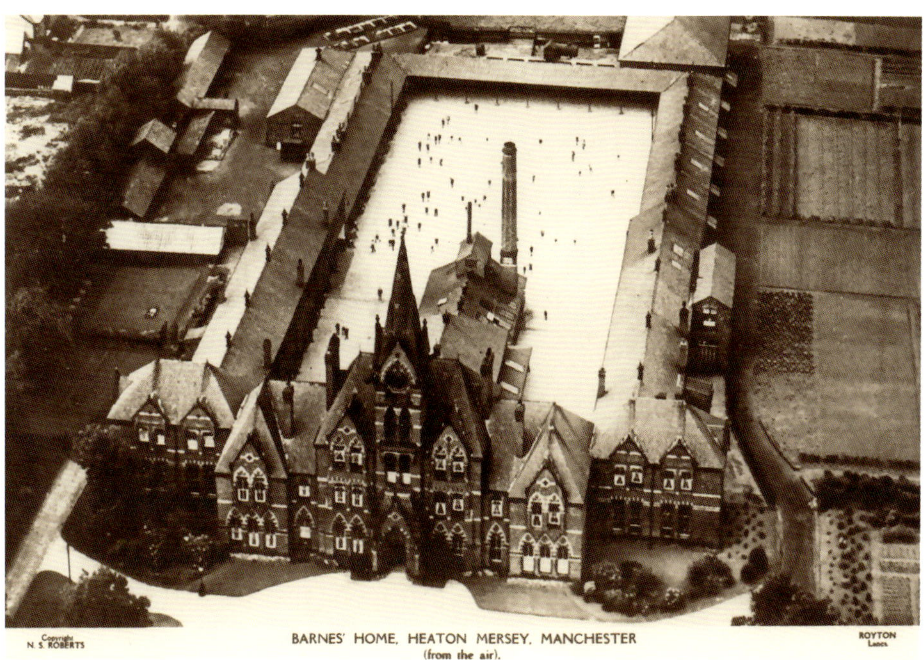

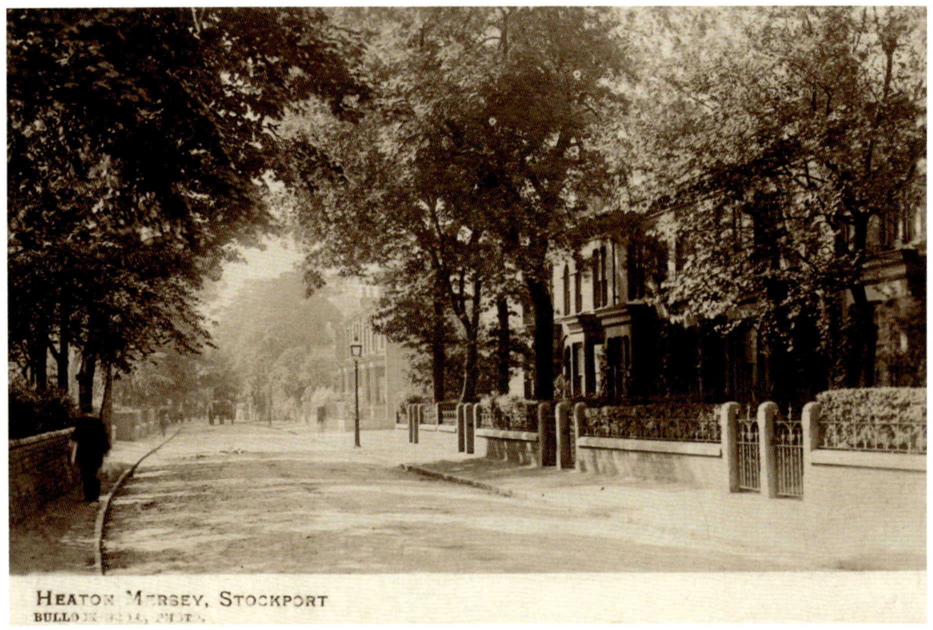

Norris Bank, 1900s

Didsbury Road would have been an important route out of Stockport as early as the 1900s. The road surface in both pictures is cobbled and rough, but traffic would have been heavy with horses straining to pull fully laden carts up the long rise past Norris Bank House and Bank Cottage to Bank Hall, at the top of the hill, and on to Heaton Mersey and Didsbury. The houses located on the rise up from Stockport would have given fine views across the town to the hills of the Peak District.

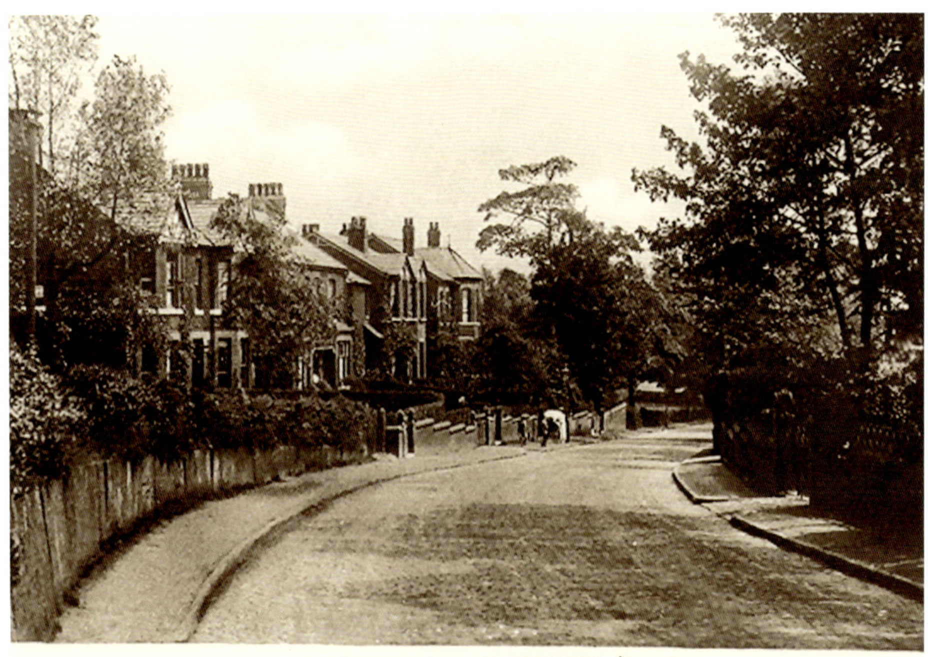

DIDSBURY ROAD, STOCKPORT (No. 8)

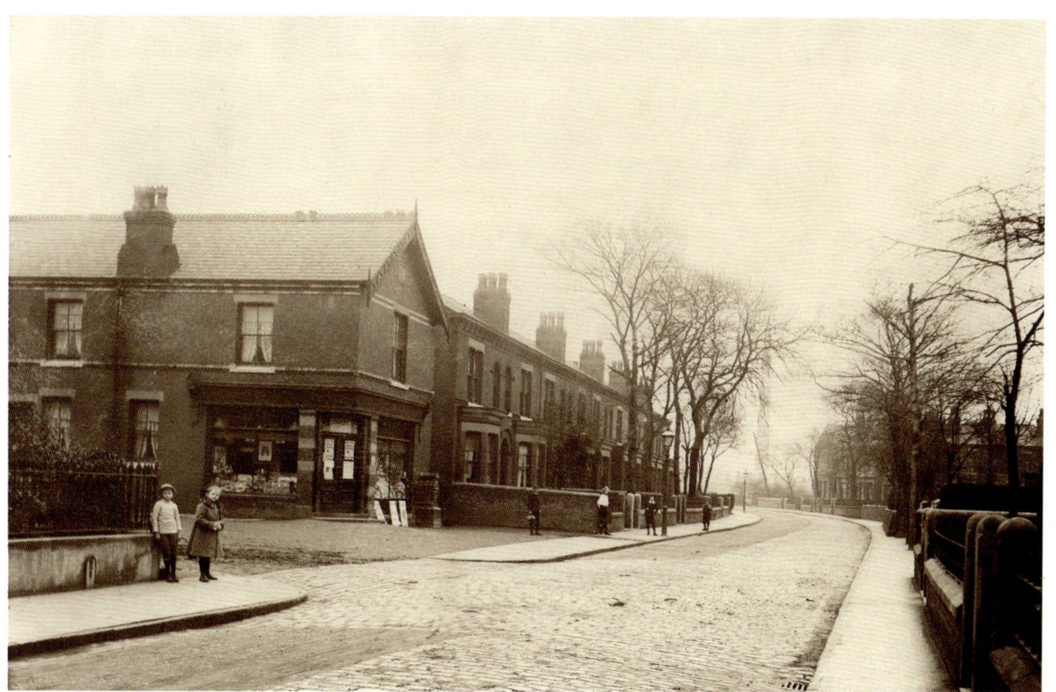

Corner Shop, Didsbury Road, Norris Bank, 1903

This photograph shows the corner shop at the junction of Didsbury Road and Norris Avenue. The shop is still there today but has been taken over for a different commercial enterprise. Corner shops were very important to the local community selling a variety of goods such as foodstuffs, agricultural supplies and hardware. A closer inspection of the photograph reveals that this particular shop is doing a good trade in seeds, which are advertised on the signs in the front door, giving an indication of the semi-agricultural nature of the area.

The shop would also have been suitably valued by the children in the picture as it undoubtedly had a good range of sweets and other 'goodies'. Bulls eyes, pear drops, liquorice sticks and humbugs would have been among their particular favourites. Tiger nuts were also very popular but not without their dangers. Although they were popular with children, because they were so sweet, they often contained a fair sprinkling of insects and grit which could play havoc with children's teeth.

Commercially produced sweets would be stocked on the shelves in large, labelled glass jars, measured out by the ounce and served in sturdy white bags. Triangular bags of broken wafers were also popular particularly if they had a marshmallow fish on top. For those children with a really sweet tooth, trays of home-made toffee were often kept on the counter and cut to the required size on demand.

The picture is a good example of a small Edwardian shop located on a corner plot at the end of a row of factory workers' houses. The doorway of the shop is situated on the corner of the plot to maximise shop floor space within and provide two display windows facing onto opposing streets.

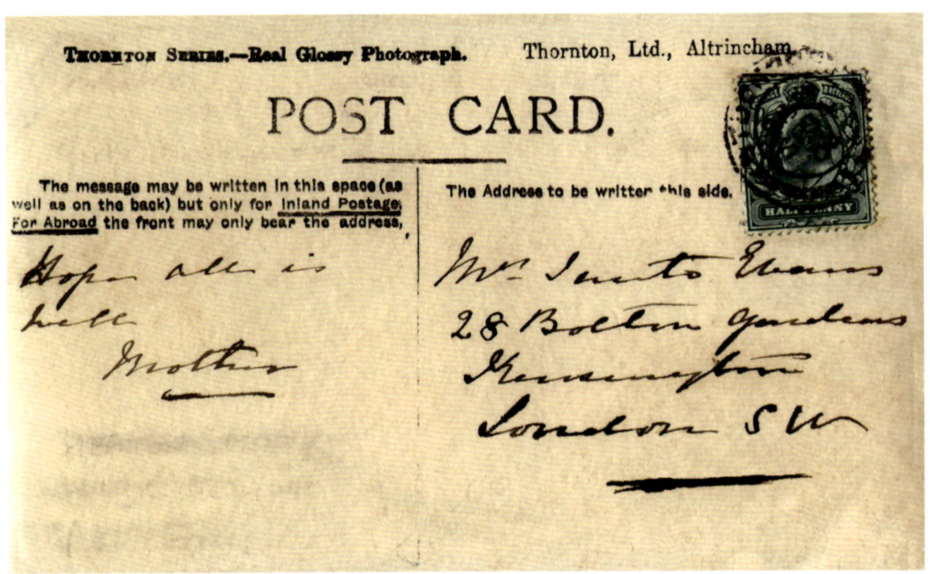

Life During the Early 1900s: Communication

The postcard provided a means of near instant communication during the late 1800s and early 1900s. The telephone had not become popular at that time, and the postal service was reliable with several collections per day and next day delivery. In some places, there might have been up to a dozen collections a day from post boxes and six deliveries a day to houses beginning in the early morning. People had confidence in the postal service knowing that messages about events happening on the next day, or in some areas on the same day, would arrive in time. Postcards sent by the residents in the Heatons around 100 years ago reveal that they contained short messages very much like the texts, tweets and emails that we send today. The comments on the postcards read; 'Hope all is well – Mother' and 'Don't forget to take out Dog License'.

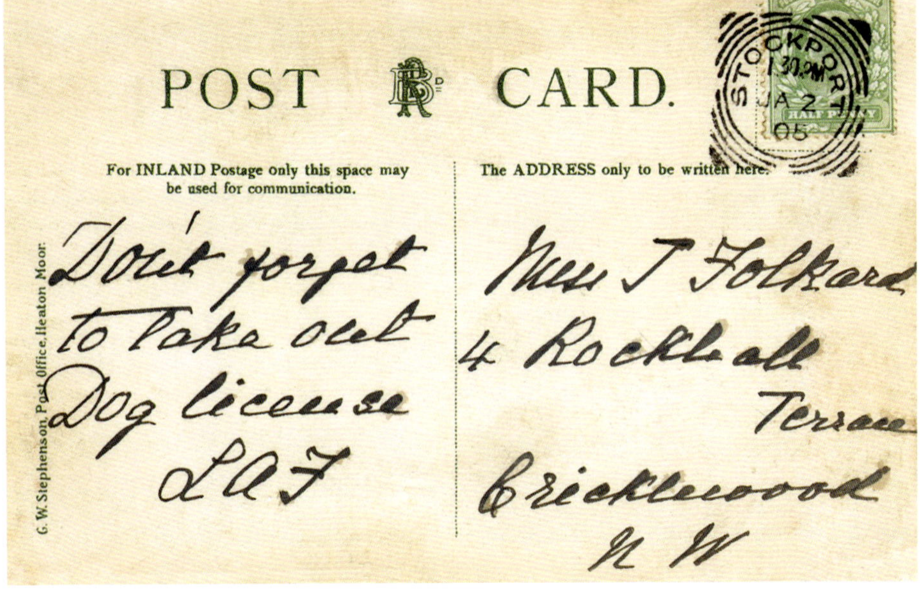

Life During the 1900s:
Communication
Continued

The postal service must
have been very reliable
in 1908 as shown on this
postcard. The card was
sent from Stockport at 1.15
p.m. on 13 August and was
received in Windermere at
7.45 a.m. on 14 August.

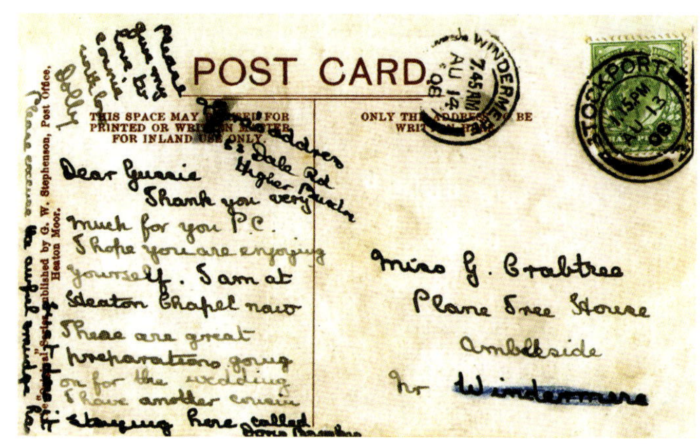

R. Freshney was explaining
to the Revd Jones just
how beautiful the area is
around Buxton saying that
it is slightly different to
Lincolnshire.

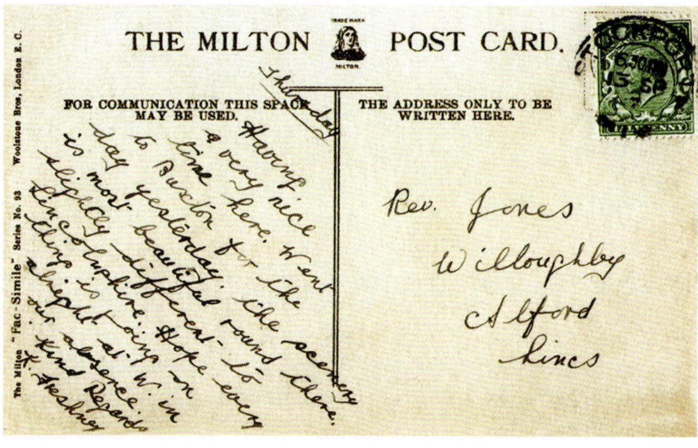

Cards were obviously
being posted from the
Heatons to other parts of
the world in 1910. Ernest
was communicating with
Hildur in Sweden.

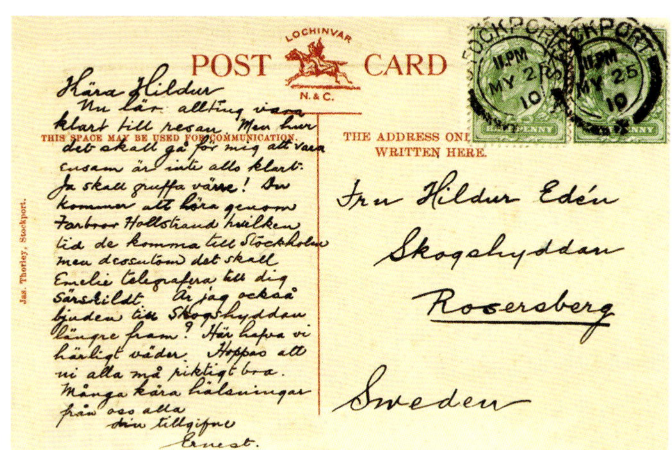

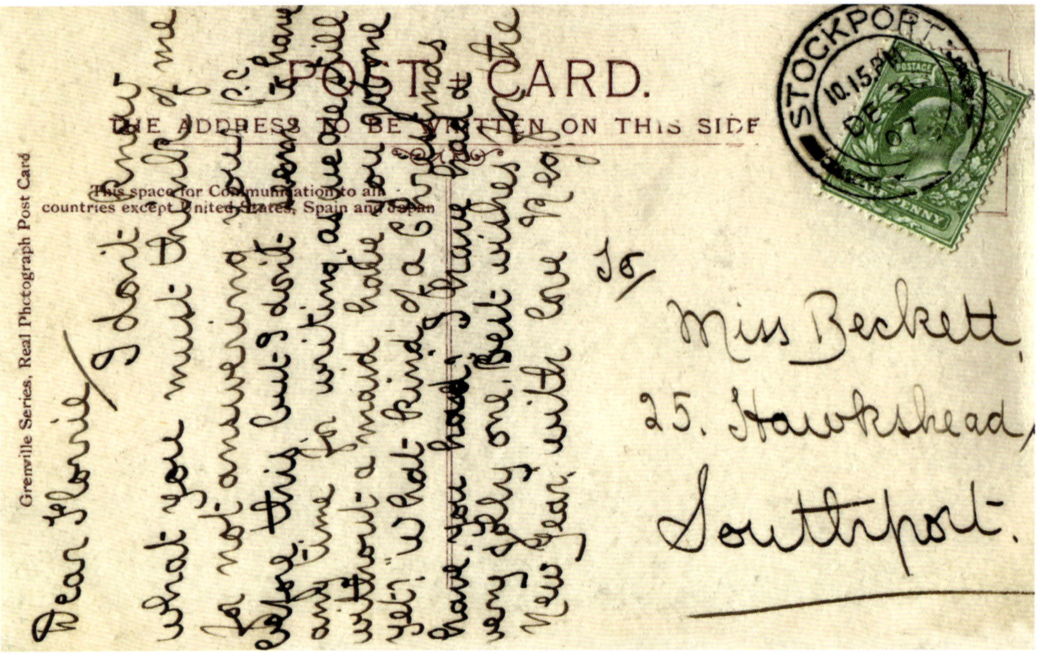

A postcard from Reg to Florrie sent on the 30 December 1907.

Life During the Early 1900s: In Service

During the 1800s and early 1900s, Victorian families were usually large in number because of high birth rates and improving life expectancy. Some households were complex in their formation with the growth in residential domestic service and lodgers as many young people, especially women, migrated to towns and cities looking for work. The man's 'breadwinner' wage was generally the norm yet, in practice, many households were dependent upon female earnings, and during the early 1900s, many women had a dual role combining a heavy domestic burden with low-paid in-service employment. However, as the nineteenth century progressed, there was a greater sharing of housework within the home, and women started to play a more prominent role in local politics. The employment statistics for 1900 indicate that there were over 1.7 million women working as domestic servants, 90% of the women's workforce at that time.

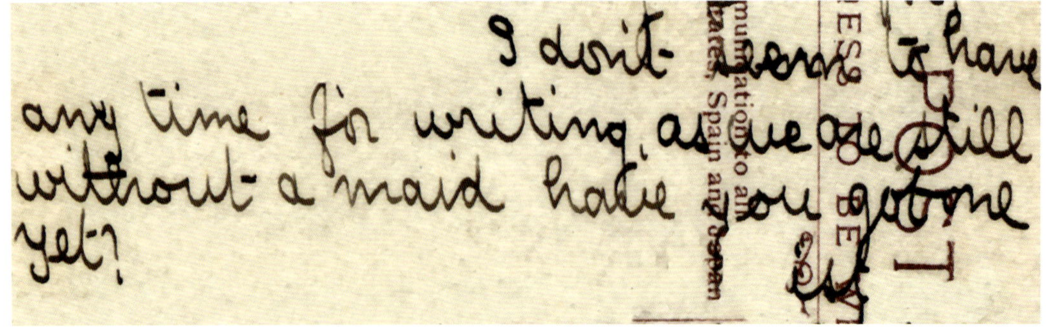

The comment on the postcard reads: 'I don't seem to have anytime for writing as we are still without a maid have you got one yet?'

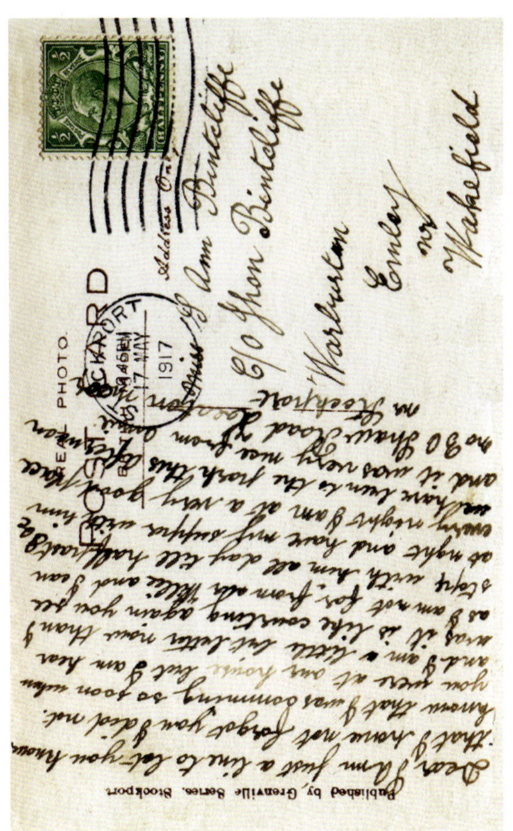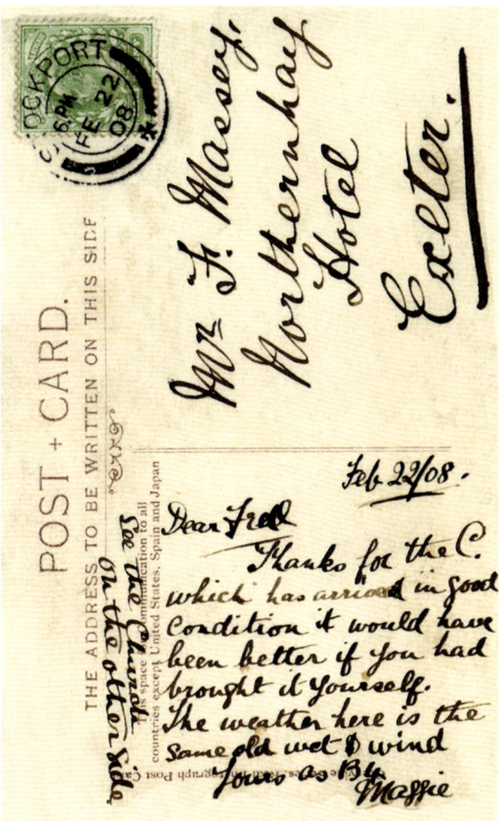

Above left: The sender says, 'I did not know that I was coming so soon when you were at our house but I am near and I am a little bit better now than I was it is like courting again.'

Above right: A postcard from Maggie to Fred saying, 'Thanks for the C which arrived in good condition it would have been better if you had brought it yourself.'

Life During the Early 1900s: Courtship

During the early era of the postcard, courtship and love were both revered, despite their strict moral code and rules of etiquette. Under this strict code of etiquette, couples invented new ways to 'play courtship'. Gifts, called 'Love Tokens', such as fans, gloves, handkerchiefs, painted miniatures and flowers were given as a sign of affection. Love letters and cards, especially Valentines cards, also played an important part allowing expression of deep emotion which society dictated was improper to be expressed otherwise. So, beginning a love relationship was much more of a challenge than it is today. The postcards show that the messages have been written sideways, hence making it difficult for those handling the card to read it.

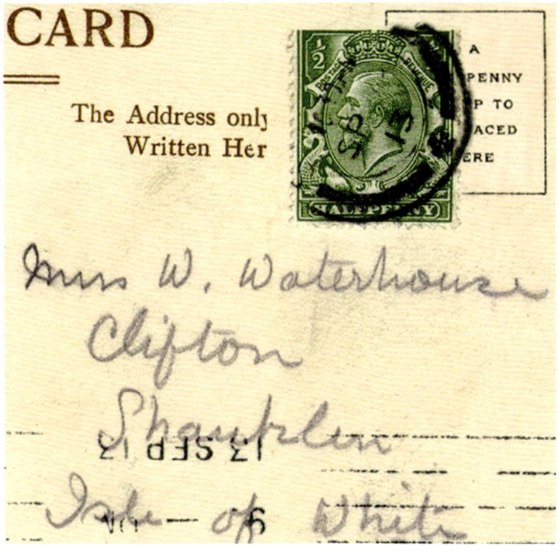

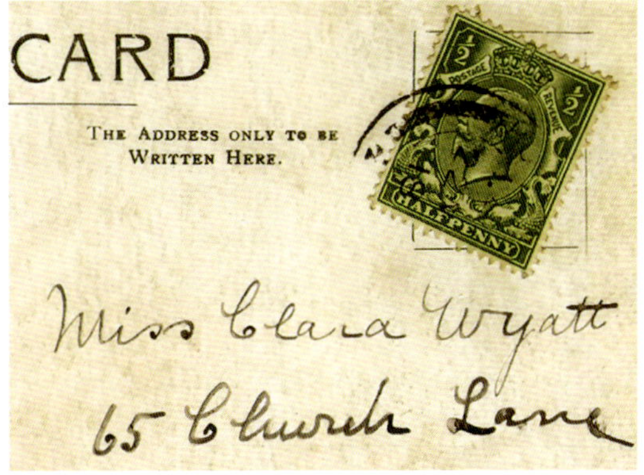

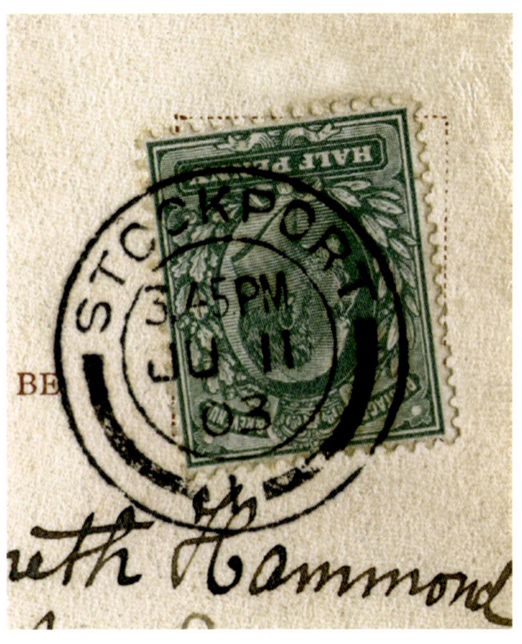

Life During the Early 1900s:
The Language of Stamps

During the late nineteenth century and early twentieth century, stamps were affixed to letters and postcards in different positions and at different angles. This became known as the 'Language of Stamps' with the position of the stamp giving a particular message to the receiver. It was therefore a convenient and simple way of expressing one's feelings. However, Post Offices around the world introduced regulations because it became a problem postmarking the stamps.

Some stamp language interpretations are as follows:

Upside down, top left corner – I love you
Upside down, top right corner – Write no more
At a right angle, top right corner – Do you love me?
At a right angle in line with surname – I long to see you
Upright in line with surname – Accept my love
Upside down in line with surname – I'm engaged
On a diagonal tilted right – Will you marry me?
On a diagonal tilted left – Yes I will!

Above: Upright in line with the surname the sender is saying: 'Accept my love'.

Middle: On a diagonal to the right the sender is asking: 'Won't you marry me?'

Below: Upside down in line with the surname the sender is saying: 'I'm engaged'.

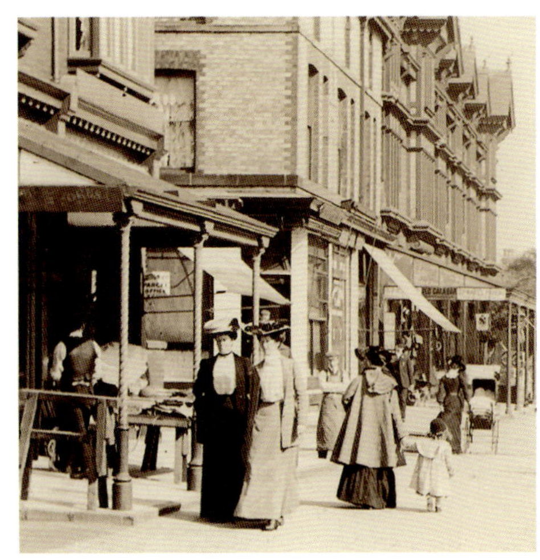

Well-dressed ladies on Heaton Moor
Road in 1907.

Life During the Early 1900s: Fashion and Transport

In European countries, during the period 1900–09, women's fashion continued with the long elegant lines of the 1890s. Broad hats and a full 'Gibson girl' hairstyle were common place. For fashionable men, the long lean and athletic silhouette look persisted. Hair was generally worn short, beards were less pointed than before, and moustaches were often curled.

Almost all commercial deliveries during the early 1900s were by horse and cart, but passengers could travel on the roads by horse-drawn bus, horse-drawn tram or later by electric tram which received its power from overhead cables. Around this time, there was a rapid development of modern transport with many inventions being developed that were making transport faster, more efficient and more comfortable than the horse-drawn vehicles.

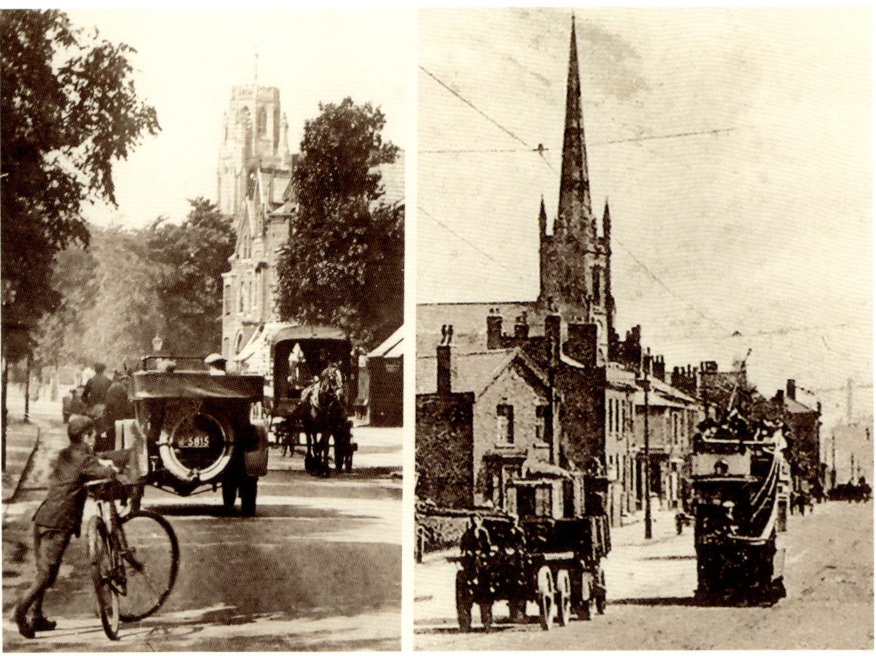

Above left: Vehicles on Heaton Moor Road in 1907 and *above right*: Wellington Road North in 1909.

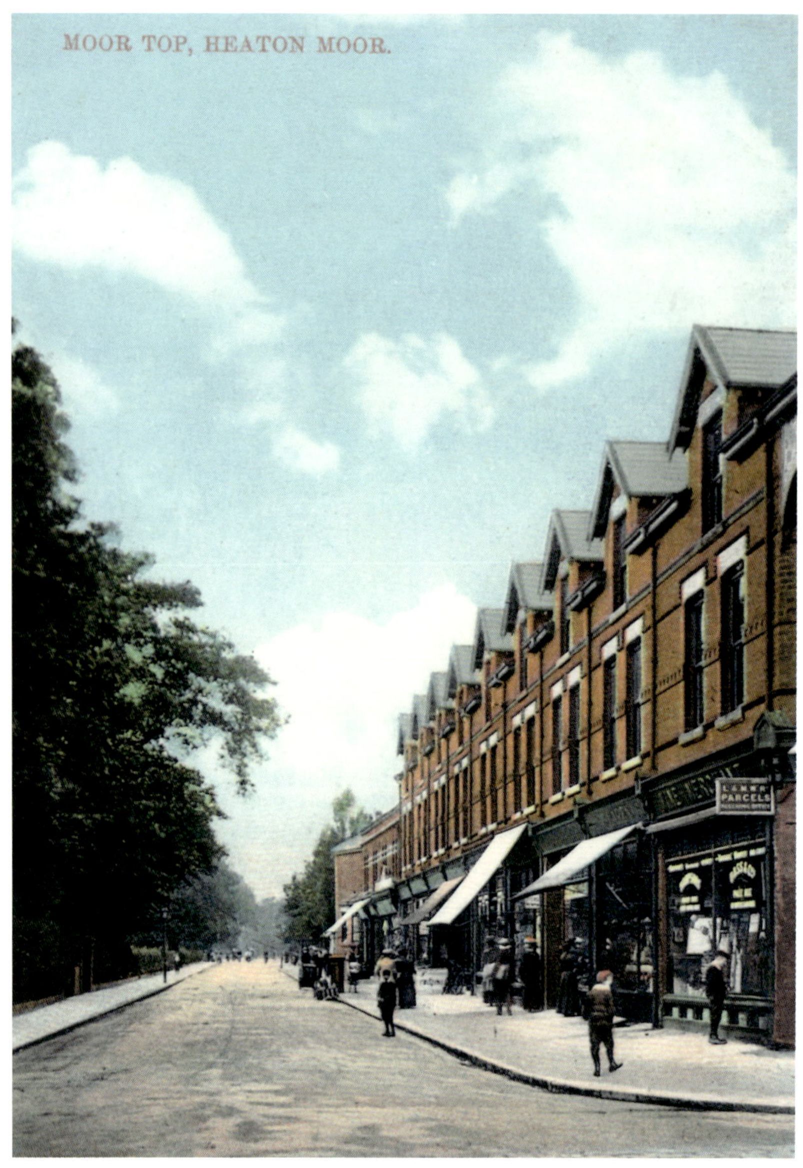

Around Heaton Mersey and Moor Top

Take any left hand turn of Didsbury Road as you pass through Heaton Mersey village and you will journey through an area that was once mainly open field and plough land eventually arriving at Moor Top, an area once known as Owler Nook.

The name certainly gives a bit of romantic mystery to the area. 'Nook', of course, is a term still used today to describe a secret corner or place of seclusion. 'Owler', however, is an old name for a smuggler, or dealer in contraband. It is also an archaic term for an illegal dealer in sheep which could be relevant to the rural nature of the area at that time. Sheep smuggling was a common practice in old England and was outlawed as early as 1367. The illegal wool trade between England and France resulted in sheep being moved to ports where they, or their wool, would be loaded onto 'owling boats'. In rural areas, like the Heatons, the animals would have been moved secretly under the cover of darkness (traditionally the time of the owl).

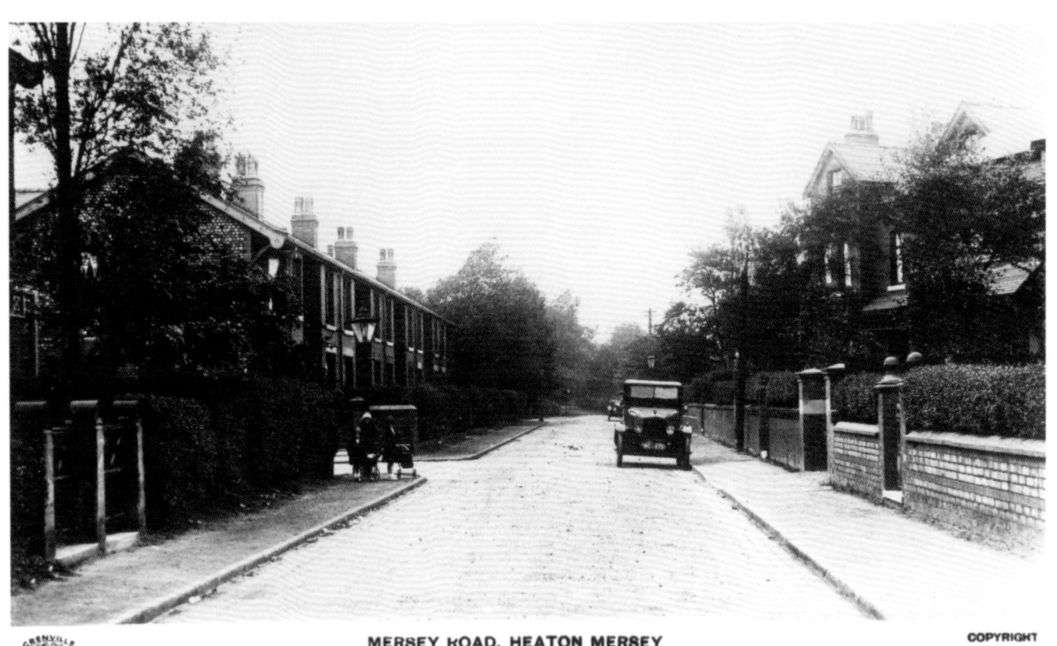

Mersey Road, 1909 and 1930s

Mersey Road has always been a popular residential road in the Heatons and is characterised by its wide variety of houses from large Victorian mansions to small terraces, all within its half-mile length. Many of the houses were built by local builder, Joseph Padmore, who acquired strips of land and constructed the terraces and some of the larger houses around the turn of the nineteenth century.

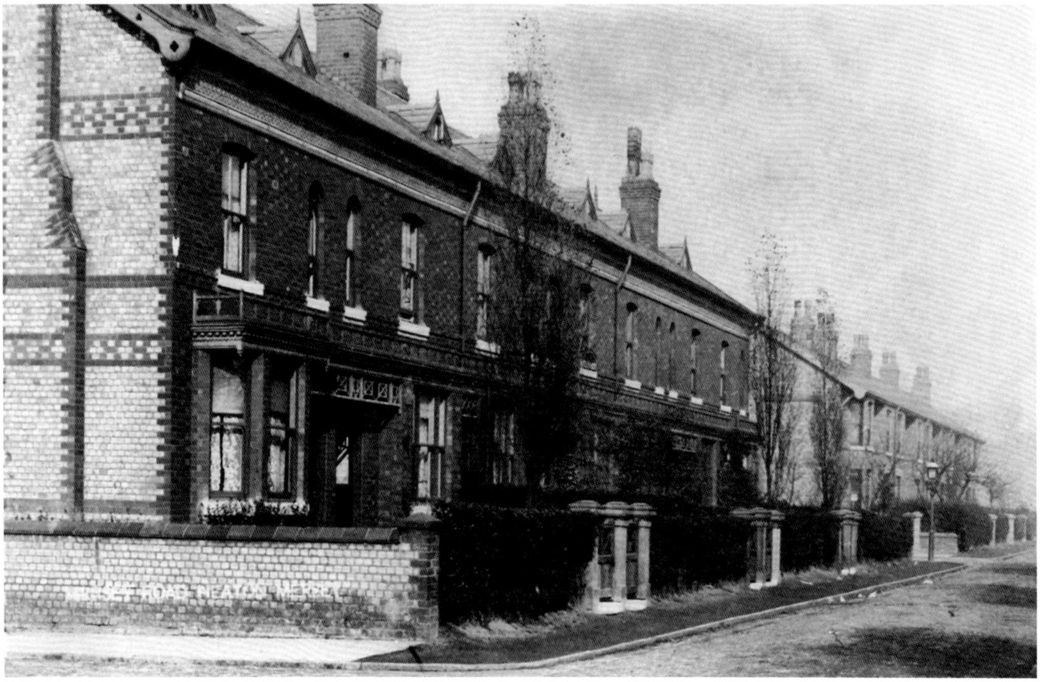

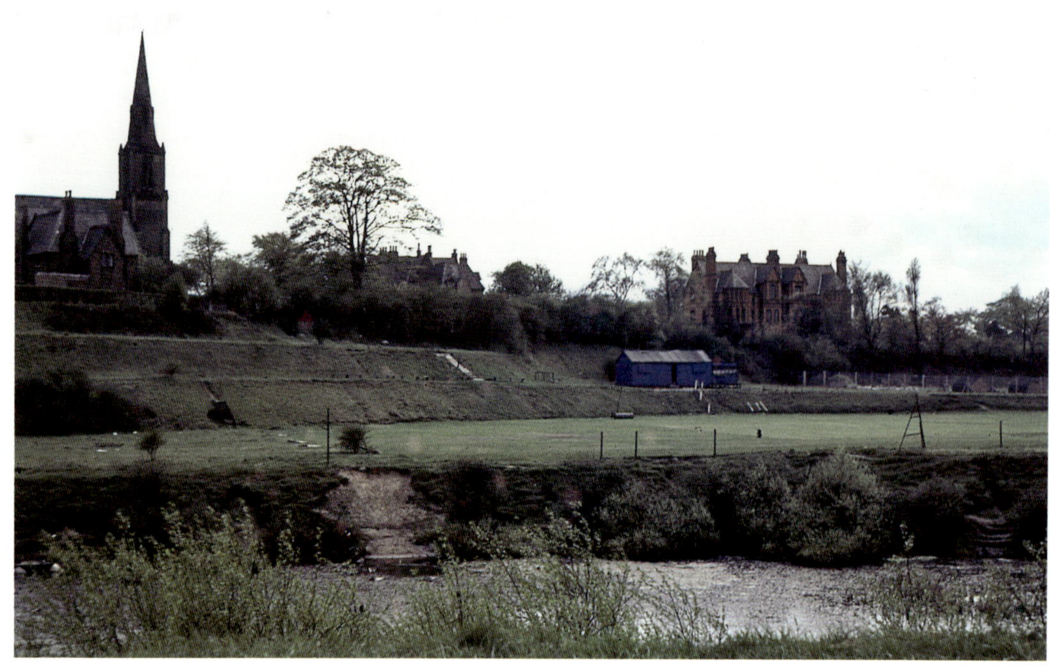

New Beech Road, 1950s and 1920s

New Beech Road is a quiet path that runs between Mersey Road and Harwood Road and, when not screened by trees and other foliage, provides an elevated view across the sports ground to Manchester and The Pennines. Residents in the early part of the century would have looked down on Peter Bailey's Brickworks, which provided most of the bricks for the construction of housing and shops in the local area. The tramlines, for transporting clay across the site, can be clearly seen in the lower picture.

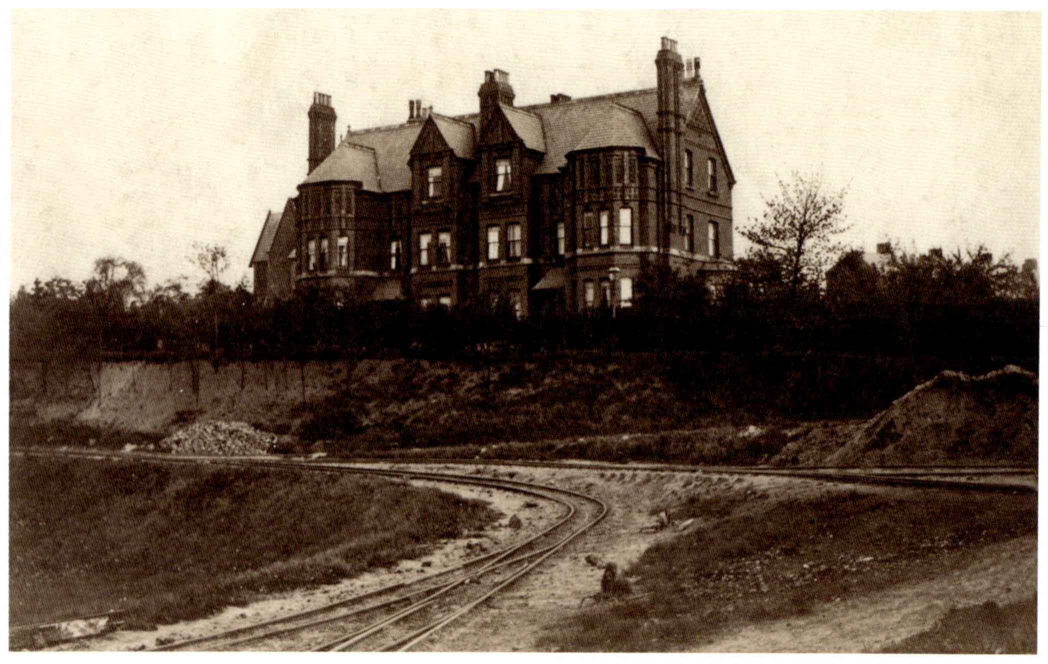

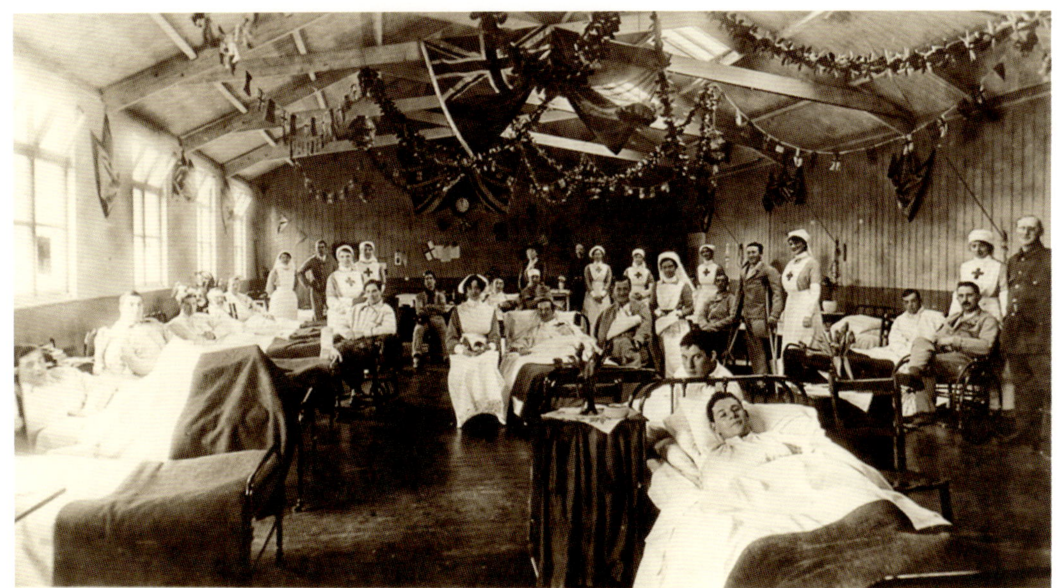

Heaton Mersey Red Cross Hospital (No. 2 Ward).

Red Cross Hospital Cavendish Road, 1916 and 1918

The Red Cross Hospital on Cavendish Road helped many servicemen from the First World War recover from the physical and mental effects of the horrors of War. Walter Brownsword, a local teacher, helped to run the organisation and was a great believer in recreational activities as a means of getting the men back to full fitness. He raised money from the local community to buy billiard tables, library books and a piano. The hospital was operational from December 1914 to January 1919.

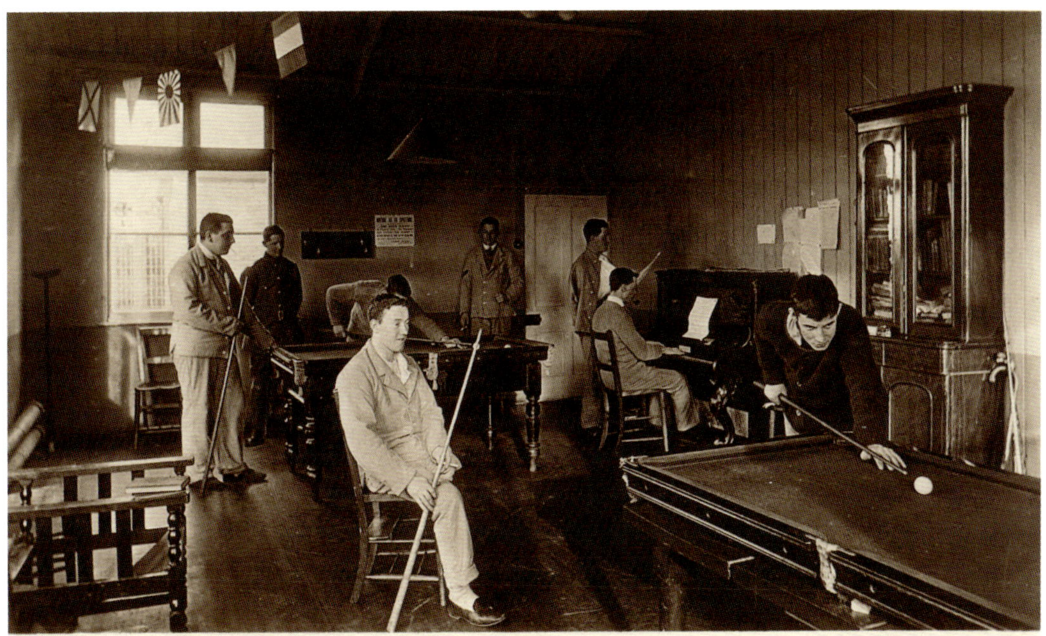

Heaton Mersey Red Cross Hospital (Recreation Room).

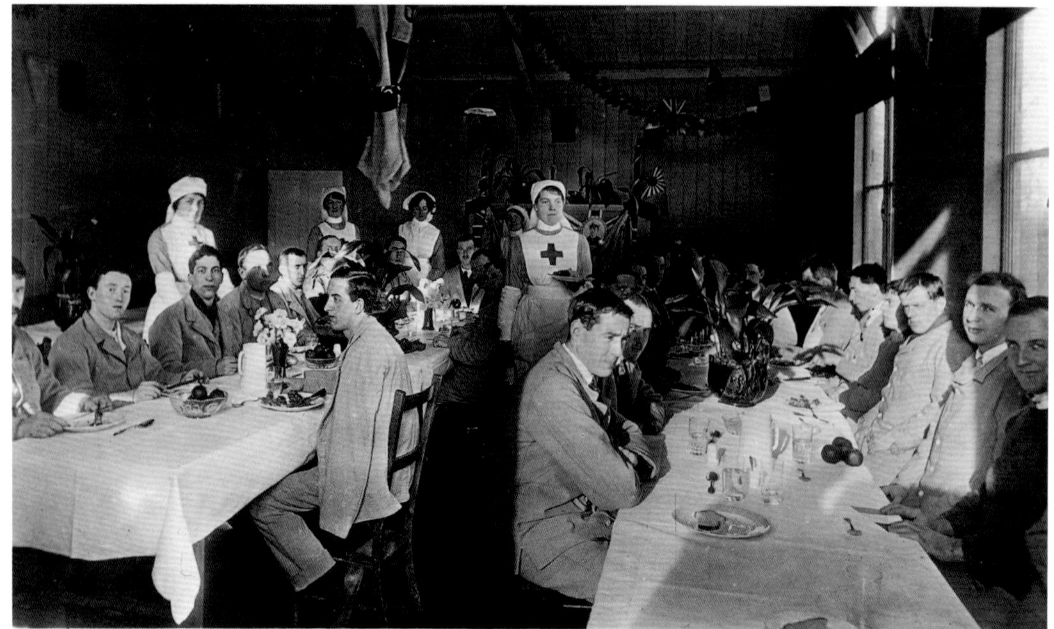

Heaton Mersey Red Cross Hospital (Dining Room).

Copyright Photo. by
T. Everitt Innes, Stockport.

Red Cross Hospital, Cavendish Road, 1918

Two more cards showing life in and around the Red Cross Hospital on Cavendish Road. The haunted look on their faces, however, tells a story all of its own. The care of the VAD nurses, and the opportunity to recuperate in the peaceful grounds, must have come as a welcome relief to the sick and injured ferried back from the horrors of the trenches. The old Methodist Church building can be seen in the background on the right of the picture.

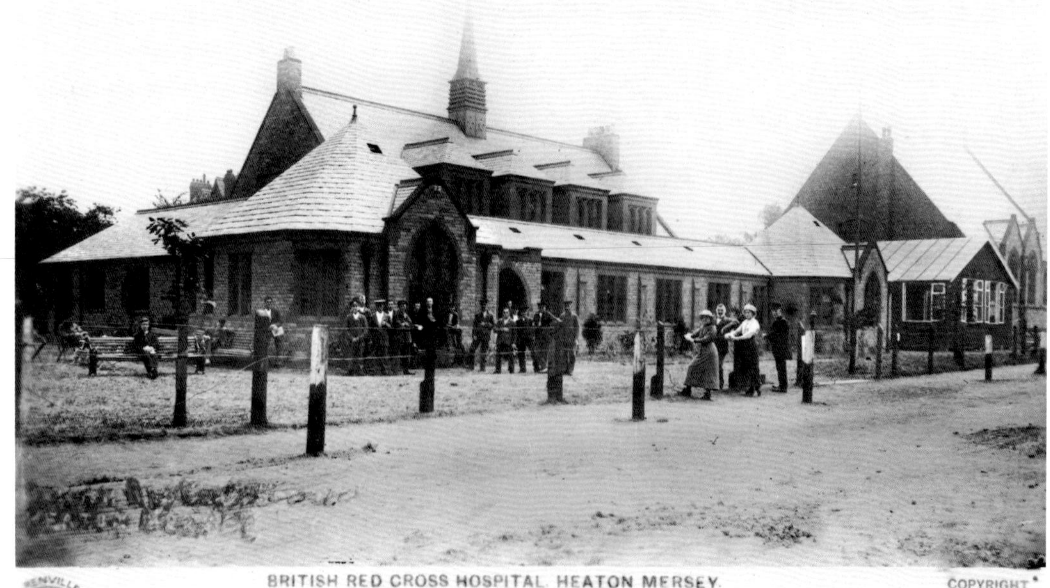

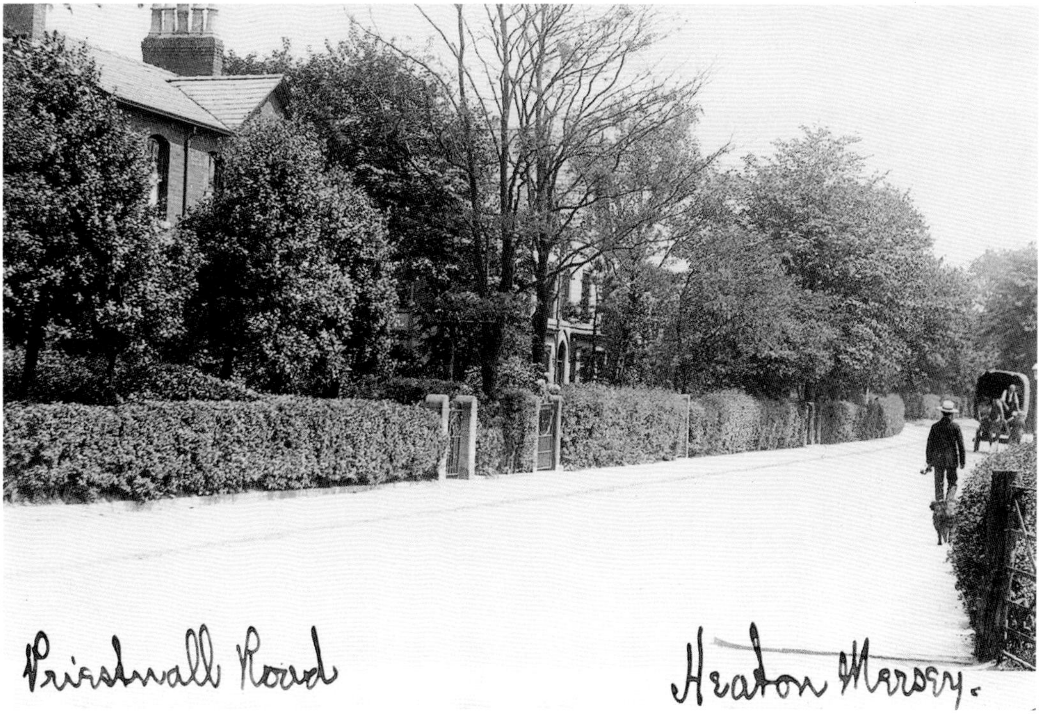

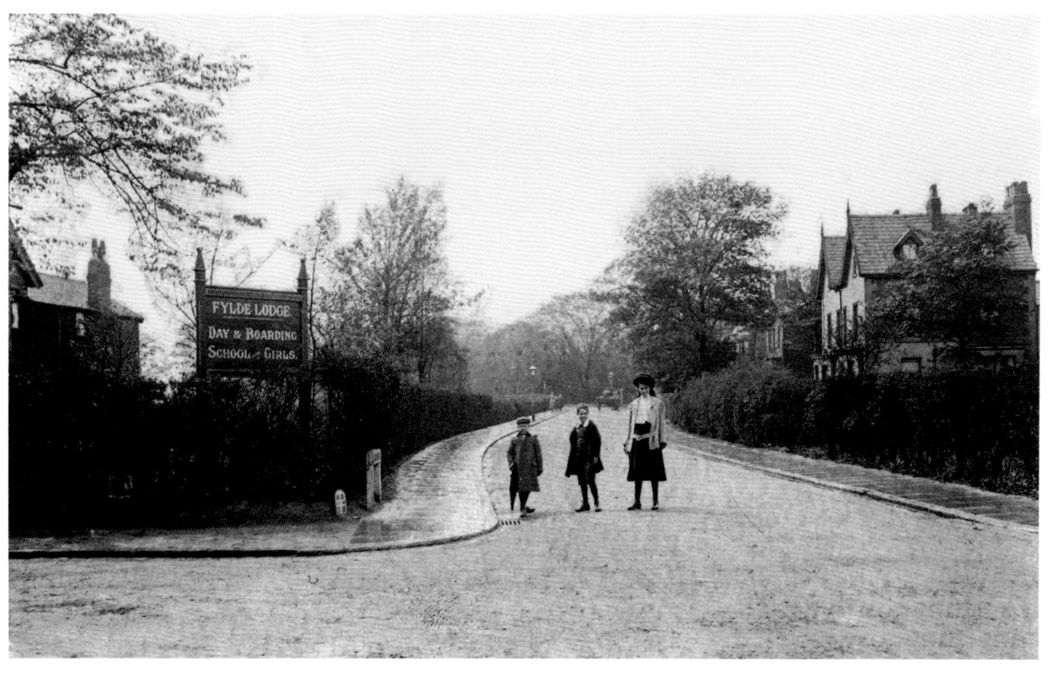

Priestnall Road, 1905 and 1907
At the turn of the nineteenth century, Priestnall Road would have been a country lane with few houses spoiling the views across open fields. The main building at its eastern end would have been Fylde Lodge School, and a walk westward would take you a quarter of a mile to the top of Mersey Road and the entrance to Priestnall Hey and Heaton Mersey Common.

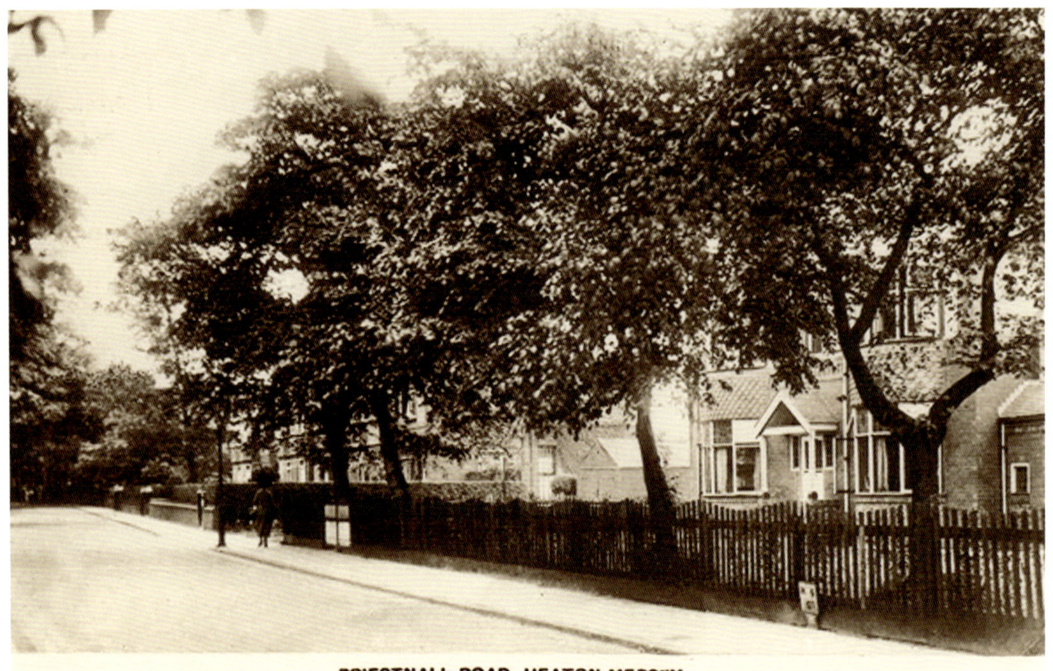

Priestnall Road, 1930s

By the 1930s, Priestnall Road was developing into a fashionable residential area with a number of 'modern' houses sitting side by side with the established Edwardian and Victorian villas. The road surface had been improved and the borders of properties firmly established. Well-kept hedges, gates and garden walls replaced the rural hedgerows of the earlier part on the century.

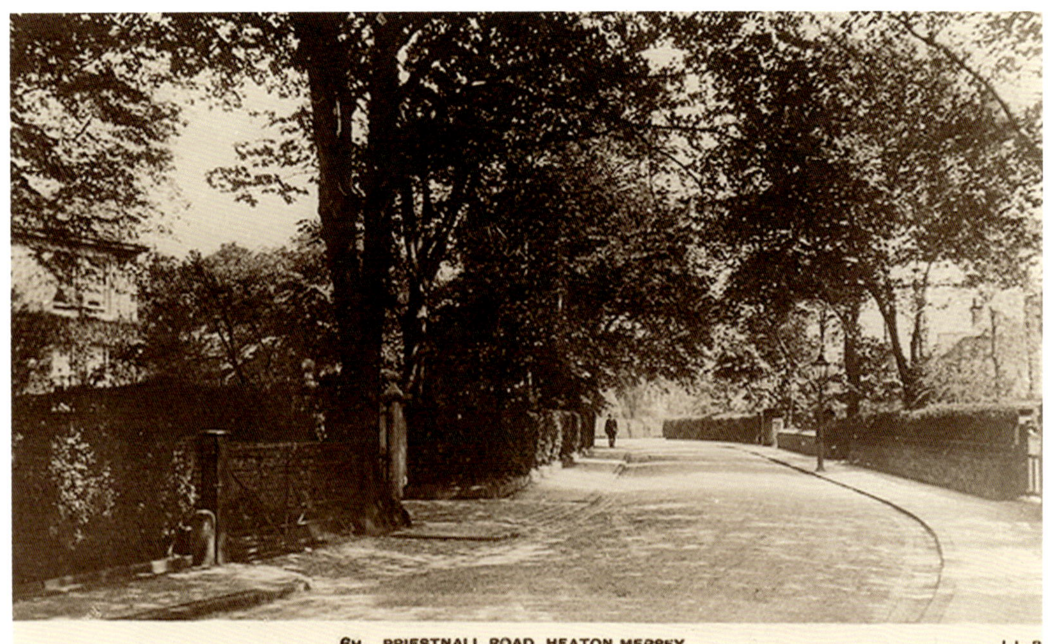

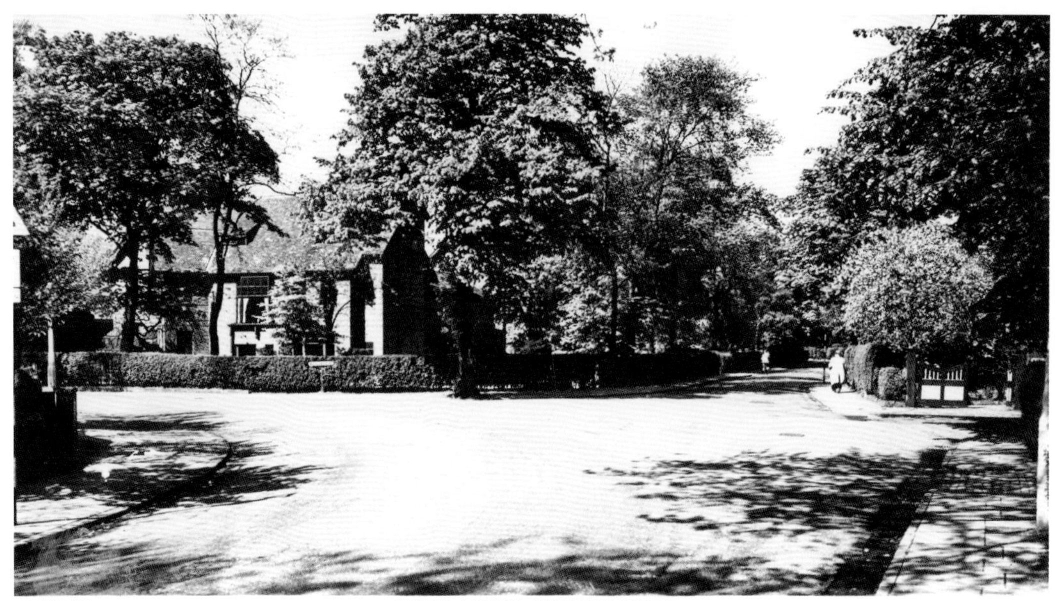

Fylde Lodge, 1904 and 1957

Fylde Lodge was originally a private house, which was converted into a school in 1893 and run by the Misses Sales for the daughters of wealthy Heatonians. The curriculum was very broad and, apart from a range of academic subjects, included singing, drawing, needlework and, at an extra cost, swimming, solo singing and elocution. In 1966, the school moved to new premises on Priestnall Road and, after educational reorganisation in Stockport, eventually became Priestnall School.

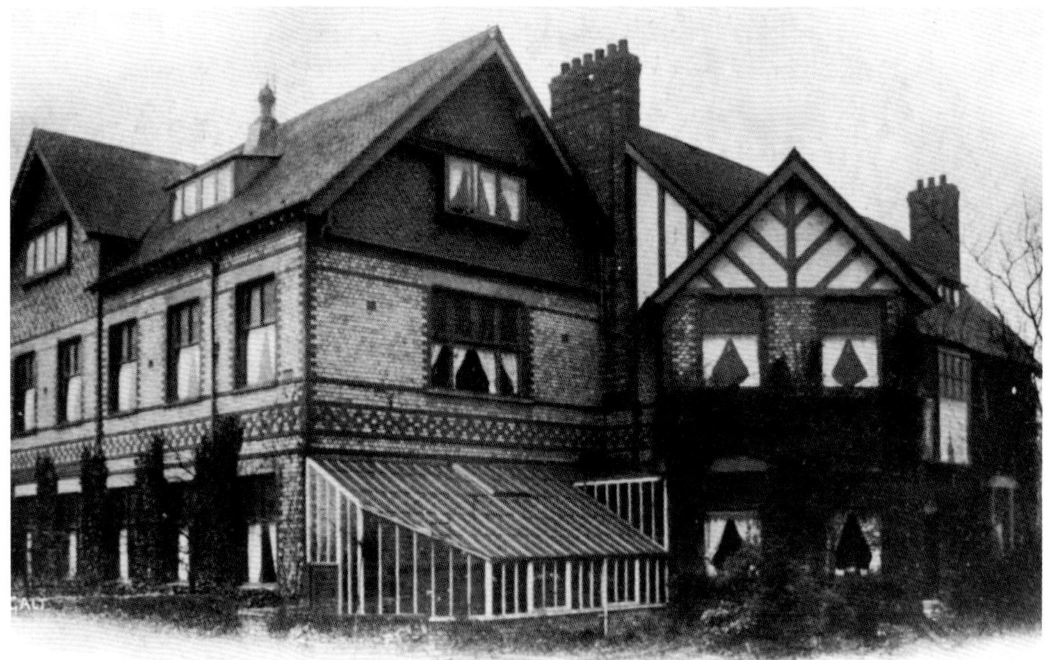

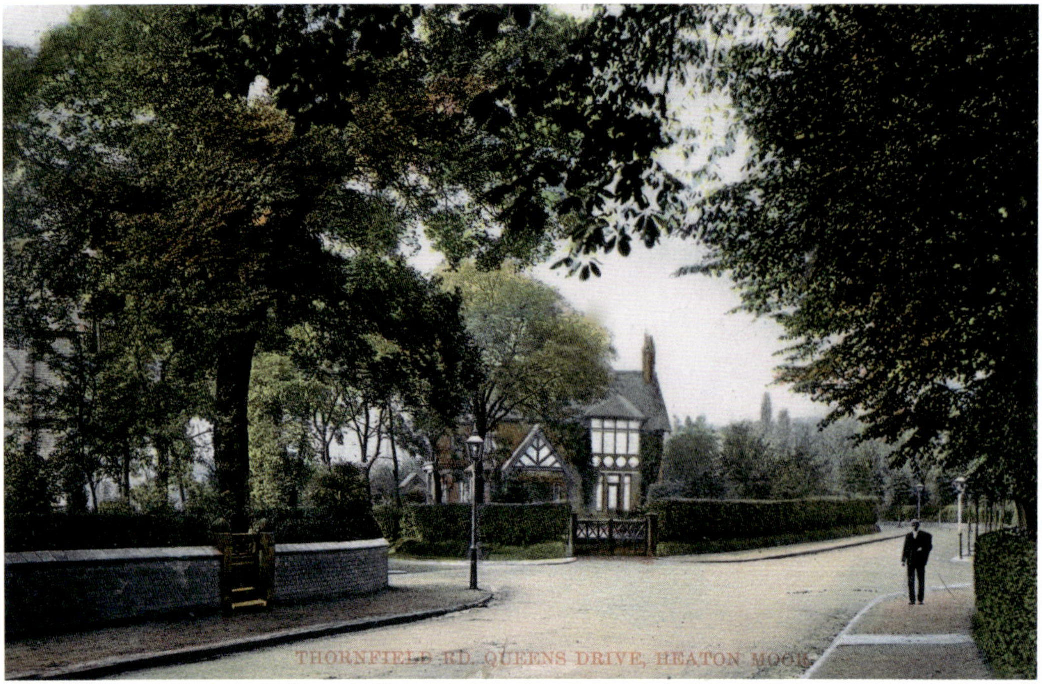

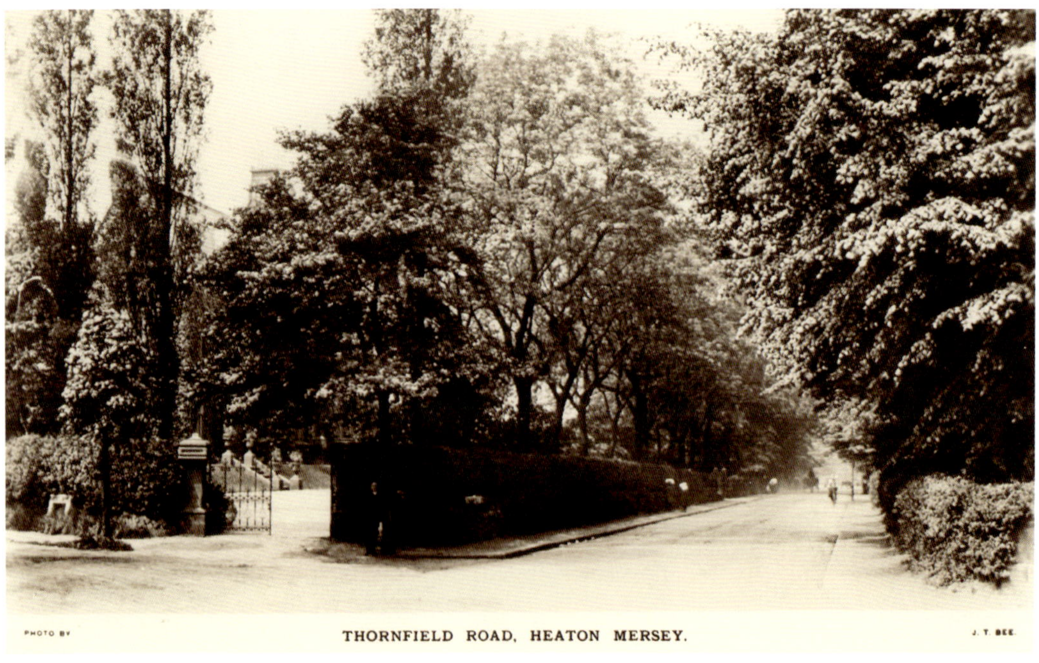

Thornfield Road, 1903 and 1920s

'Thornfield' was the name given to a large house on Didsbury Road built by a local brass founder, Matthew Curtis. He lived there until his death in 1887, and although his family continued to live in the house, it was eventually demolished in the mid-1930s. The family name lives on, however, in the names of two local roads (the other being Curtis Road at the junction with Thornfield Road near Heaton Moor Park entrance).

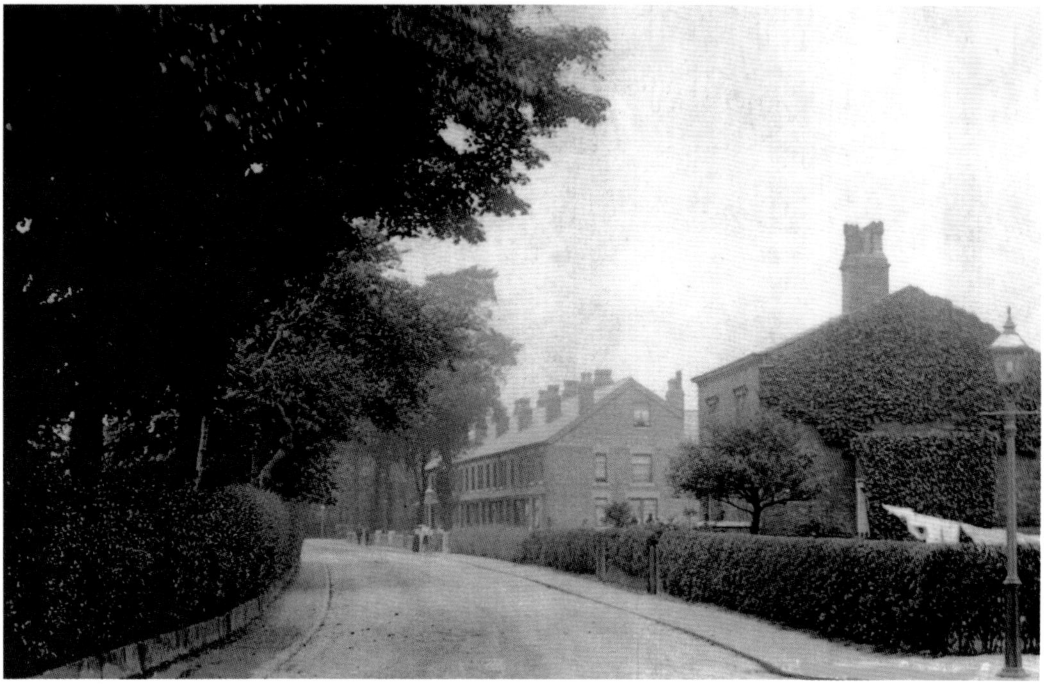

Bank Hall Road and Moorside Road, 1907
At one time, Bank Hall Road was the main road linking Didsbury Road to Heaton Moor
Road, but the building of Moorside Road resulted in a more direct route to the Heatons and
established Moor Top as an important shopping area in its own right. The sweep of Bank Hall
Road formed the northern boundary to Barnes Industrial School that stood on Didsbury Road.

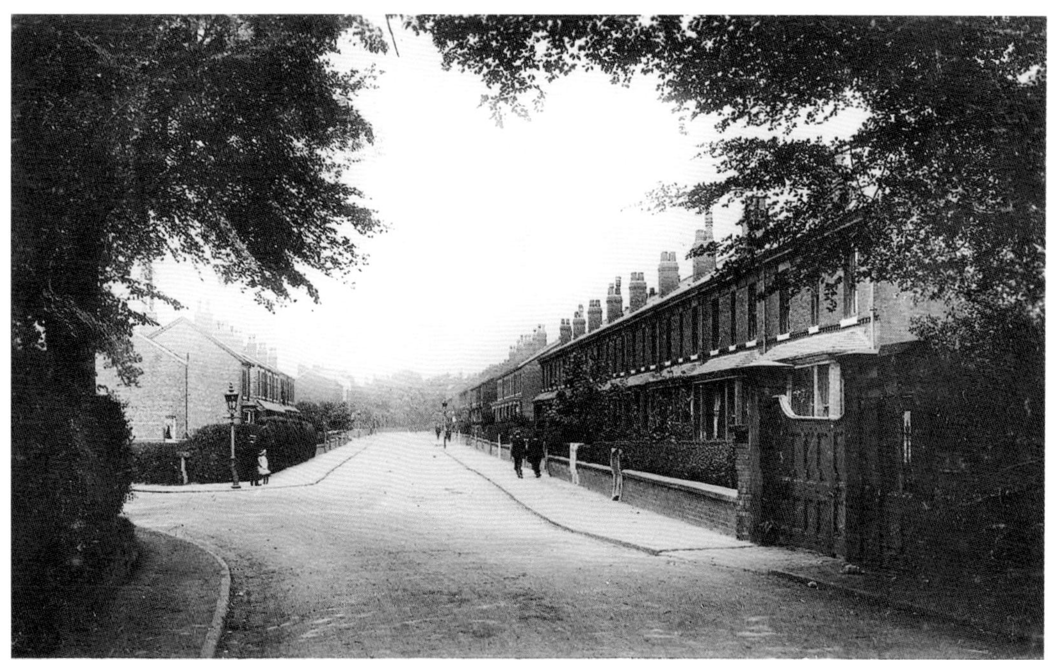

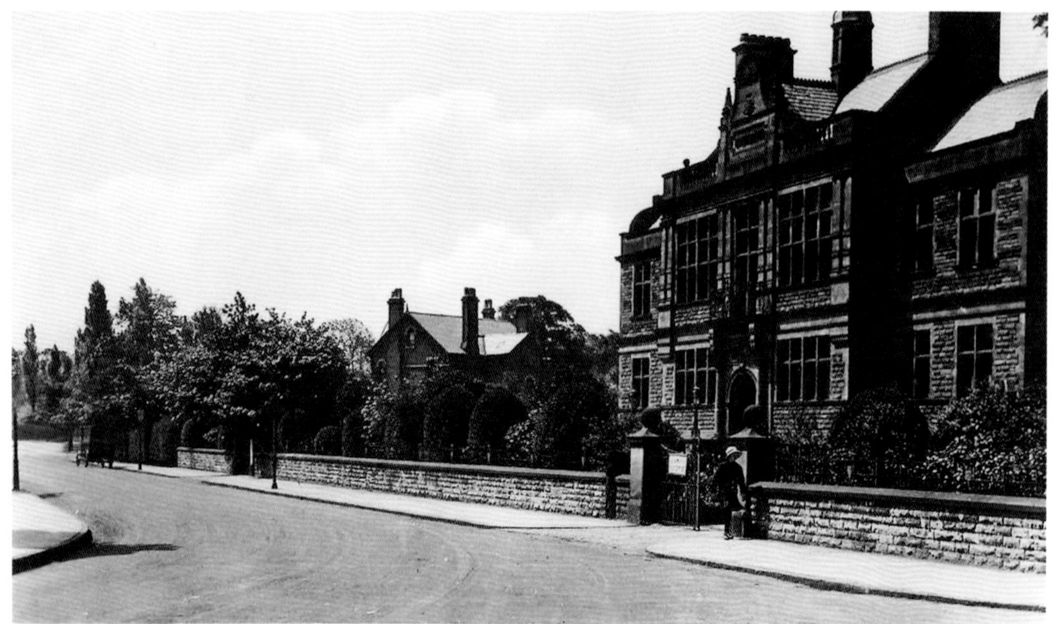

Thornfield Road Council Offices, 1906 and 1944
The old Heaton Moor Council Office Buildings on Thornfield Road have changed little over the years. The building was originally the premises of Heaton Norris Urban District Council but in its later years was home to Heaton Moor Infants School. At one time, it also hosted Cellars Youth Centre, providing a range of activities for young people in the area.

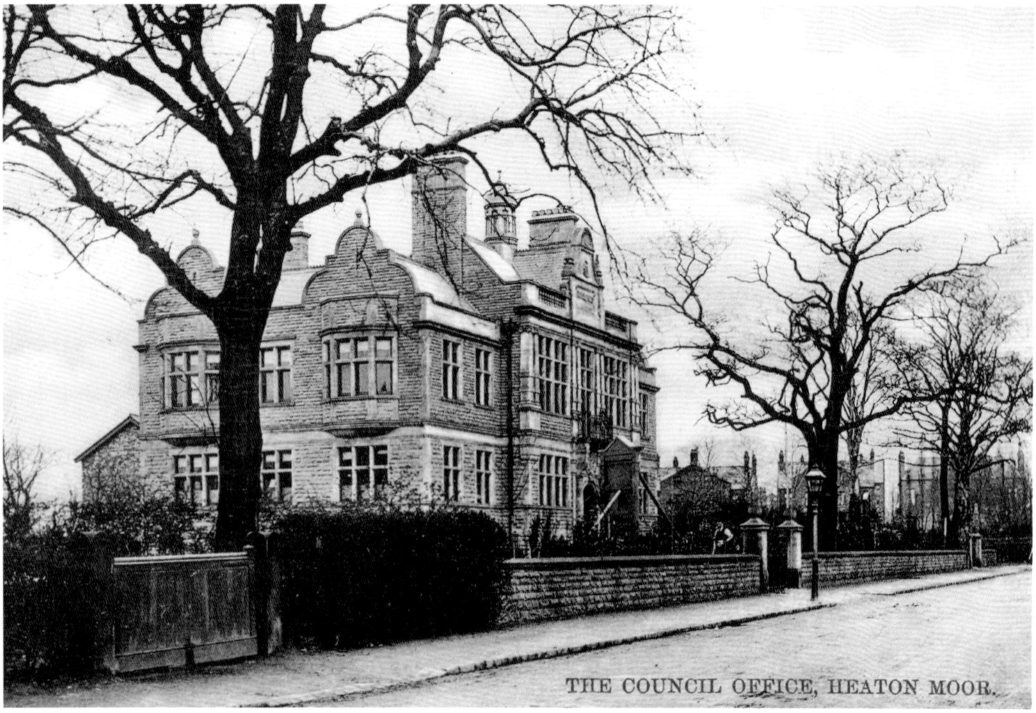

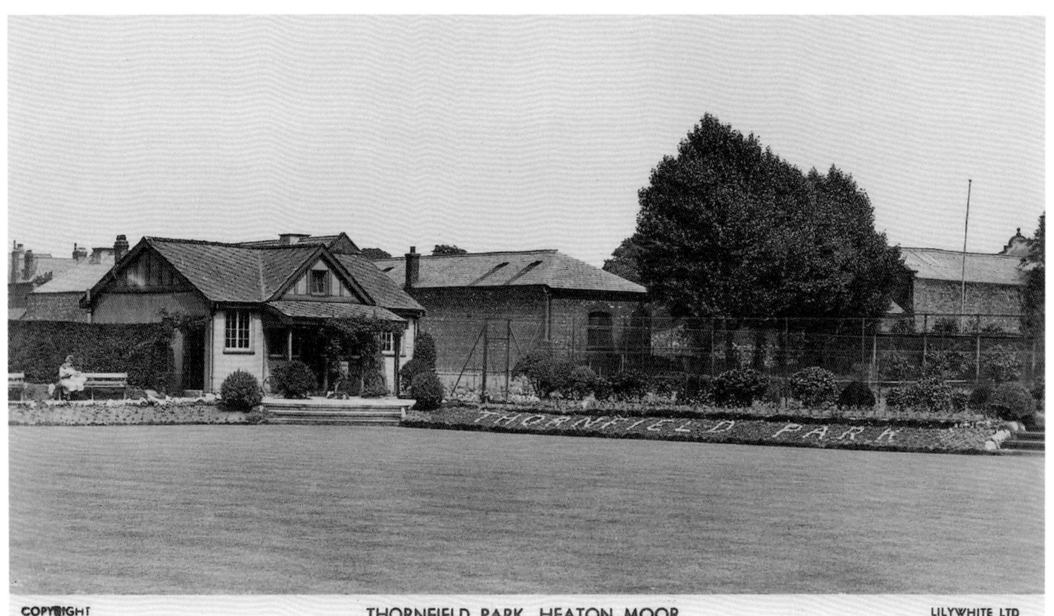

Ventnor Road, 1905, and Thornfield Park, 1930s

The residents of Ventnor Road, and the other nearby terraces of red brick houses, would have been well served by Thornfield Park. The park was not open at the time of the Ventnor Road photograph but was formally opened to the public on 1 June 1913, the Heatons Recreational Grounds Committee having seen the importance of establishing a second haven of green space in their semi-rural community. A sum of £664 was obtained to landscape the grounds, lay down tennis courts and a bowling green and construct a bowling pavilion, all of which still survive to be enjoyed today.

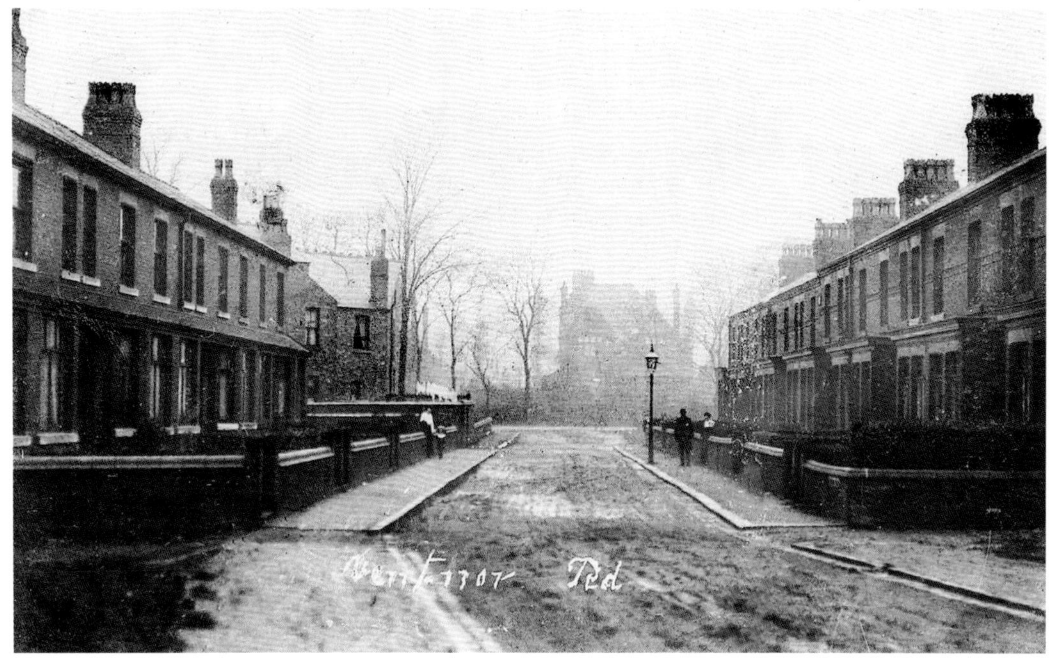

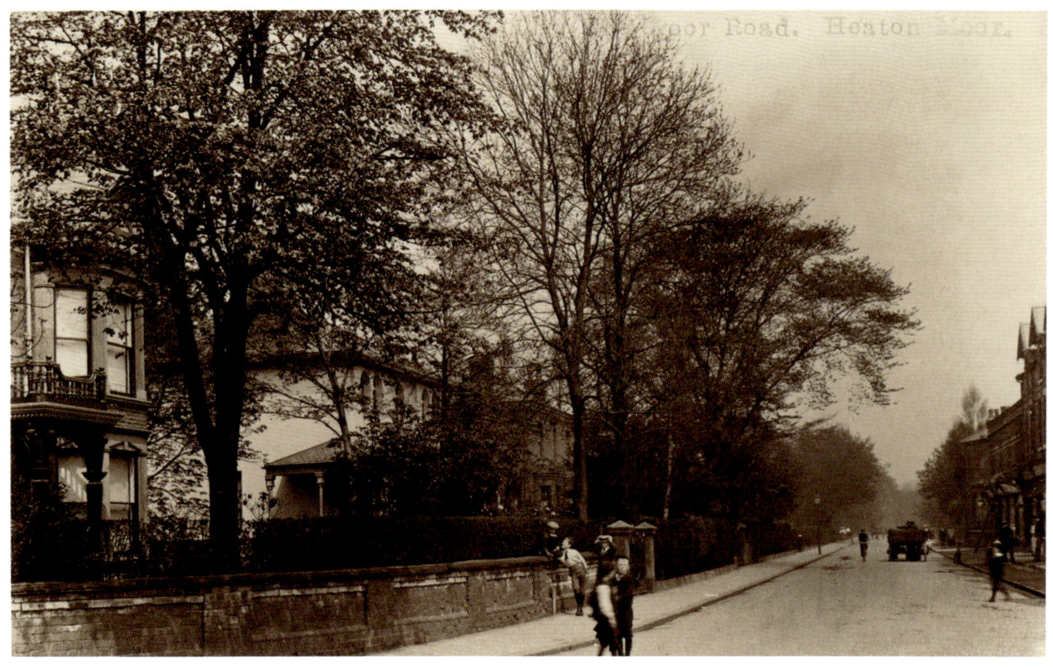

Moor Top, 1909 and 1910

These two cards show how much this corner of the Heatons has changed since the 1900s. The three fine houses in the top card are Dunbar, Berne Cot and Beech House. The top of Berne Cot (built in Colonial style by a member of the Bengal Lancers) is still visible today above the modern shop frontages. In the picture below, the Victorian houses in the centre have undergone a similar transformation with their frontages also given over to modern development.

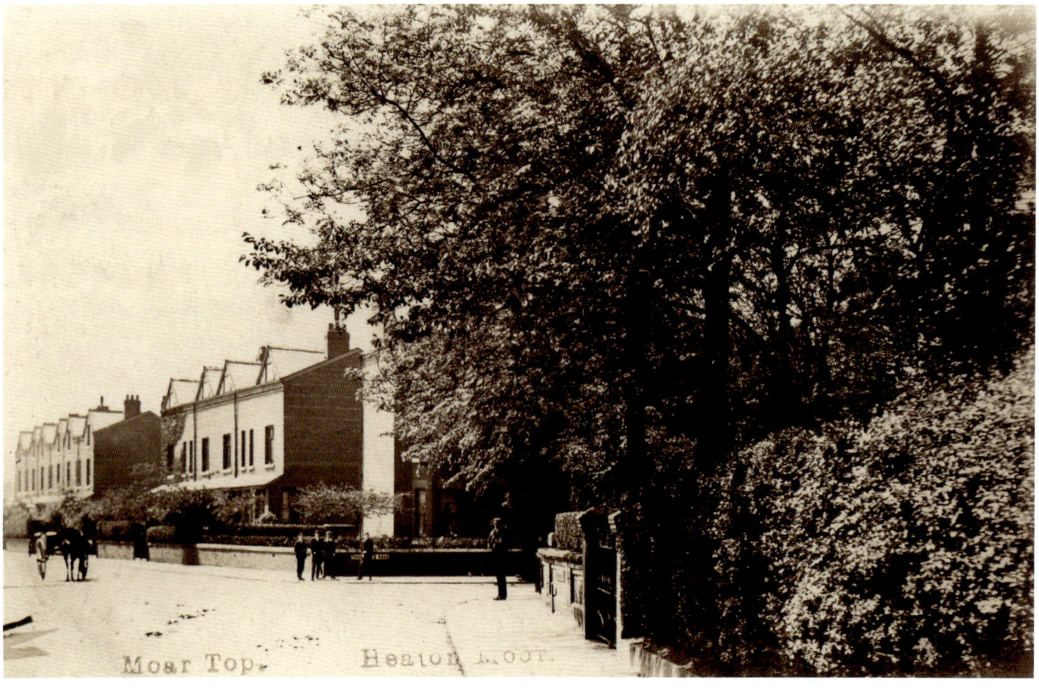

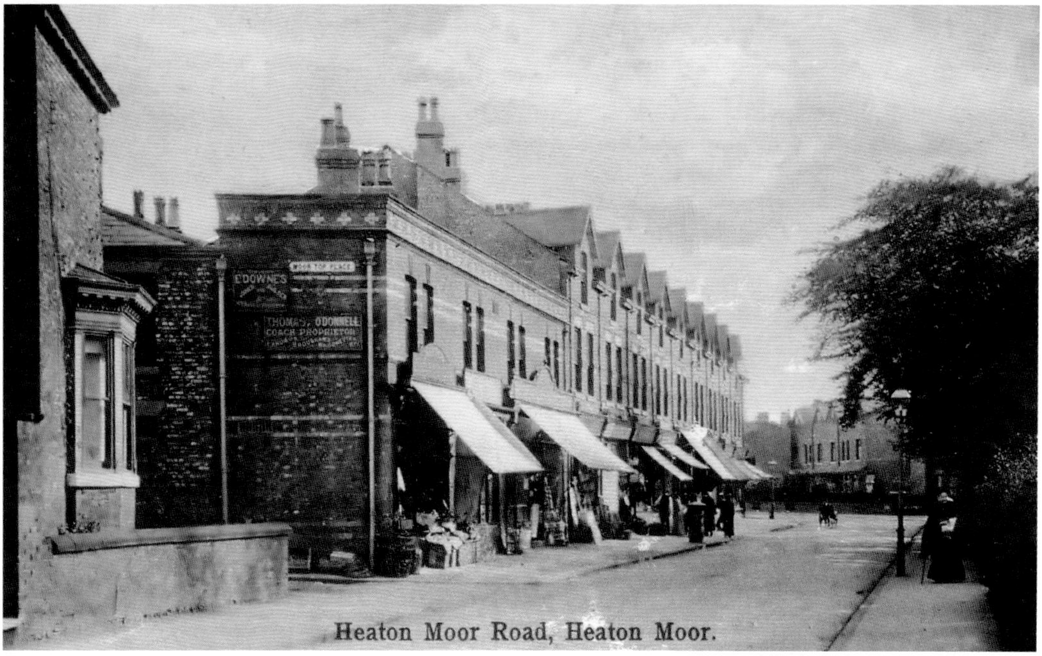

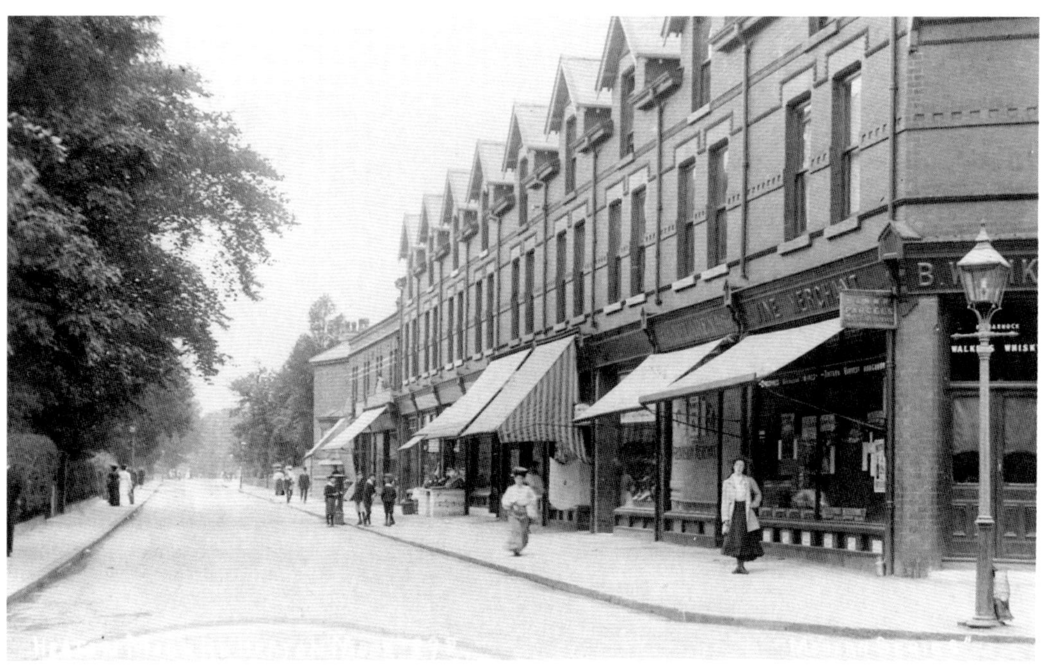

Moor Top Shops, 1906 and 1907

The area formally known as Owler Nook developed its own character with the first shops appearing around 1872. They provided a good range of services and included a grocer's, wine merchant's, baker's, butcher's and a stationary and newspaper shop. The shop on the corner, in the picture below, also offered a parcels service for the LNWR. The boys in the centre are congregating around a postbox, possibly outside the post office, before it relocated to nearby Moorside Road.

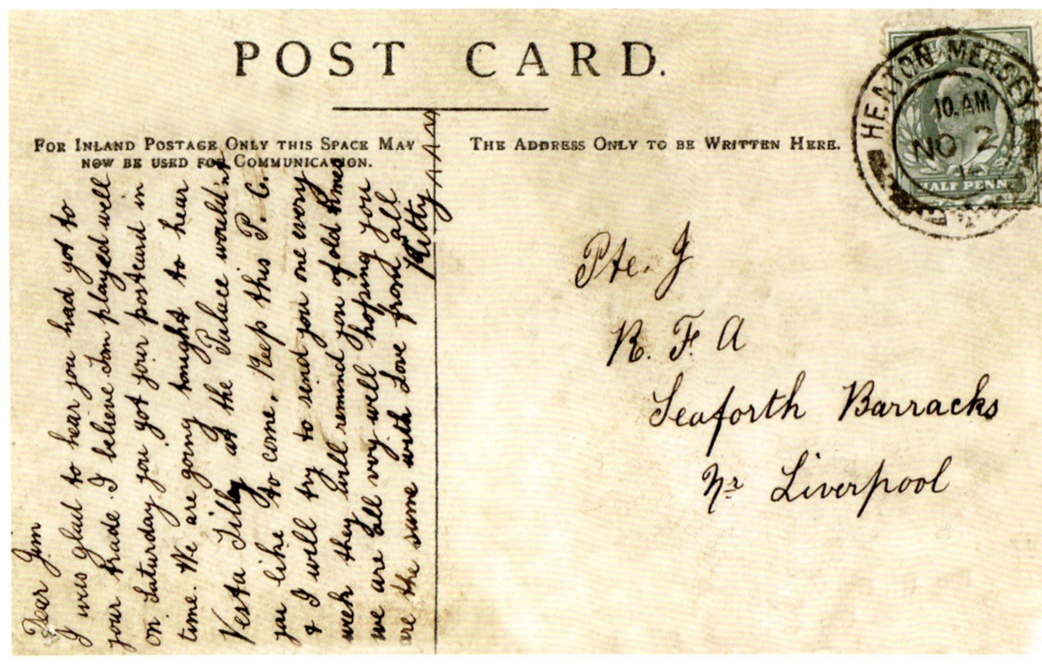

A postcard sent from Kitty to Jim on 2 November 1914.

Entertainment: Vesta Tilley

Matilda Alice Powles, 13 May 1864–16 September 1952, was an English music hall performer, male impersonator and singer who was better known as Vesta Tilley. Her father, Harry Ball, was a comedy actor and music hall chairman who encouraged his daughter to appear on stage before the age of four. Vesta played the principal boy in many pantomimes before taking on the role of a male impersonator. The communication on the postcard shows that Kitty is going to attend the Palace Theatre, Manchester, to see Vesta Tilley. The postmark on the stamp shows a date of 2 November 1914. Vesta visited the Palace Theatre during the Autumn/Winter period of 1914 not only to perform but also to act as a music hall recruiter for the Army.

The comment on the postcard reads, 'We are going tonight to hear Vesta Tilley at the Palace wouldn't you like to come.'

Pte. J

R. F. A

Seaforth Barracks

Nr Liverpool

It is quite ironic that Kitty was sending this card to Jim to invite him to the show: 'wouldn't you like to come'. He was already a private in the Royal Field Artillery based at Seaforth Barracks in Liverpool. Vesta Tilley would probably have been recruiting men for the army during the show. Seaforth Barracks was a major recruiting centre for Liverpool troops during WW1 covering the Bootle, Litherland, Seaforth and Waterloo areas.

Entertainment: Vesta Tilley Continued

The First World War had started so men were required to sign up to take the 'Kings Shilling'. Vesta, and many other performers around the country, would use the interval time during shows to encourage men to sign up for the war as conscription was not introduced until 1916. She would walk down the theatre aisle, draped in a Union Jack, during the interval, encouraging men to follow her onto the stage where the recruiting officers were waiting for them. It was probably an emotive time especially with her singing songs such as 'We Don't Want To Lose You But We Think You Ought To go' and 'In Dear Old England's Name'.

She married Sir Walter Frece (sometimes spelt Freece), a music hall impresario who had founded a chain of music halls. He was also the composer of many of her songs. However, he wanted to become a Member of Parliament and Vesta's profession, at that time, was not seen as respectable. He gained a seat and became a Conservative Member of Parliament for Ashton-under-Lyne, Lancashire, in a by-election in 1920, and he regained this seat at the general election in 1922. His majority was only 239 in 1923, so he decided to find a safer seat for the 1924 general election where he became an MP for Blackpool. Vesta retired in 1920, having spent fifty-two years performing on stage. Her farewell tour took one year between 1919 and 1920 with her final performance at the Coliseum Theatre in London at the age of fifty-six years. The proceeds of this one-year tour went to the charities that she supported and was involved with.

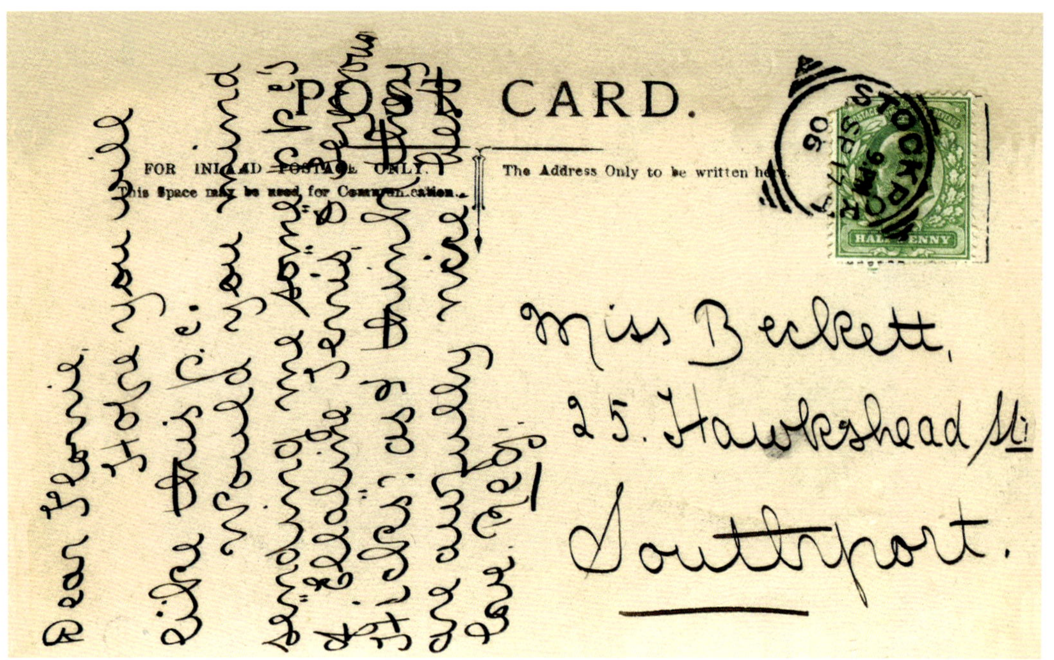

The postcard was sent on 6 September 1906. Reg asks Florrie: 'Would you mind sending me some portrait picture cards (p.p.c.'s) of Ellaline Terriss and Seymour Hicks as I think they are awfully nice'.

Entertainment: Seymour Hicks and Ellaline Terriss

Seymour Hicks (1871–1949) was a famous British actor who made his stage debut at the age of sixteen and made his last film appearance in the year of his death 1949. During his early career, he was a music hall performer, playwright and actor appearing on stage relentlessly, often with his wife Ellaline Terriss (1893–1949). He later turned his skills to the screen becoming a screenwriter, producer and actor manager appearing in three of the early silent films. Hicks decided to produce his own films in 1923, and during his first film, 'Always Tell Your Wife', which had been one of his stage plays, he fired the director and hired a young unknown director by the name of Alfred Hitchcock. In 1905, he commissioned the building of the Aldwych Theatre and, in 1906, the Hick Theatre, both from the wealth he had accrued during the years 1887–1904. The Hick Theatre later became the Globe Theatre (1909) and finally the Gielgud Theatre (1994). He was knighted in 1934, Sir Edward Seymour Hicks, for his services to stage and film.

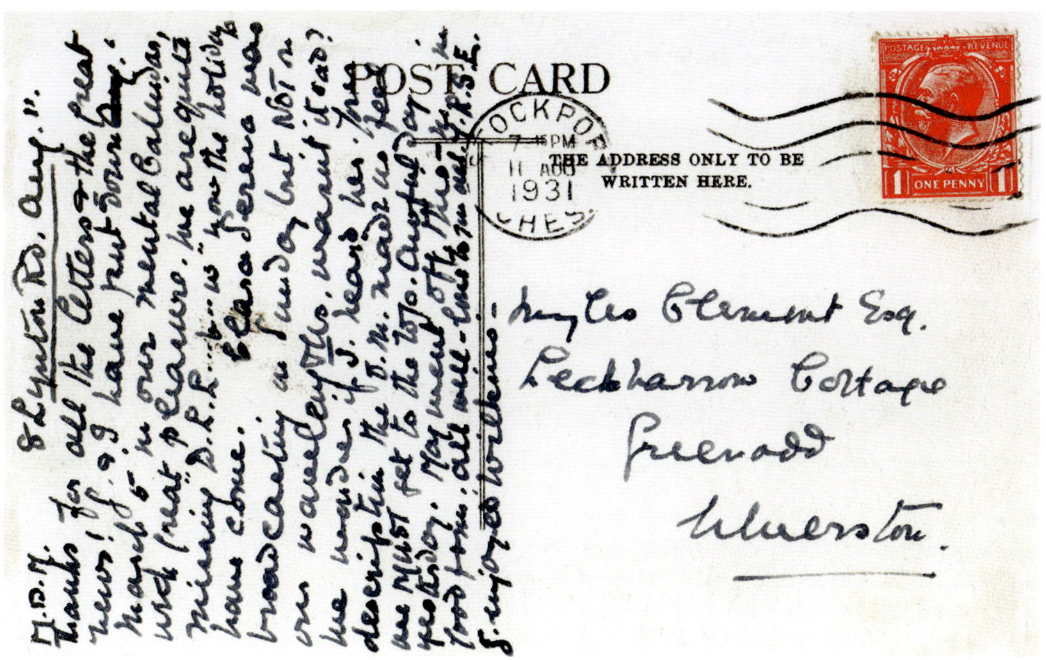

The postcard was sent on 11 August 1931.

Entertainment: Clara Serena

The comment refers to Clara Serena, 1890–1972, who was a singer, contralto and daughter of Lutheran parents, Herman Franz Kleinschmidt and Ida Wilhelmine Mathilde. Clara was registered as Clara Serena Hulda. Her parents, who had migrated from the German free city of Bremen in 1836 to Australia, encouraged Clara with her musical skills. She won a scholarship in 1908 to the Royal College of Music in London and qualified in 1911 with a diploma. She took the name of Clara Serena in 1913. Clara returned to Australia at the outbreak of the First World War returning again to London in 1922 to make her operatic debut. Her linguistic ability enabled her to sing fluently in many languages. She spent her later years back in Australia and died in 1972, at the age of eighty-two at Aldersgate village, Felixstow, South Australia.

The comment on the postcard reads: 'Clara Serena was broadcasting on Sunday but NOT on our wavelengths, wasn't it sad? We wonder if J heard this'.

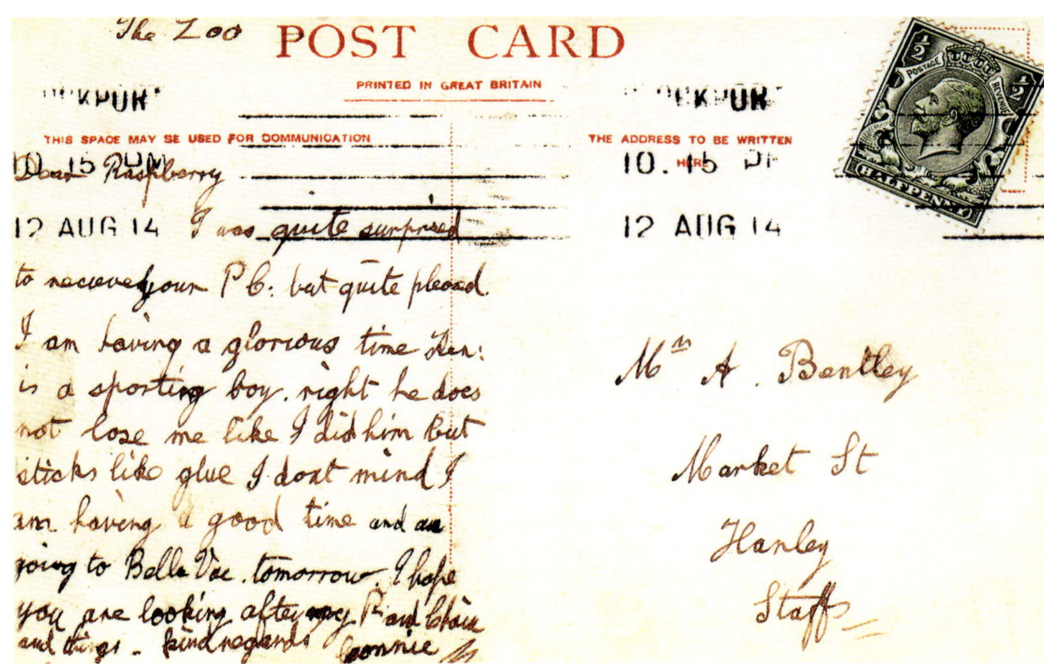

The postcard was sent on 12 August 1914.

Entertainment: Belle Vue

Belle Vue Zoological Gardens operated in Manchester for 145 years opening in 1836 and finally closing in 1981. During its heyday, the zoo, amusement park and annual circus would receive two million visitors annually. The complex was constructed using bricks from Bailey's Brick Works in Heaton Mersey, and as a publicity stunt, elephants were used to transport the loads to the construction site in Longsight. Nowadays there are very few remains to suggest that Manchester's 'Showground of the World' ever existed.

The message reads, 'am having a good time and am going to Belle Vue tomorrow.' It mentions 'The Zoo' written at the top of the card.

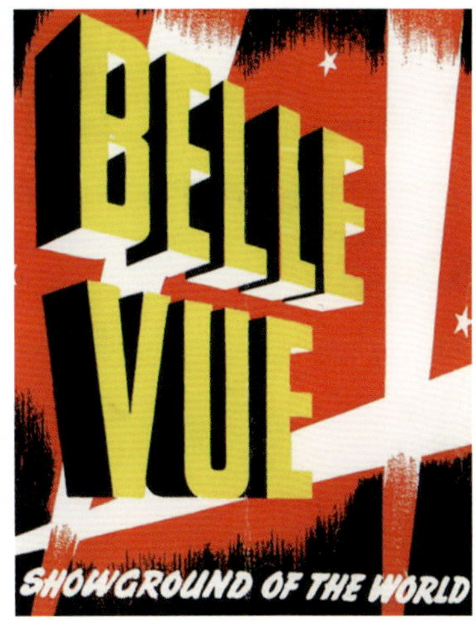

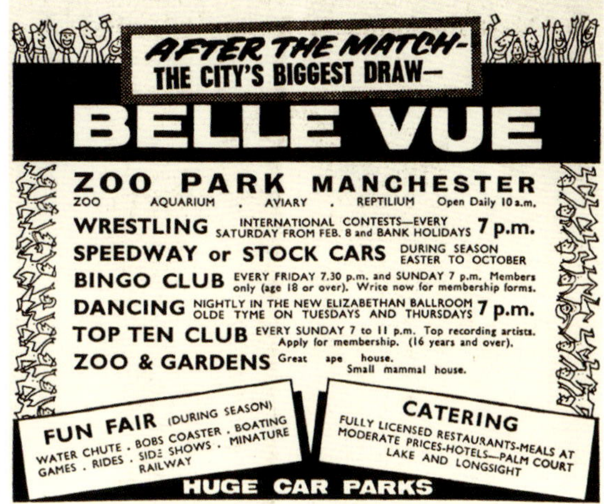

The 1947 Belle Vue Guide.   A later Belle Vue advertisement.

Entertainment: Belle Vue Continued

In the 1878 Guide to the Zoological Gardens, it states that the gardens will be open every day with a full programme of attractions. The pleasure grounds were extensive covering over fifty acres that included a museum of natural history, large lakes with pleasure boats and steamers. The Great Hall was decorated by Danson and Sons of London and included galleries and refreshment rooms, affording covered space for 4000 visitors. In 1878, a new maze had been specially designed and modelled from Hampton Court in London. The Belle Vue Band played every day throughout the summer and on Monday, Wednesday and Saturday during the winter.

The actual advertisement for the refreshment rooms stated:

'Capable of accommodating Thousands at one time with Tea, Wines, Spirits, Ale, Porter, Cakes, Gingerbeer, Salads, &c., adjoin the Great Hall and visitors are furnished with Hot Water for Tea, Tea Cups and other requisites for 2d. each, in the extensive rooms set apart for that purpose'.

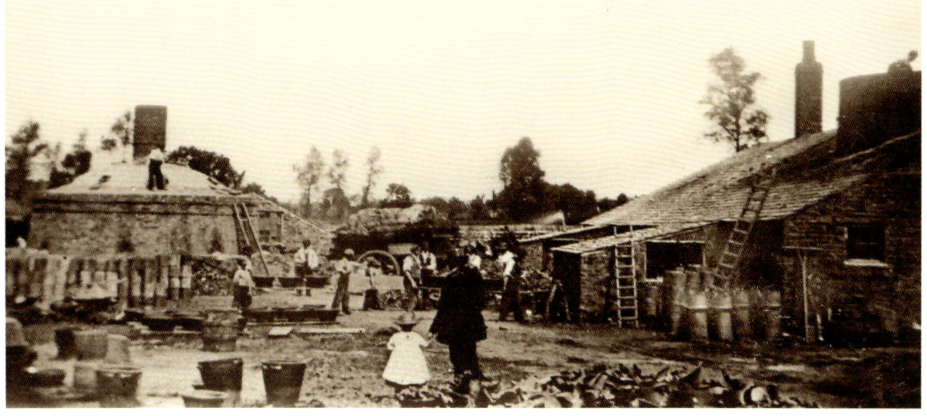

Bailey's Brickworks, in Heaton Mersey, provided many of the bricks for the building of Belle Vue.

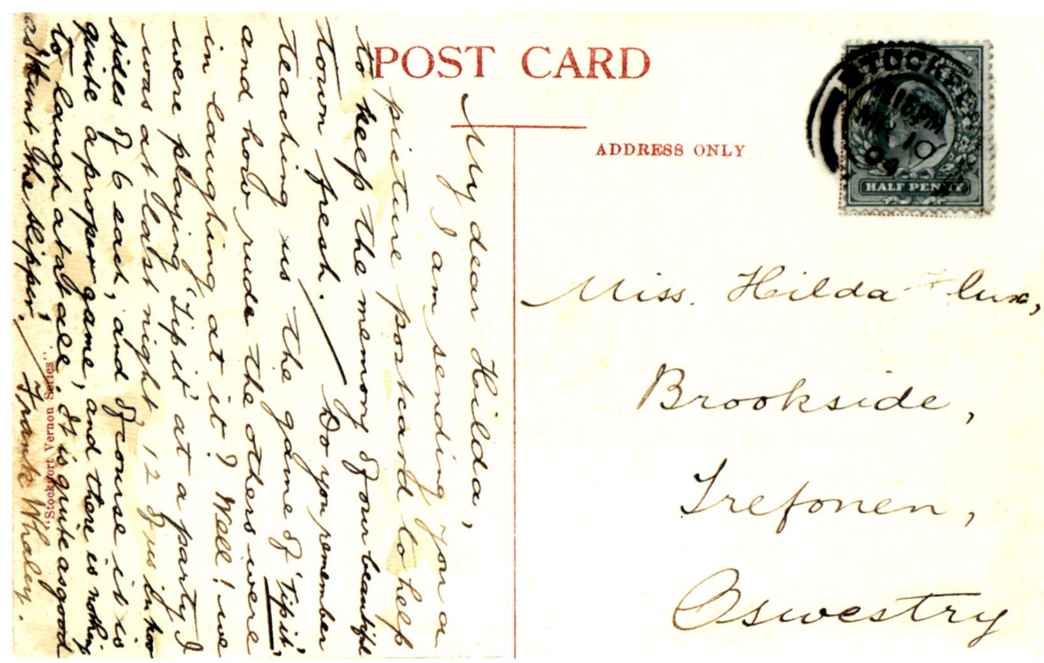

The postcard was sent on the 10 March 1904.

Entertainment: Pastimes

During the late nineteenth and early twentieth centuries families were among the first ever to have an abundance of free time and among the last to pass that time without television. Families were very fond of playing parlour games, a number of which have since been forgotten, but some have been passed down to successive generations and some remain in a slightly different guise. The most popular games included Tip It (as mentioned on the postcard), Charades, Squeak, Piggy, Squeak! Snapdragon, Blind Man's Bluff and Hunt the Slipper. Other interactive activities included card games, euchre and bridge, and board games such as dominoes, checkers and chess.

The message states, 'Do you remember teaching us the game of 'Tip it', and how rude the others were in laughing at it?'

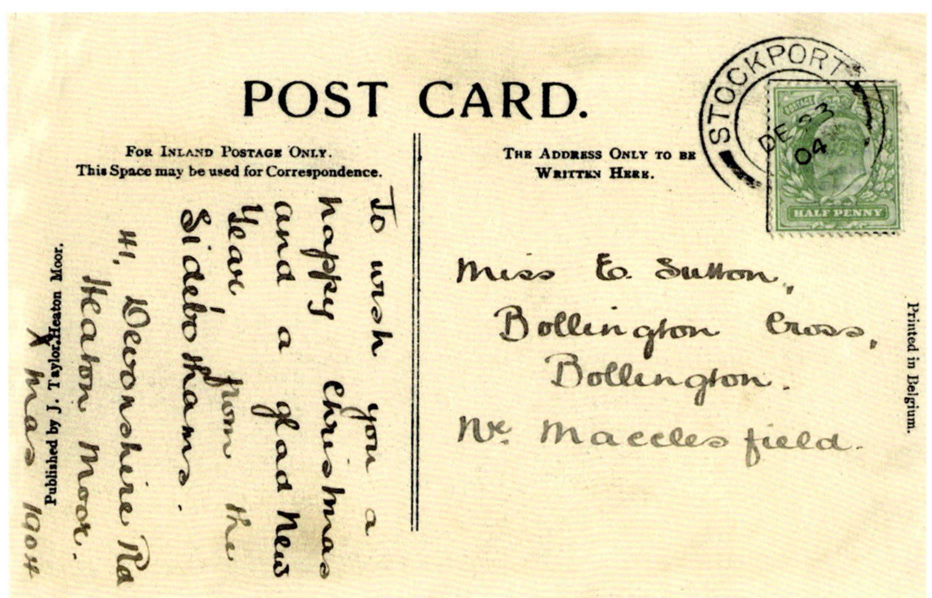

Entertainment: Christmas Time

The two postcards on this page were sent at Christmas time. The bottom card was posted at 8 p.m. on 24 December 1908 with the sender relying on the postal service to deliver it on Christmas Day morning. From the mid-1800s, Christmas traditions were becoming established with the familiar components of the modern Christmas including St Nicholas, Santa Claus and Christmas trees. Edwardian Christmas celebrations ranged from the simple and home-made to the shop-bought decorations and gifts. Between 1900 and 1920, Christmas became increasingly commercial, and there was a dramatic increase in the giving of gifts to children and people having Christmas trees. Christmas stockings that were hung on the bed or hearth first appeared during the mid-1800s, and the 'Book of the Home' described how to decorate a Christmas tree in the early 1900s.

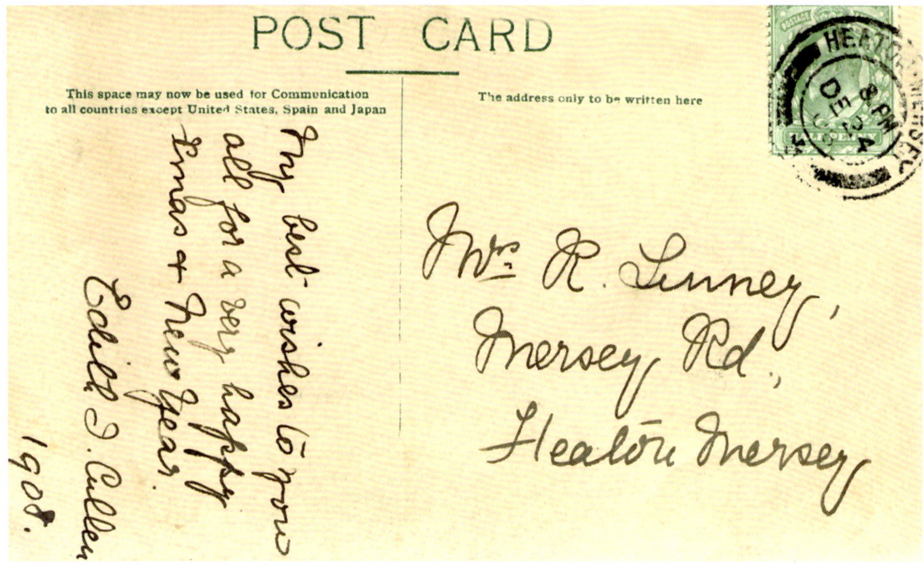

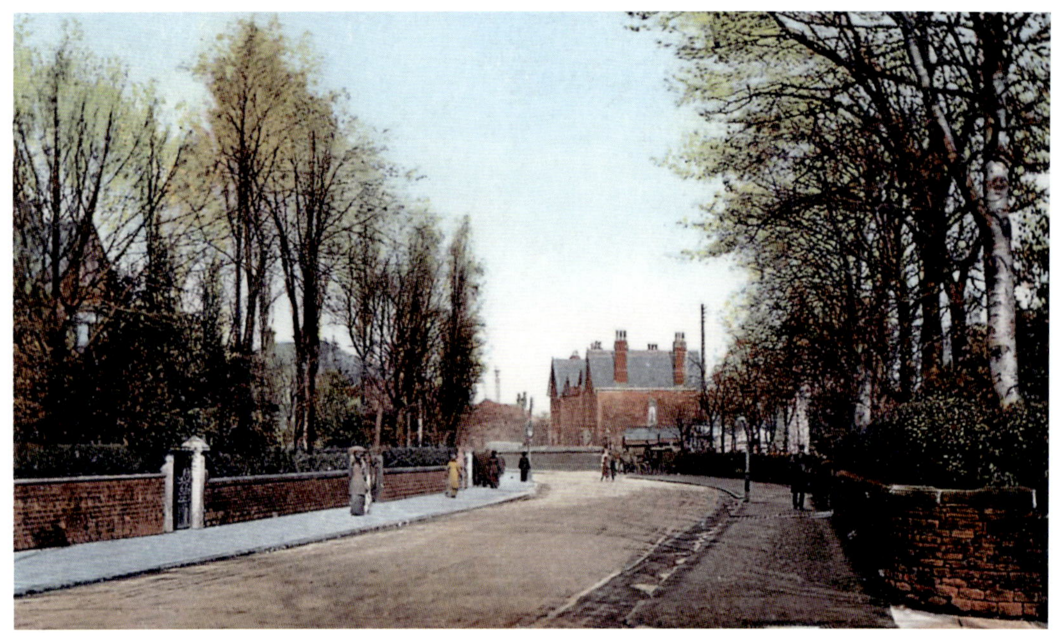

Around Heaton Moor

The area of Heaton Moor is centred mainly around Heaton Moor Road. It developed as a popular residential area in the late nineteenth century when the coming of the railway to Heaton Chapel Station opened up the area for residential development appealing to wealthy families who had business connections in Manchester and Stockport. The building of parks, libraries, shops and a cinema made the area a desirable place to live, away from the pollution and congestion of inner city areas. With building increasing in the 1930s, the area was marketed by one local developer as 'having that quiet reserve with just that degree of friendliness which will make you want to live there for always'.

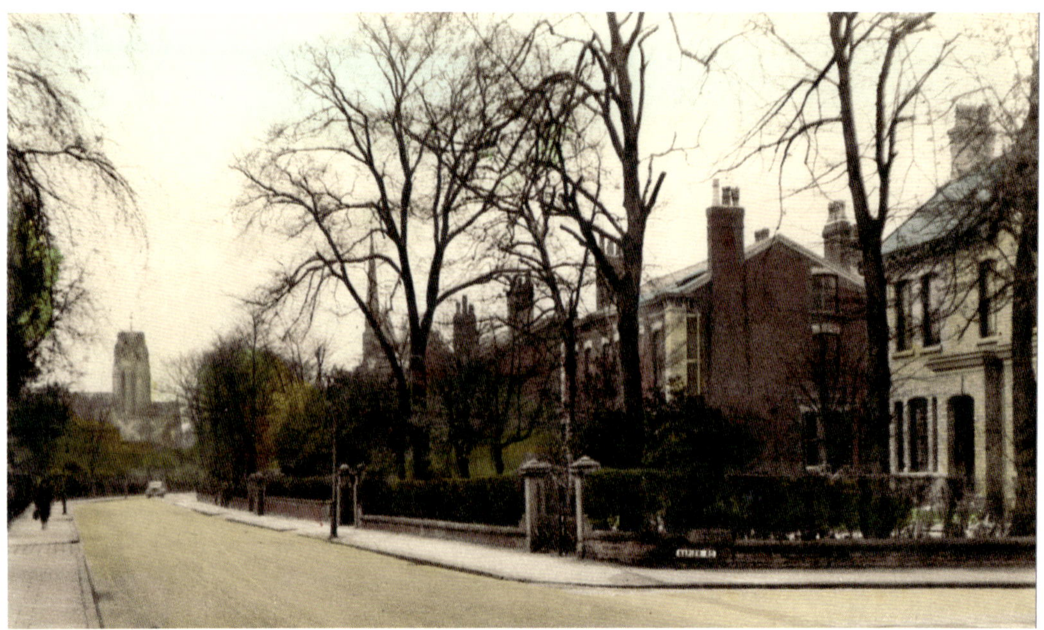

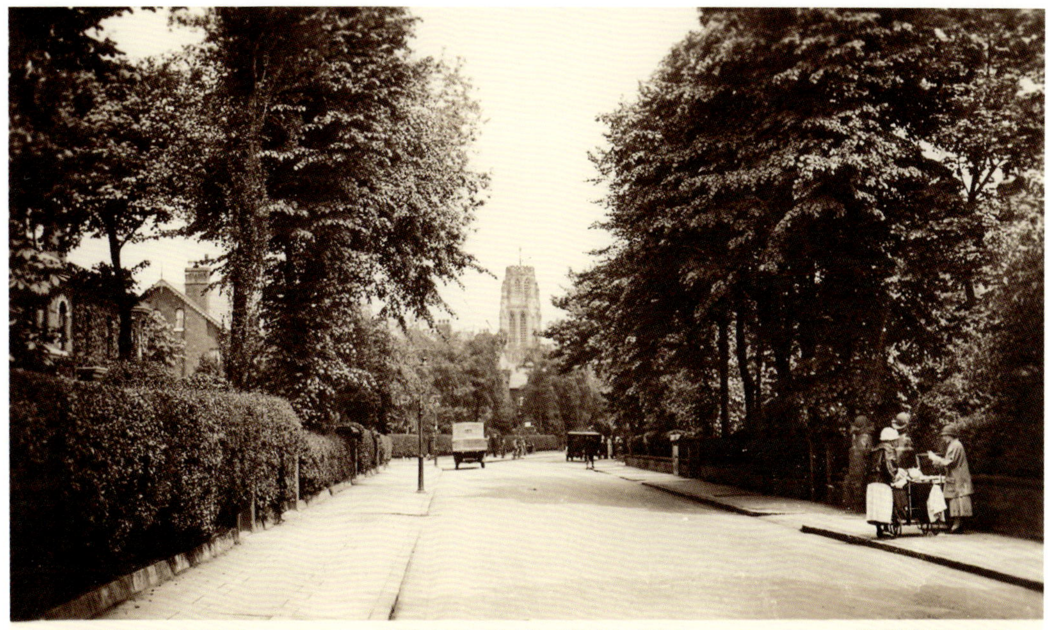

LILYWHITE PROCESS COPYRIGHT.   HEATON MOOR RD., HEATON MOOR.   WHITES SERIES H M 23

Heaton Moor Road, 1927

St Paul's Church has always been a landmark along Heaton Moor Road with its fine tower rising above the tree-lined thoroughfare. Heaton Moor Road was free of heavy traffic in those days, and these two cards show local nannies out and about on their daily business but still finding time to stop and chat among the pleasant surroundings of Heaton Moor village. The horse-drawn cab may well have been one of those that regularly ferried residents to and from Heaton Chapel Station.

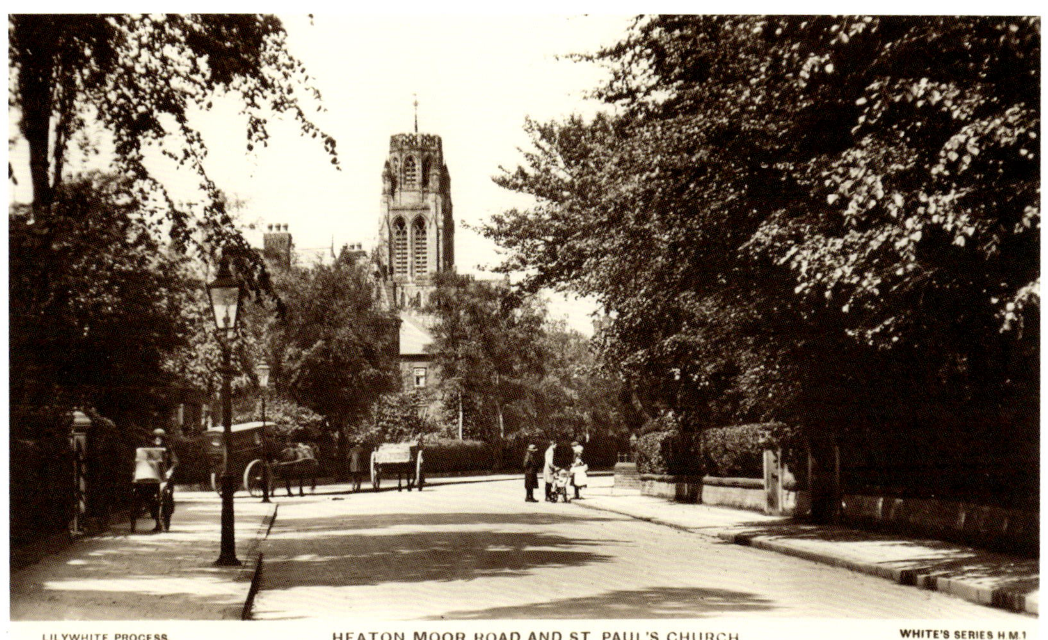

LILYWHITE PROCESS COPYRIGHT.   HEATON MOOR ROAD AND ST. PAUL'S CHURCH   WHITE'S SERIES H M.1

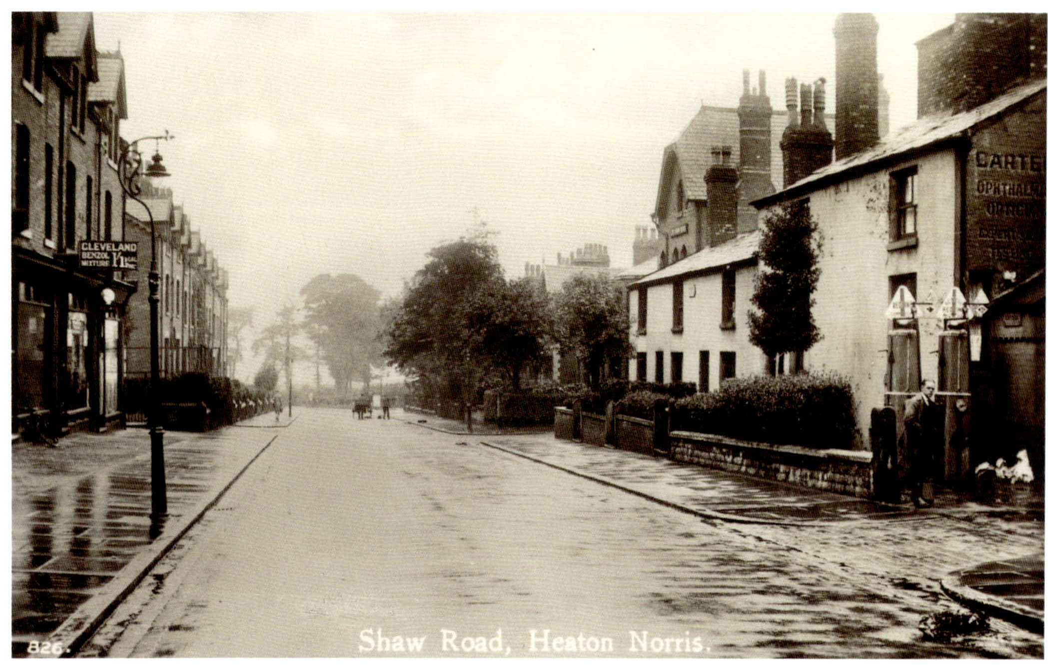

Shaw Road, 1920 and 1924

Shaw Road has always been a popular shopping area in the Heatons and, at one time, led down to Shawfold Farm and open fields, A petrol station can be seen on the right of the earlier picture selling Benzol Redline, possibly paid for in the shop on the other side of the street which is advertising Benzol Mixture at 1*s* 6*d* a gallon. In the later picture, the Lancashire and Yorkshire Bank is well established on the corner of Heaton Moor Road.

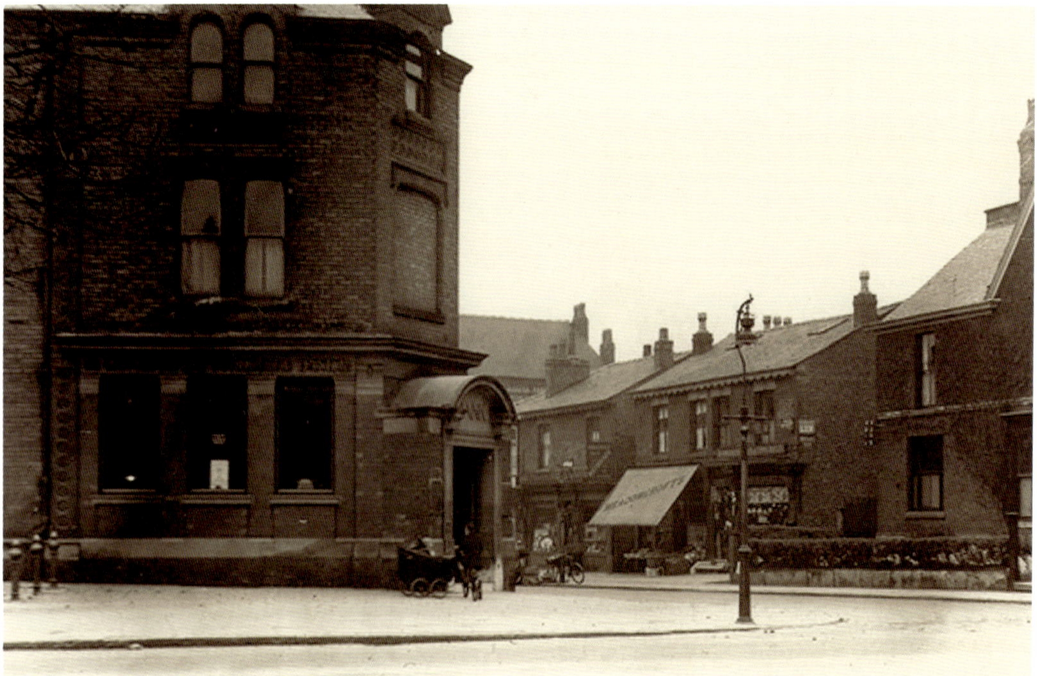

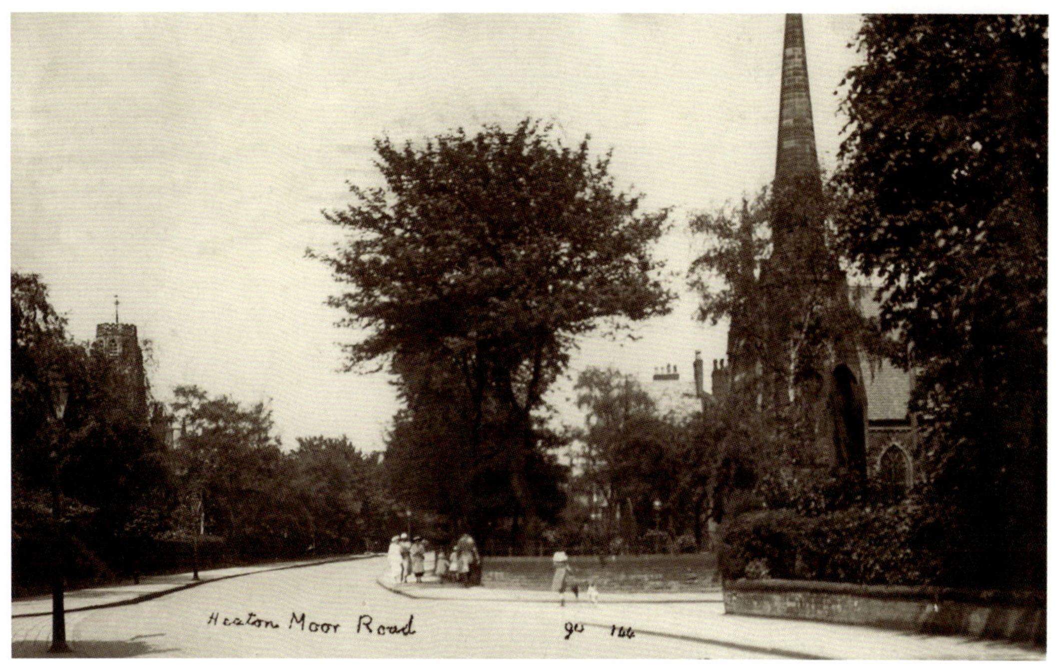

Heaton Moor Methodists Church, 1920s

Heaton Moor Methodist Church was built in 1894 but was pulled down and rebuilt in the early 1980s. It was redesigned by local architects in a more modernistic style incorporating the original stained glass window and stone tracery. The window is an impressive feature that can be clearly seen from Heaton Moor Road. Today the Methodists now worship in partnership with the United Reformed Church.

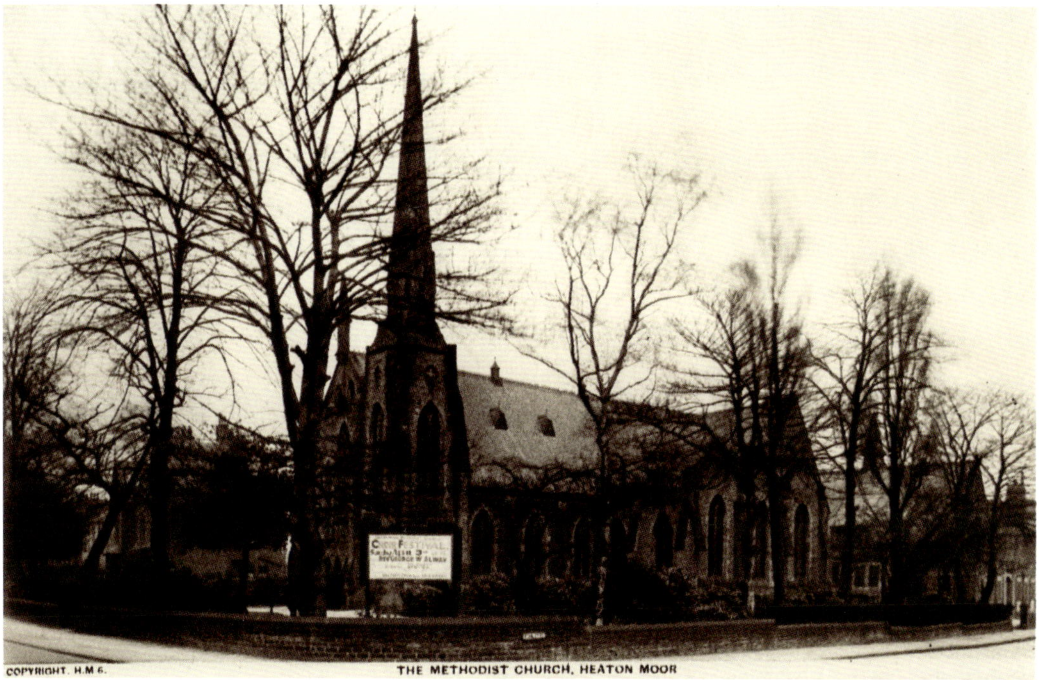

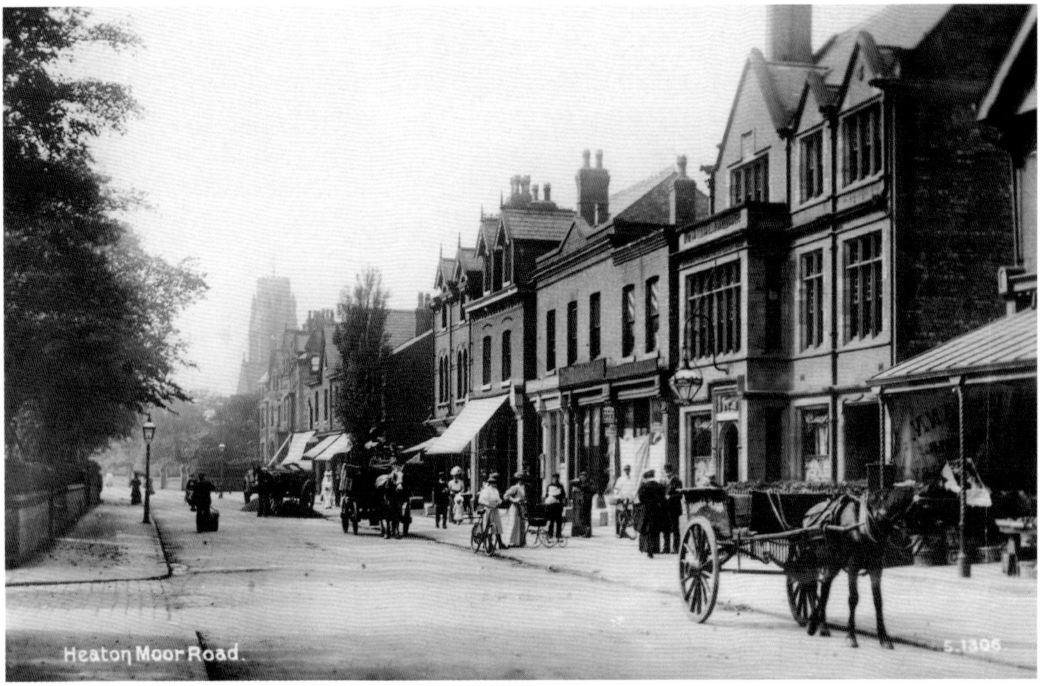

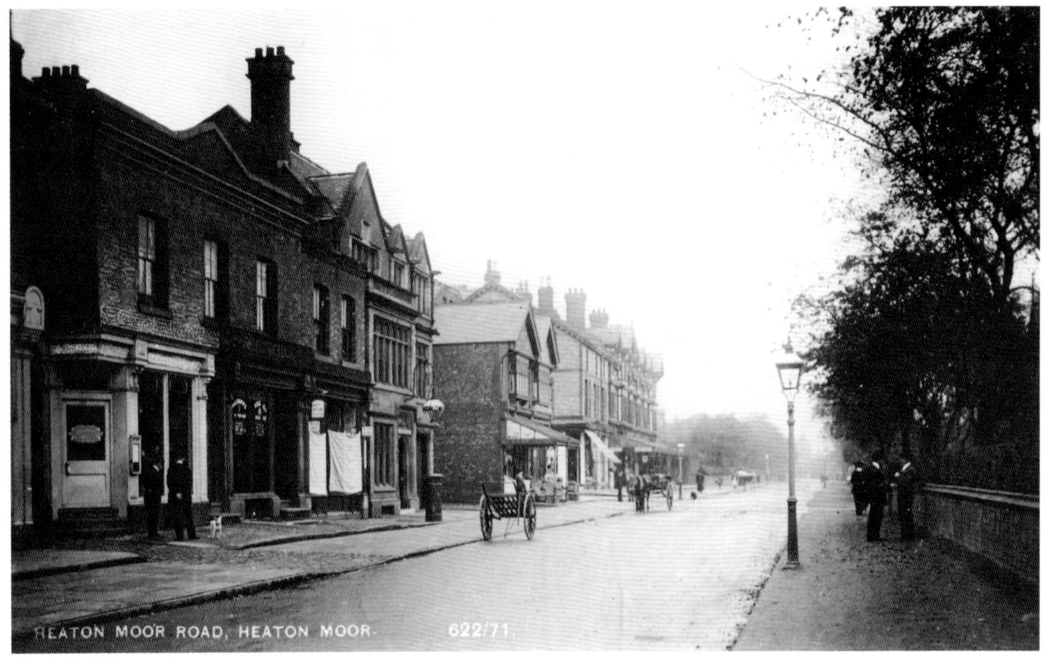

Heaton Moor Road, 1905

These cards, from around the same year, give a good impression of the range of shops available to the new wealthy classes who were moving into the area. The shop with its windows covered by white cloth is a post office and small lending library, and the post box occupies the same position it does today. The gap in the shops, next to the Plough Inn, can still be seen. The space is now filled by a local supermarket constructed after the shops with verandas were demolished.

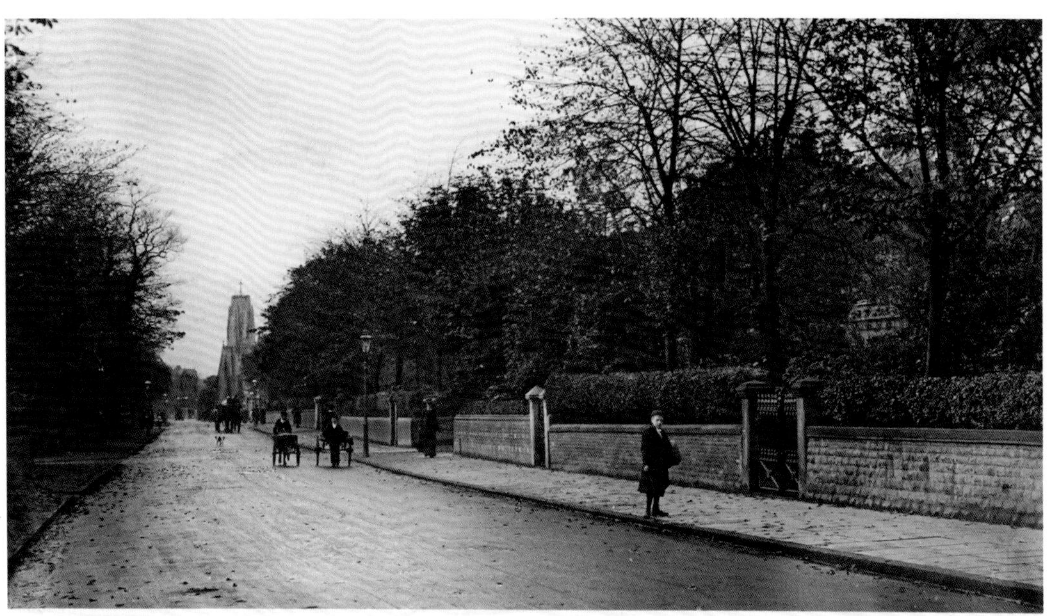

Heaton Moor Road, 1906 and 1913

These two cards picturing a busy Heaton Moor Road in the early 1900s show handcarts being used on the highway. Use of such carts was common in in the early years of the century and, as Heaton Moor was a wealthy area, Edwardian ladies would not want to carry home their shopping. Young boys would often be employed to deliver goods by hand or, by handcart, if they were making several deliveries locally.

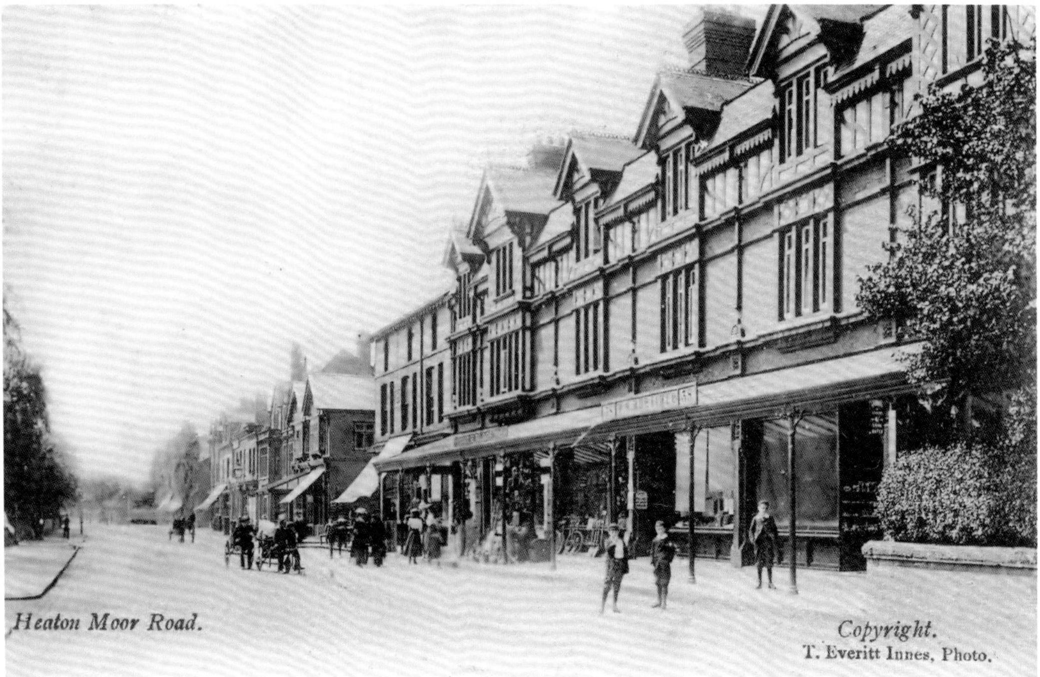

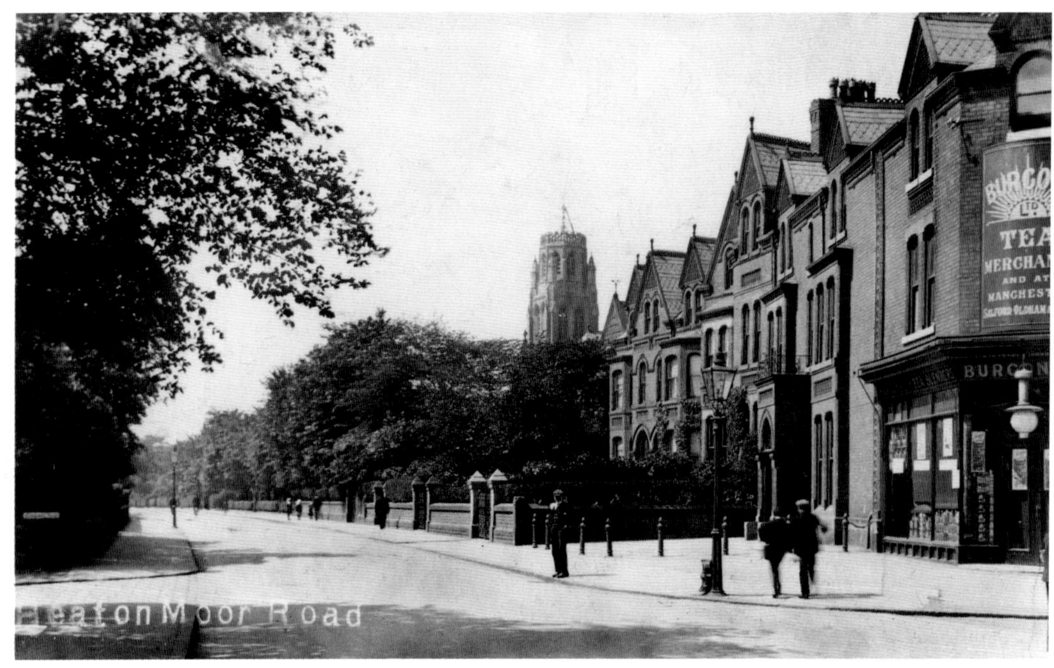

Heaton Moor Road, 1907 and 1918

These two cards show the establishment on the corner of Shaw Road which was Burgons Tea merchants. They had branches across the North West including shops in Salford, Oldham and Bolton. Within the shop, the Tea Department proclaimed to offer 'a greater variety than that of any other house' and sold what they termed '3 Capital Ts', the Kintuck Blend, Burgon Blend and Special Blend, which were all available for customers to sample in the café.

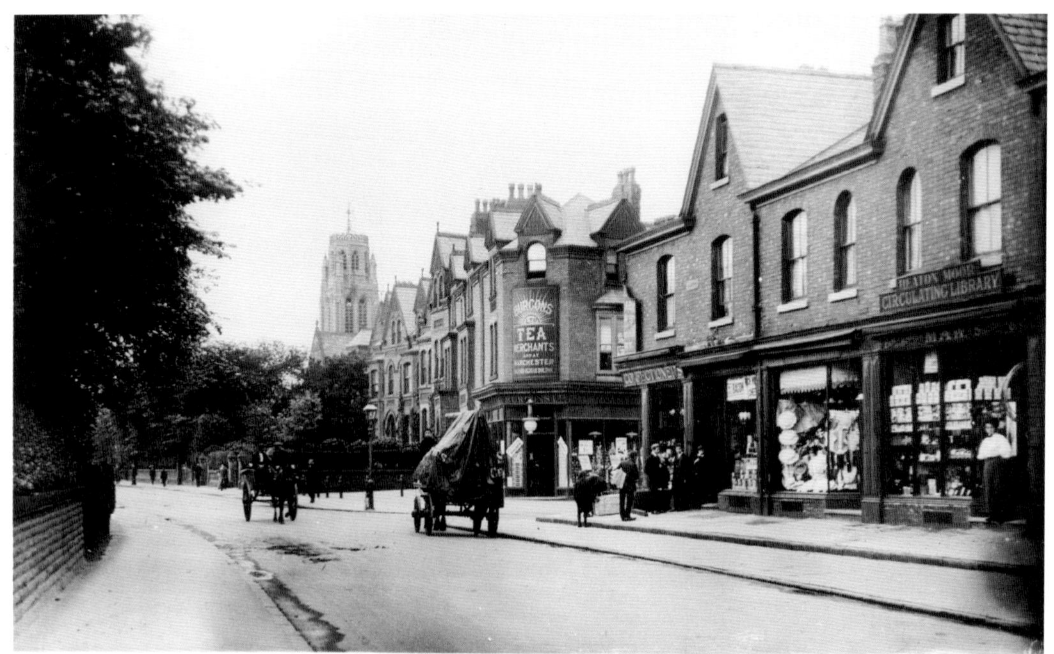

HEATON MOOR RD., HEATON MOOR.

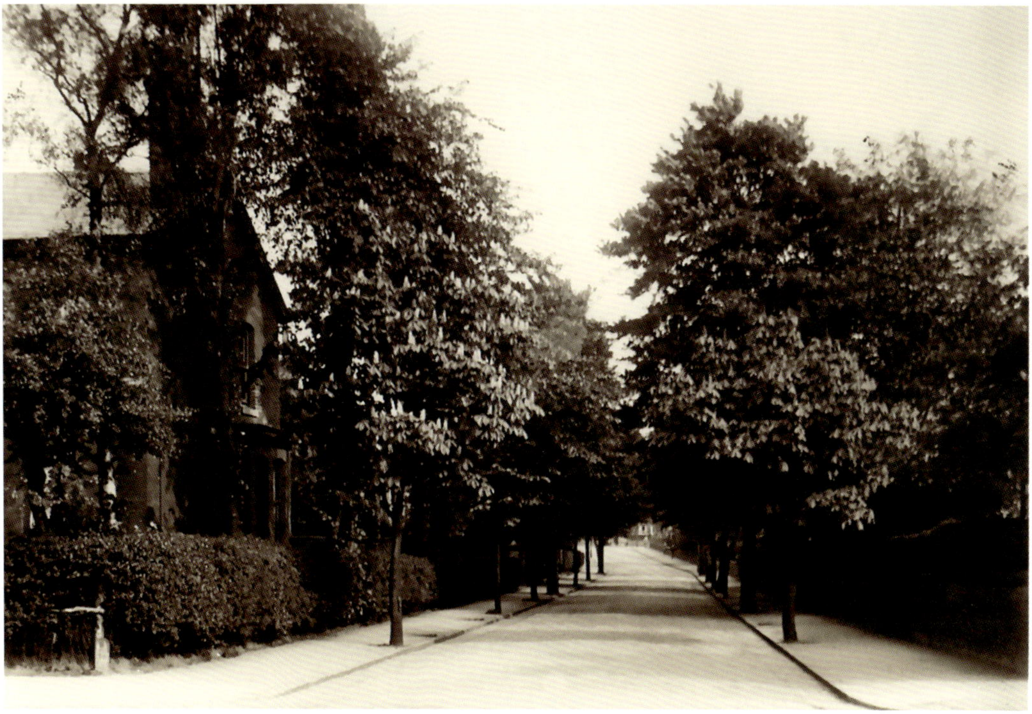

Gibsons Road and Peel Moat Road, 1920s

With the coming of the railway, an extensive building programme developed resulting in many residential roads being constructed as branches from the main Heaton Moor Road. Lying close to the railway, both Gibsons Road and Peel Moat Road were home to some of the fine Edwardian and Victorian residences which would have been in demand for those prosperous families wishing to be within walking distance of Heaton Chapel Station.

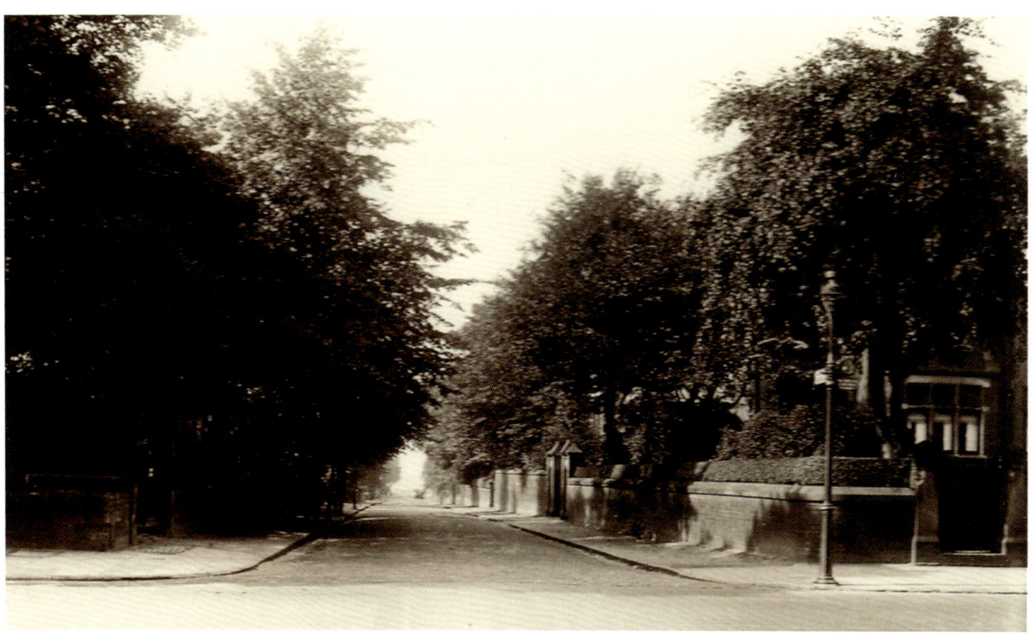

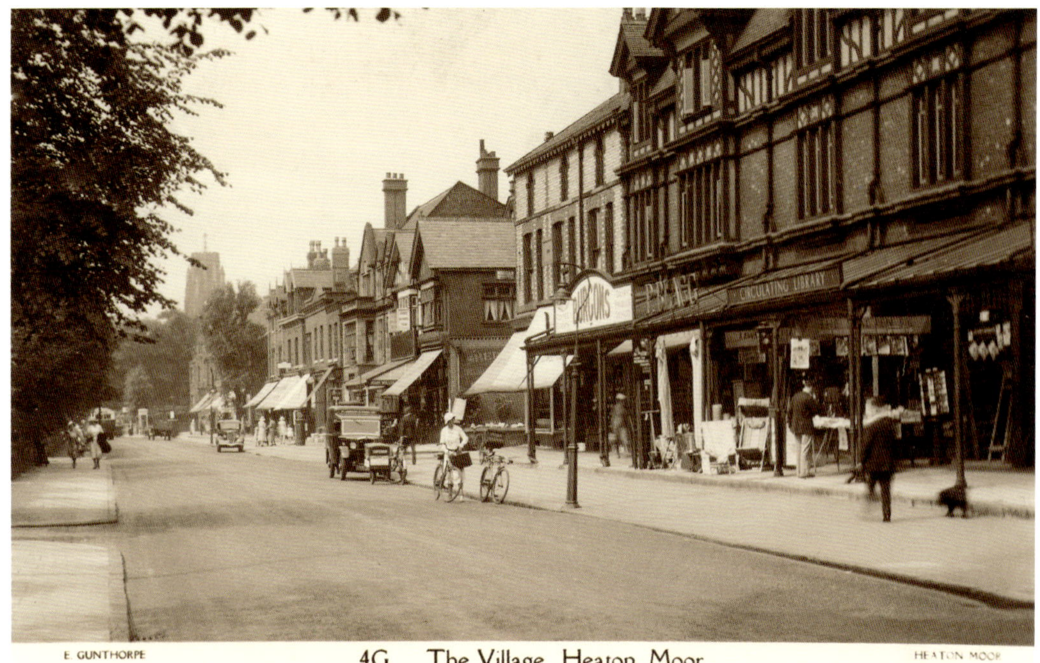

4G.   The Village. Heaton Moor.

Heaton Moor Road, 1937 and 1968

In the 1930s, Heaton Moor Road was still relatively traffic free with most people going about their shopping on foot or by bicycle. By the 1960s, however, the area was already busy with motor traffic, and part of the wide pavement had been cut back to accommodate vehicle parking. The glass and metal verandas have mostly survived except for the ones which were demolished to build the square, concrete, more functional construction, on the corner of Portland Grove.

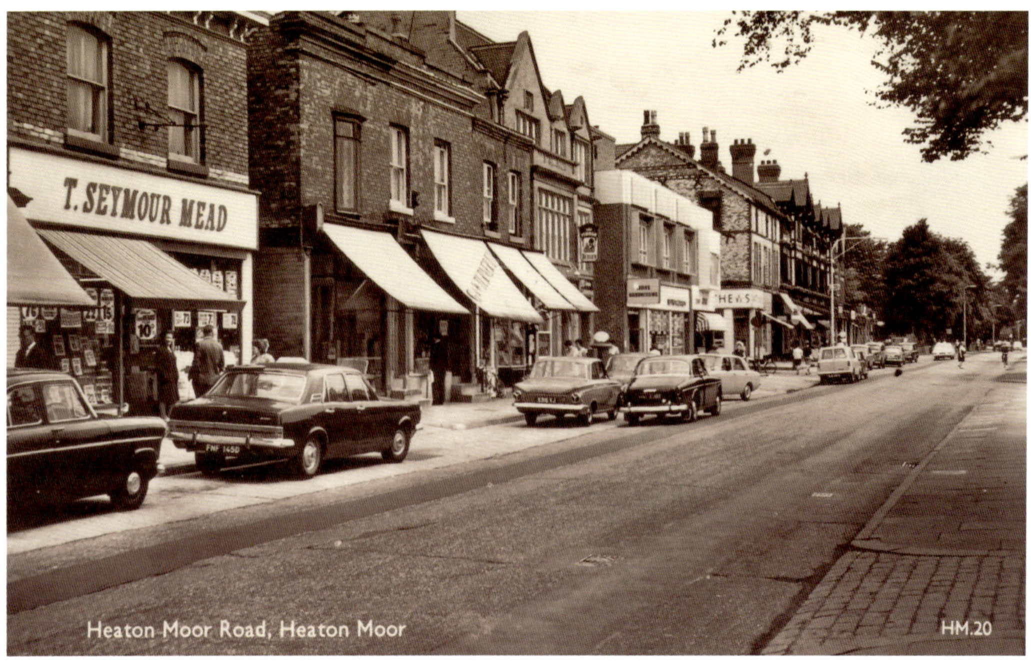

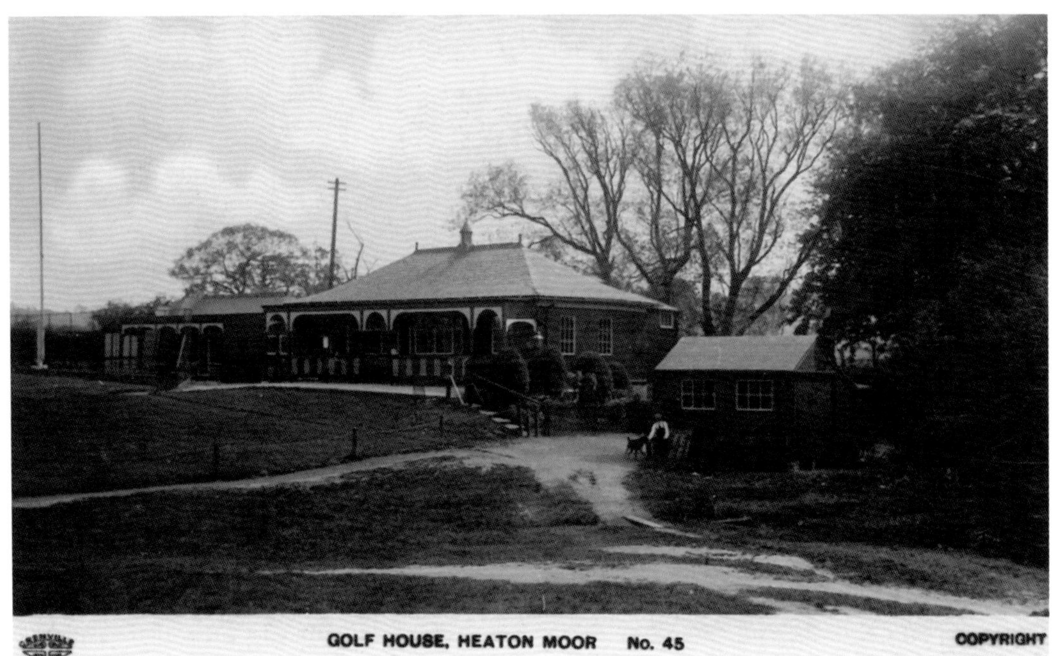

Heaton Moor Golf Club, Early, 1900s

Heaton Moor Golf Club was opened in 1892 and was built on land surrounding Mauldeth Hall to the north-east of the Peel Moat settlement. The layout of the course is just under 6000 yards and is populated with attractive tree-lined fairways. A round of golf can take in the historical location of the course as the 15th hole requires golfers to actually drive over Peel Moat, which is designated by English Heritage as a site of historical significance.

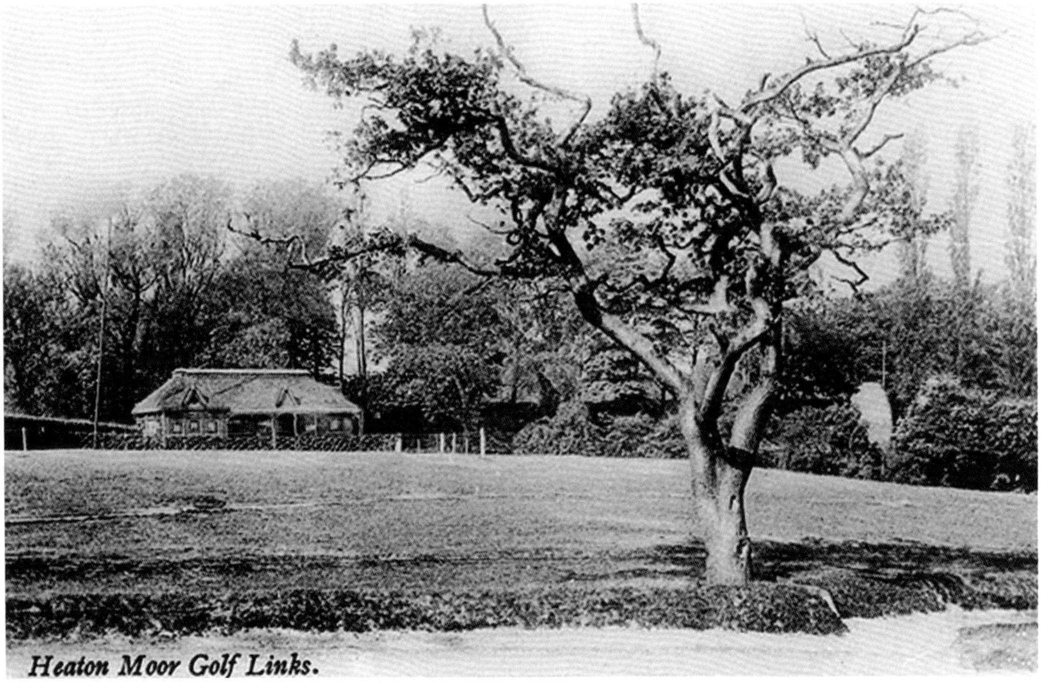

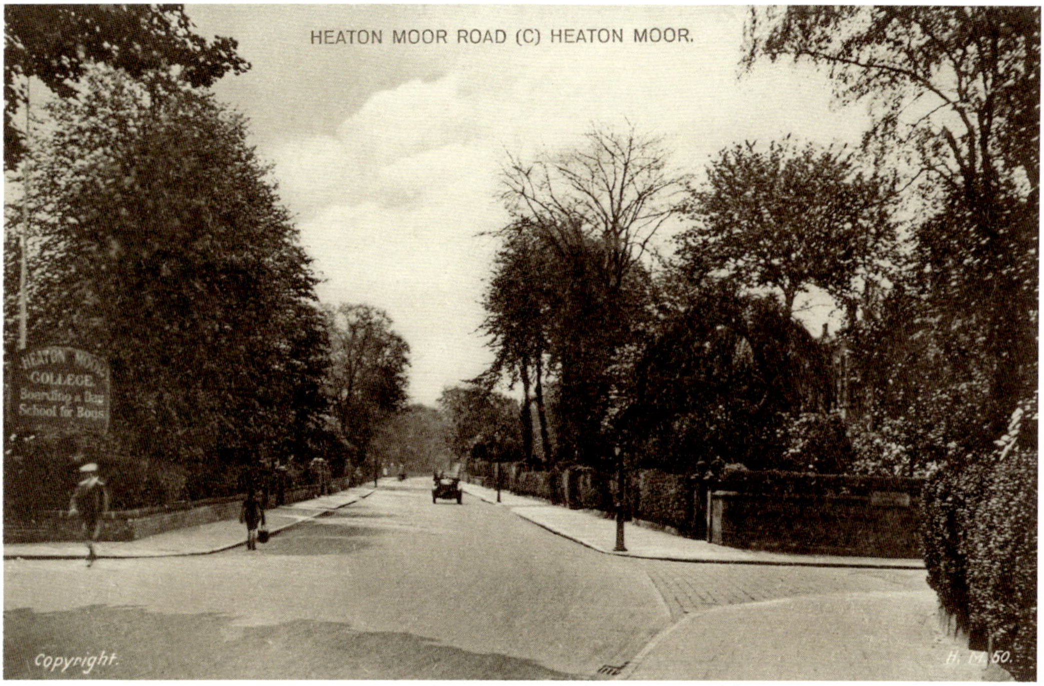

Heaton Moor College, 1931

Heaton Moor College was situated on the corner of Stanley Road and Heaton Moor Road. It was a boarding and day school for boys from four years of age. It provided a 'Sound Education On Modern Lines' and offered tuition for 'Professional, Preliminary, Matriculation and Civil Service Examinations'. In its prospectus, it boasted that its entire staff was made up of graduates and that the Preparatory Department was run under the supervision of a 'Highly Qualified Mistress'.

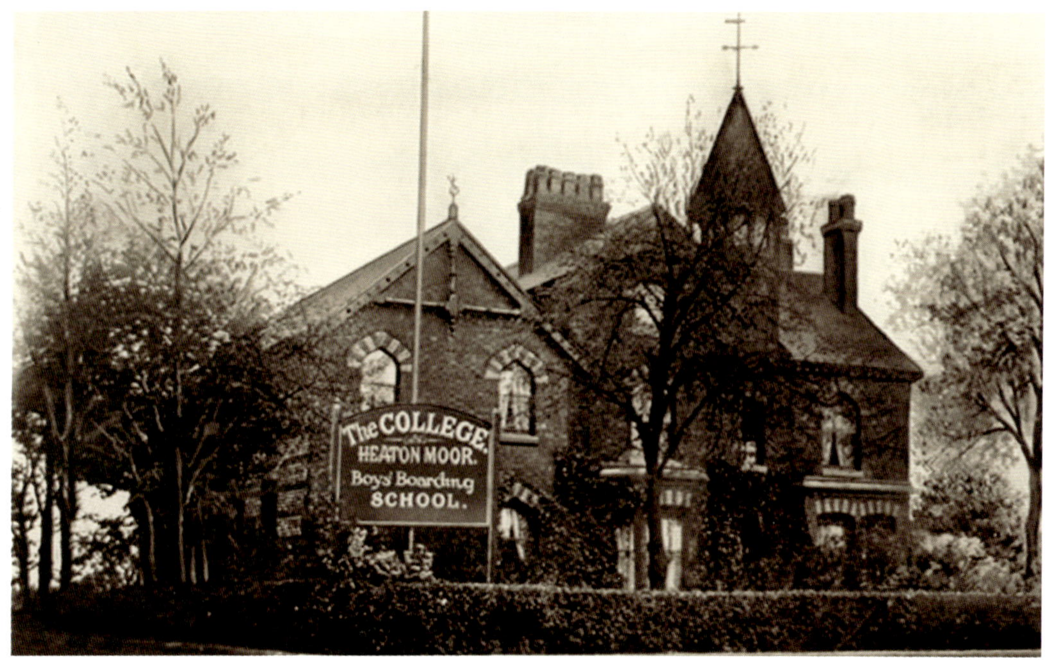

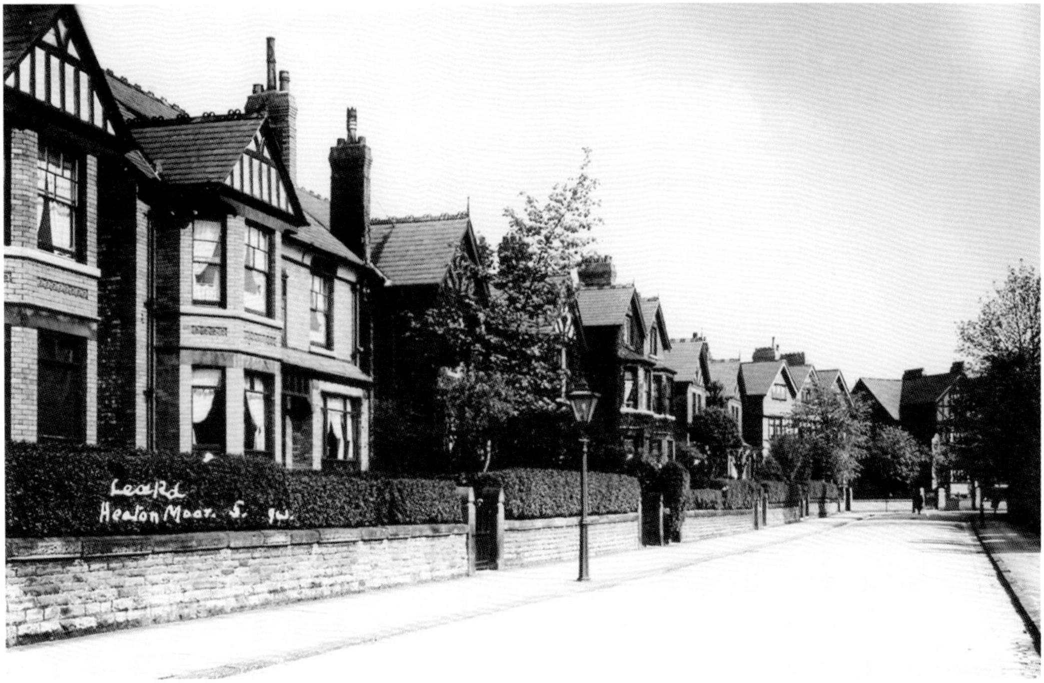

Lea Road, 1930s and 1950s

The dwellings constructed in Lea Road were typical of the grand Victorian or Edwardian houses built close to the railway station in the early part of the twentieth century. By the 1950s, however, more modern designs had started to appear on the opposite side giving the road its familiar appearance of today. The lack of cars is noticeable on both pictures with garden walls and gates intact with no drives needed for motor vehicles.

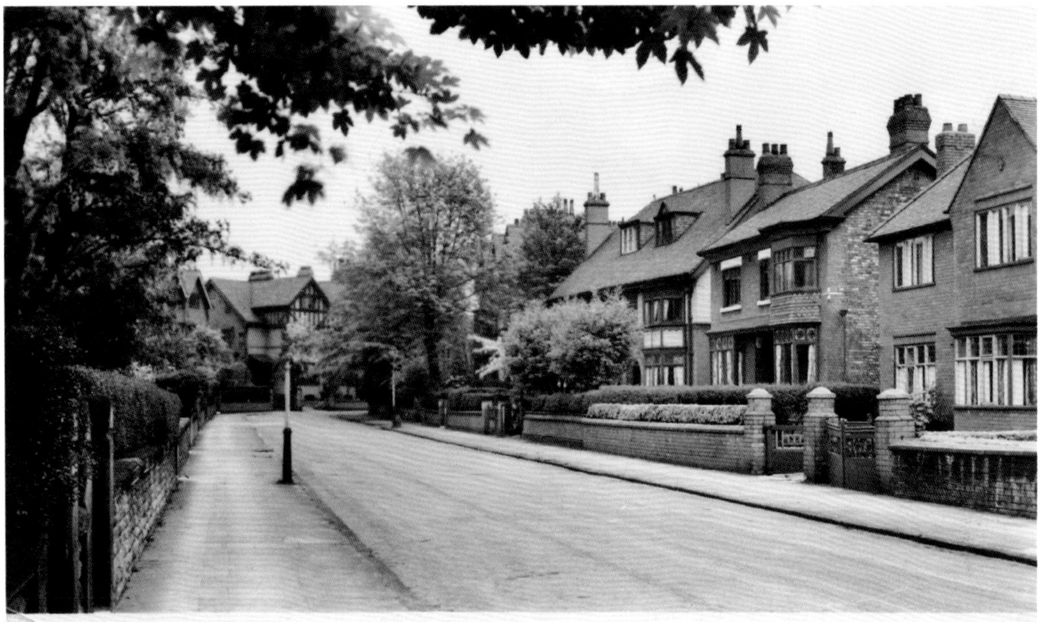

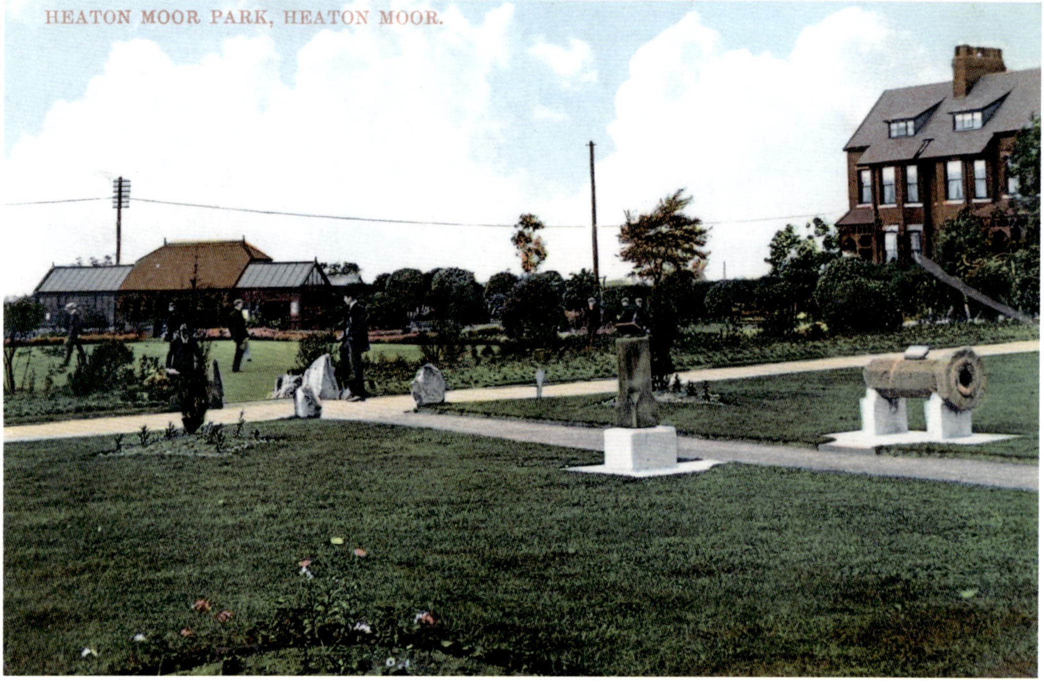

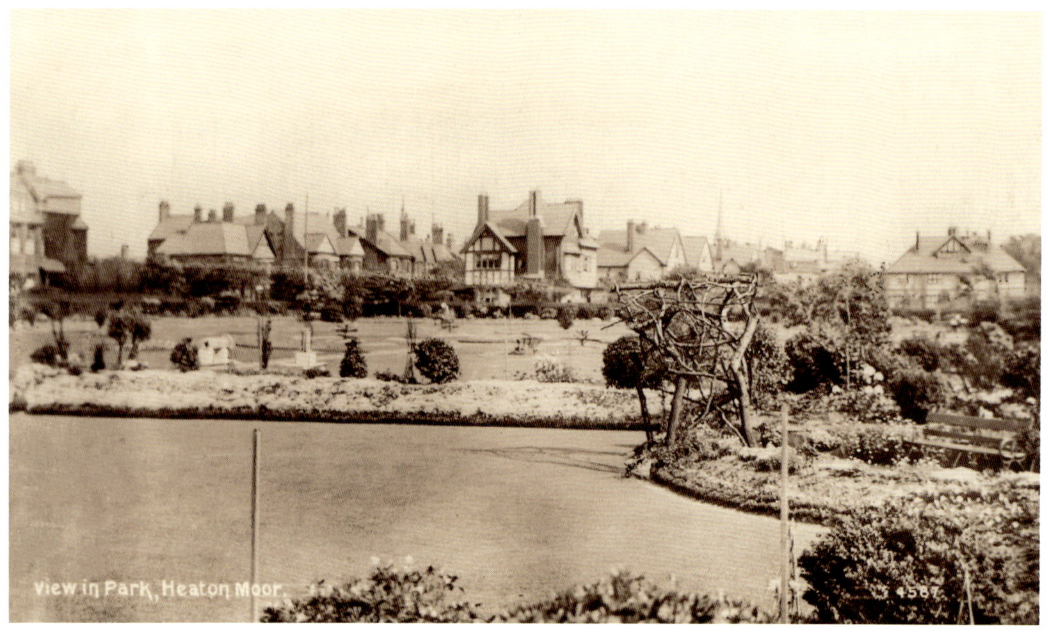

Heaton Moor Park, 1908

In 1894, Lord Egerton of Tatton donated approximately four acres of land that was to be placed into a charitable trust to allow play, pleasure and recreation for the people of the Heatons. Heaton Moor Park was officially opened in 1897 as part of the Diamond Jubilee celebrations for Queen Victoria. Mr Thomas Shann, Chairman of the Recreation Grounds Committee, opened the park gates with a golden key. The bowling greens were constructed by 1910 and the tennis courts in place by 1922.

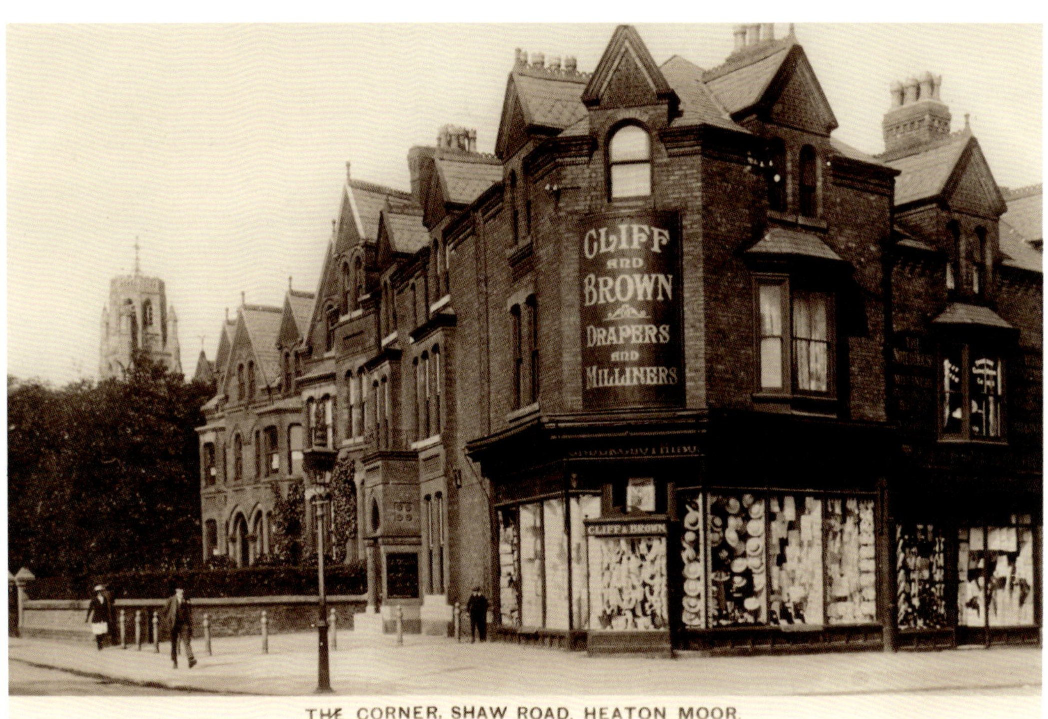

THE CORNER, SHAW ROAD, HEATON MOOR.

Cliff and Brown's Draper's and Milliner's, 1918

Theses premises at the top of Shaw Road have been home to a number of businesses over the years but, at the time of the photograph, dated August 1918, it was a thriving concern selling a wide selection of hats and other soft garments. Hats were a popular fashion item for the Edwardians and Victorians. Huge broad brimmed hats were especially fashionable and were often trimmed with masses of feathers and, occasionally, stuffed birds. Hummingbirds were a popular choice but were quite expensive, so the cheaper option was to decorate them with ribbons, bunches of blackberries, cherries or artificial flowers.

The majority of hats on display in Cliff and Brown's appear to be white. Wearing white in Edwardian times was a symbol of wealth, as whites needed laundering, which meant employing maids who would spend hours scrubbing out stains.

Hats were also an important accessory to men's wear. A good hat was considered to be the sign of a gentleman, and men returning from the Great War would have been expected to wear a hat for a period of time as part of the demobilisation process. A man's outfit, minus a hat, would be deemed inappropriate for a gentleman, and men had many styles of hats to choose from, whether elegant or casual. The reason bowler hat is often seen on postcards from the time was that it was considered unsuitable for formal occasions but fine for everyday casual wear.

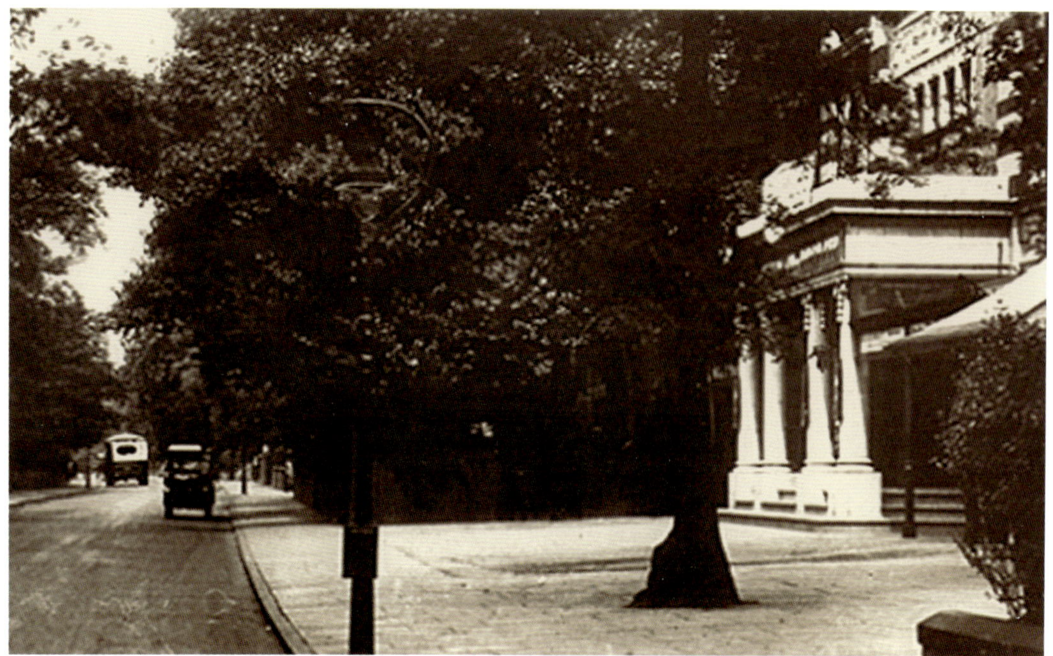

The Savoy Cinema, 1930s

The Savoy was opened by the Mayor of Stockport in March 1923. It had a balcony and seated over a thousand people. Audiences flocked to see its first screening, a silent production of *The Virgin Queen* starring Diana Manners, with accompanying music from Constance Cross's Ladies Orchestra.

This new entertainment gave the people of the Heatons a view into worlds previously unknown to them, and they would certainly have revelled in the action and drama surrounding the life of Elizabeth 1. Diana Manners, or later, Diana Cooper, Viscountess Norwich, had the widespread reputation as the most beautiful young woman in England and appeared in countless profiles, photographs and articles in newspapers and magazines. She died aged ninety-three, in 1986, having starred in silent movies' 'talkies' and some of the first colour films.

In 1938, it was badly damaged by fire and had to be closed for some months. With the coming of the Second World War, it provided much needed light entertainment and screened regular newsreels from the conflict in Europe. It was also occasionally used as an evacuation centre for local families whose homes were under the most threat of bomb damage.

After the war, the cinema managed to survive despite the coming of television and the associated drop in cinema audiences. In 1971, it underwent a complete facelift with its balcony being removed and the front boxed in to provide a covered foyer and waiting area. At the time, its advertising claimed it was the 'ultimate in luxury theatre going' and it continued to provide a quality social amenity for Heatons' residents.

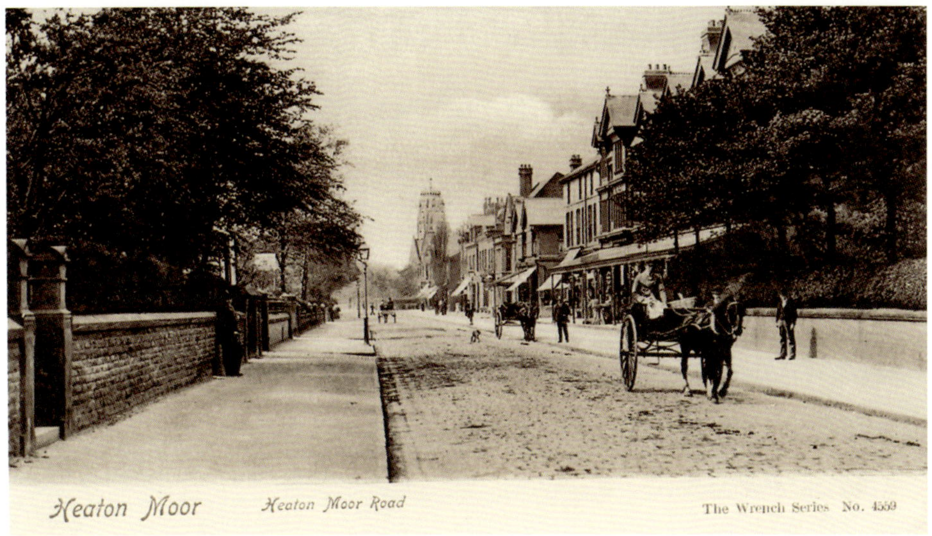

Hansom Cabs. Heaton Moor Road, 1903

This postcard shows Hansom Cabs plying their trade along Heaton Moor Road in the early 1900s. The Hansom Cab was a horse-drawn carriage designed and patented by Joseph Hansom in 1834. The original factory was situated in Hinckley, Leicestershire, and the vehicles were originally called the Hansom Safety Cab as they were designed to combine speed with safety and had a low centre of gravity which made for stable cornering.

They enjoyed immense popularity as their light design allowed them to be pulled speedily by one horse making journeying far cheaper than having to employ a larger, four-wheeled coach. At the height of their popularity, there were around 7,500 in use in English cities, and by the late nineteenth century, they had been successfully exported to many countries around the World.

They continued to be widely used in the United Kingdom until 1908 when petrol cabs (Taximeter Cars) began to creep onto British streets, and by the 1920s, they had almost disappeared. The last licence for a horse-drawn cab in London expired in 1947.

They would have been a common site around The Heatons especially along Heaton Moor Road, which was the main thoroughfare leading to Heaton Chapel Station.

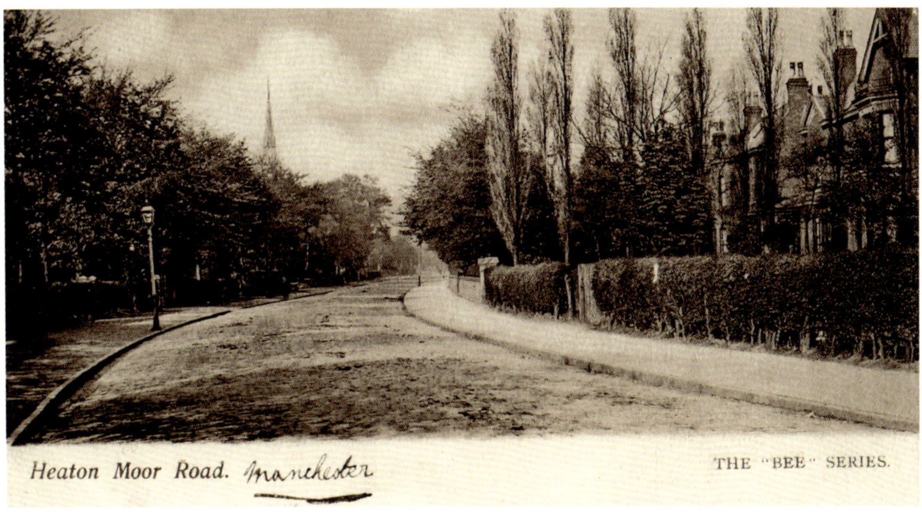

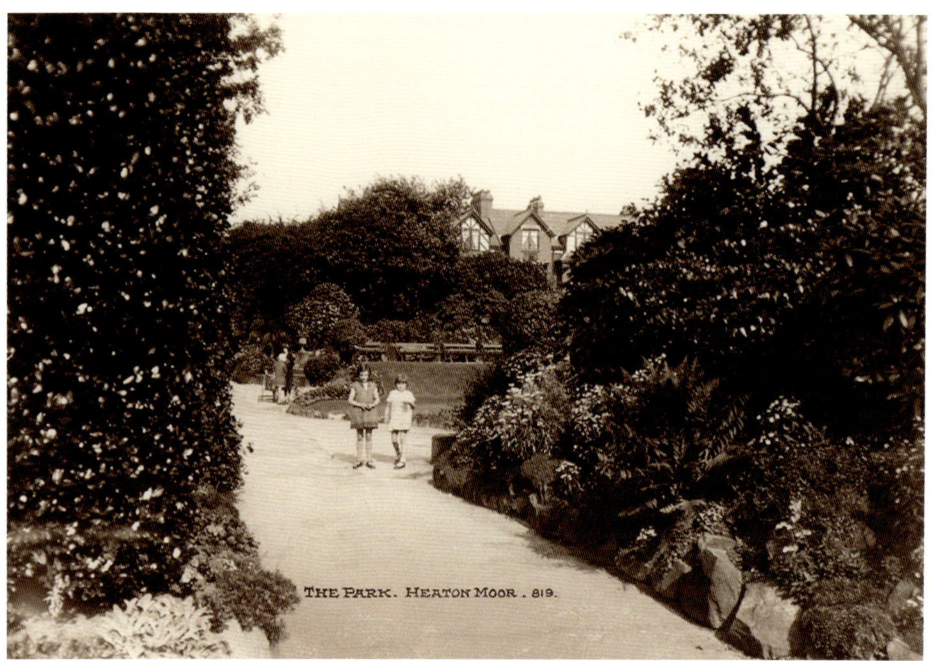

Postcard History: Photography

The two photographs, which were used for postcard production, were both taken by local photographer J. L. Brown of Stockport Road, Ardwick Green, *c.* 1920. These images were produced on glass plates, a process that allowed for a reduced exposure time and high-quality duplication, known nowadays as negatives. Photographic processes went through many changes, from 1839, when Louis Daguerre introduced his Daguerreotype process, to 1889 when the Eastman Company introduced the first commercially available transparent roll film. Around this time, photography started to become available to the masses especially when Kodak introduced the first 'easy-to-use' box camera advertising it with the slogan: 'You press the button, we do the rest'.

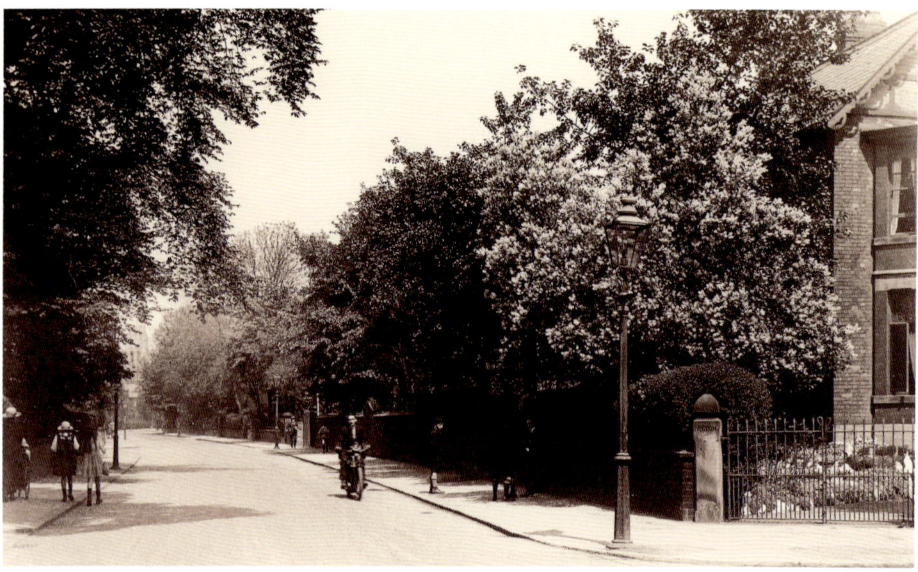

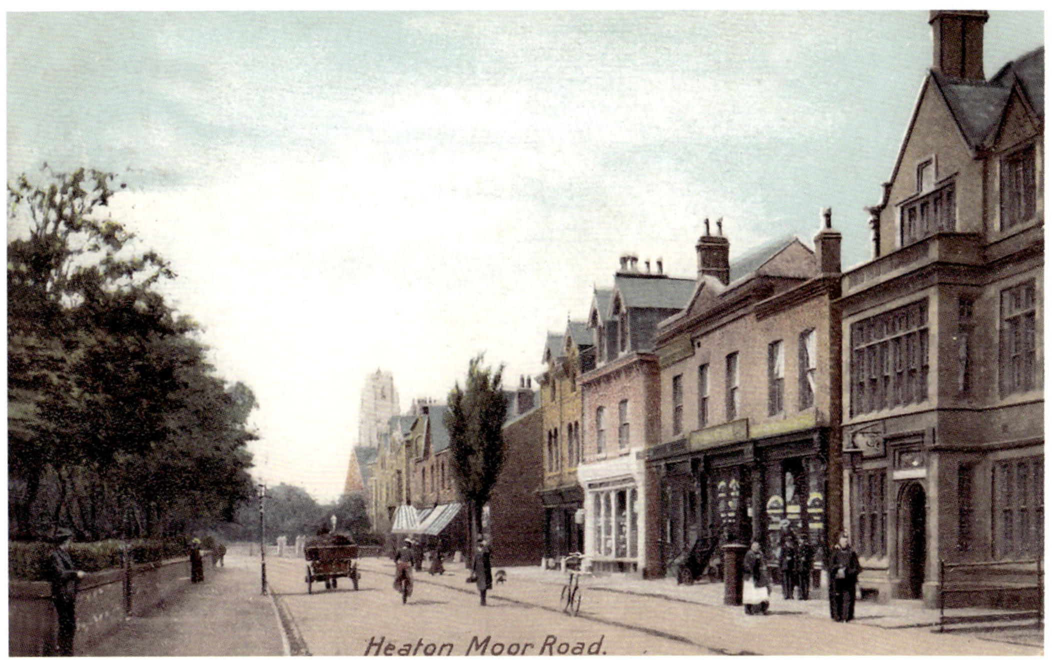

Heaton Moor Road.

Postcard History: Colour Tinting

In an attempt to create more realistic images, photographers and artists started to hand-colour monochrome photographs. The photograph would be painted by hand usually taking place in the photographer's studio prior to production. The paints that were used were oil-based and transparent, and their chemistry was such that many of the colourists, usually women, were to suffer illness as a result of licking their brushes to form a point. The top postcard, 1905, shows a view along Heaton Moor Road looking towards St Paul's Church and the bottom one, also of Heaton Moor Road, 1907, showing the Congregational Church are both examples of colour-tinted postcards.

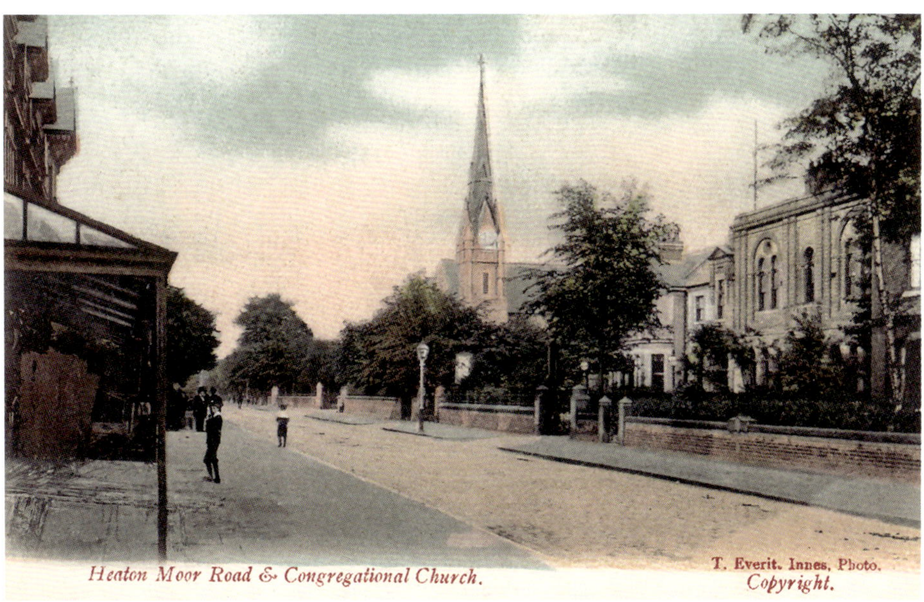

Heaton Moor Road & Congregational Church.

T. Everit. Innes, Photo.
Copyright.

When the Crown Inn was built in 1820, it was set back from the neighbouring buildings because of the two poplar trees growing in front of it. The photograph was taken in 1910 when Joseph Rigby was the licensee and the records, dated 1923, show that he was still there.

The trees were felled in 1930, and the Inn was extended to bring it in line with its neighbouring buildings. The Plough, further along Heaton Moor Road, was rebuilt in 1886 as a replacement for a hostelry of the same name which stood on the site. Above the door is a representation, in sandstone, of a ploughing scene.

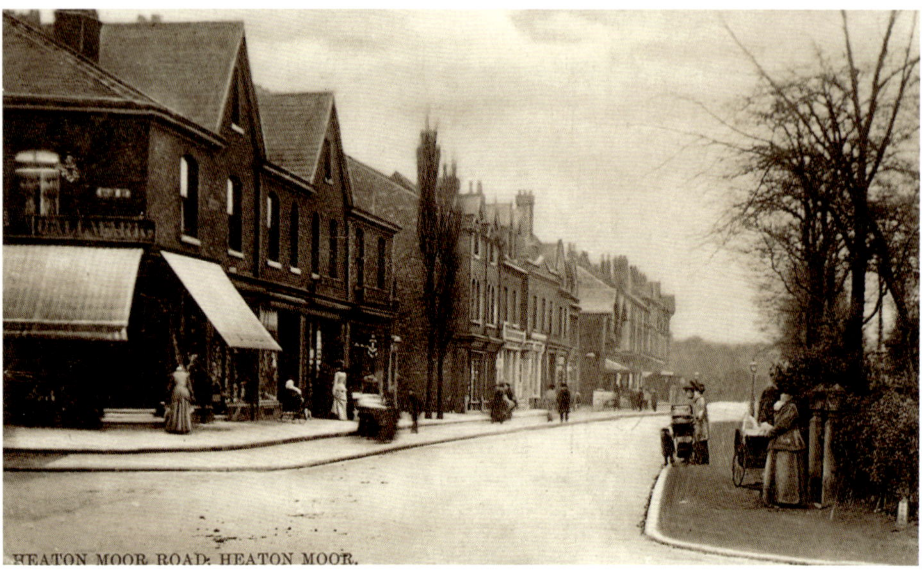

The Crown Inn, on Heaton Moor Road in 1908, was originally set back from the road and behind the two poplar trees.

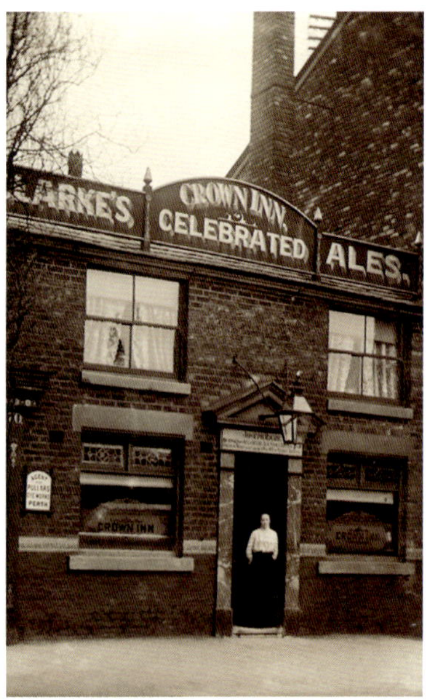

The landlady of the Crown Inn posing for the photographer, *c.* 1910.

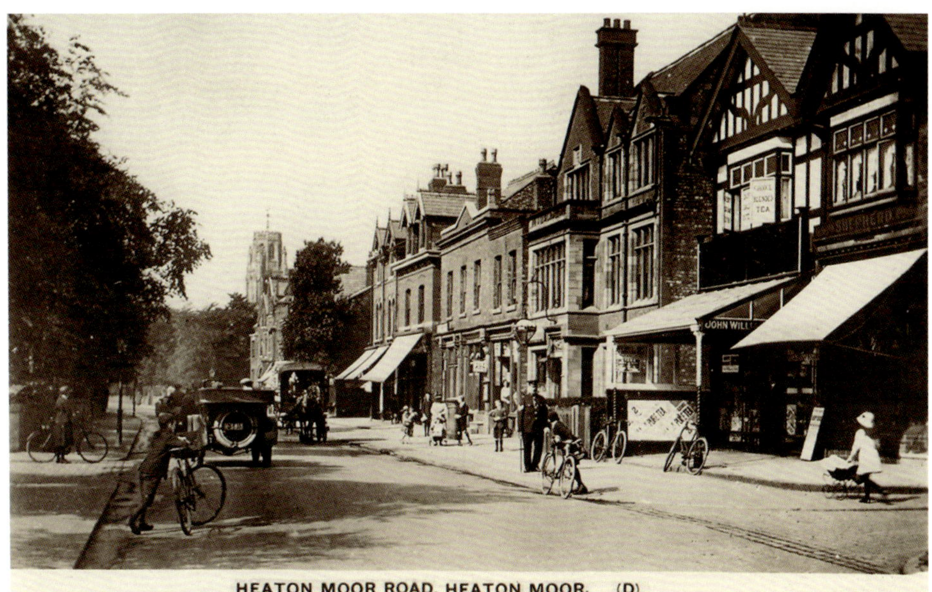

The residents of Heaton Moor in 1907, posing for a photograph.

Postcard History: Posing for Photographs

People have always been the most popular subjects for photography since the camera was introduced. The early photographers did not have the sophisticated equipment, that we can all own nowadays, but they still had to work with light and exposure, use composition, choose backgrounds and relax and pose their subjects without them moving. Exposure times were a bit longer than they are today, so the photographer would pose people in the street making them standstill until he had finished. A popular shot of the time was one where shop owners, sometimes with their employees, would pose in front of their premises just like J. Bullen, the Tailor, did in around 1900. The photographs would then be used to produce postcards.

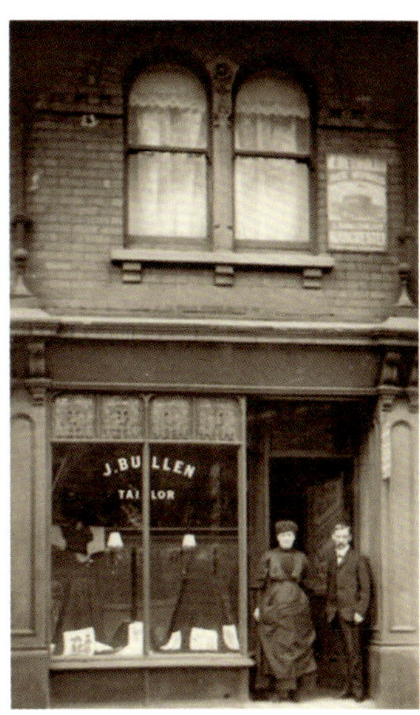

J. Bullen, Tailor, standing outside his shop at 66A, Heaton Moor Road, Heaton Moor.

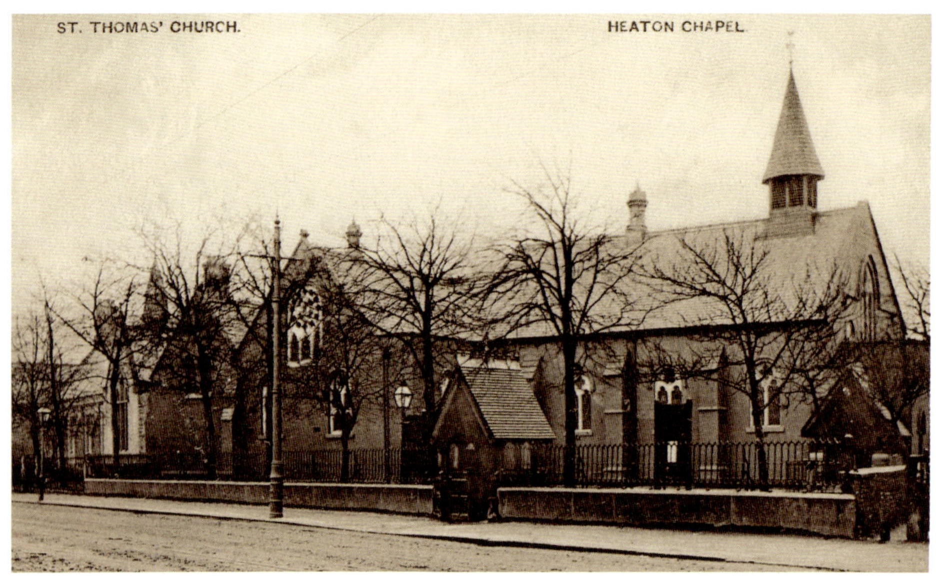

Around Wellington Road and Heaton Chapel

The area of Heaton Chapel sits mainly to the east of Wellington Road and can rightly claim to be the place where the Four Heatons really began. The four areas we know today started to develop their own identities around the mid-1700s, when the building of St Thomas' Church on Manchester Road resulted in the area becoming known as Heaton Chapel. The land was donated by a local Yeoman named Thomas Collier, and the Church was built in 1755, with consecration taking place some ten years later in 1765. The new building was first used as a chapel of ease, a subsidiary institution acting simply as an outpost for local churches, but after seventy years in this roll, St Thomas' was assigned its own parish, making it the parish church for the entire Heatons. Prior to this, congregations had been expected to walk to chapels in Manchester or Stockport which were some distance away.

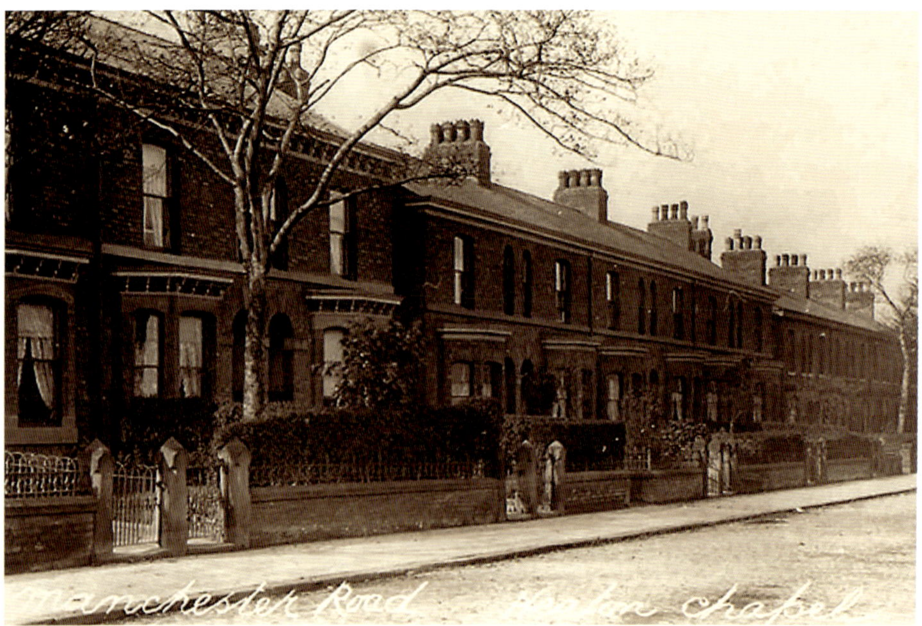

Christ Church, 1908, and St Thomas' Church, 1913

These churches stand at either end of Stockport's stretch of the A6 but, whereas St Thomas' continues to flourish today, Christ Church stands semi-derelict with only its tall spire still remaining. In 1977, it had the misfortune to catch fire during the lengthy fireman's dispute. By the time an emergency fire engine arrived, considerable damage had been done to the structure and the building was irreparable. The five clock bells made by Warner in 1896 were stolen in the aftermath.

CHRIST CHURCH, HEATON NORRIS

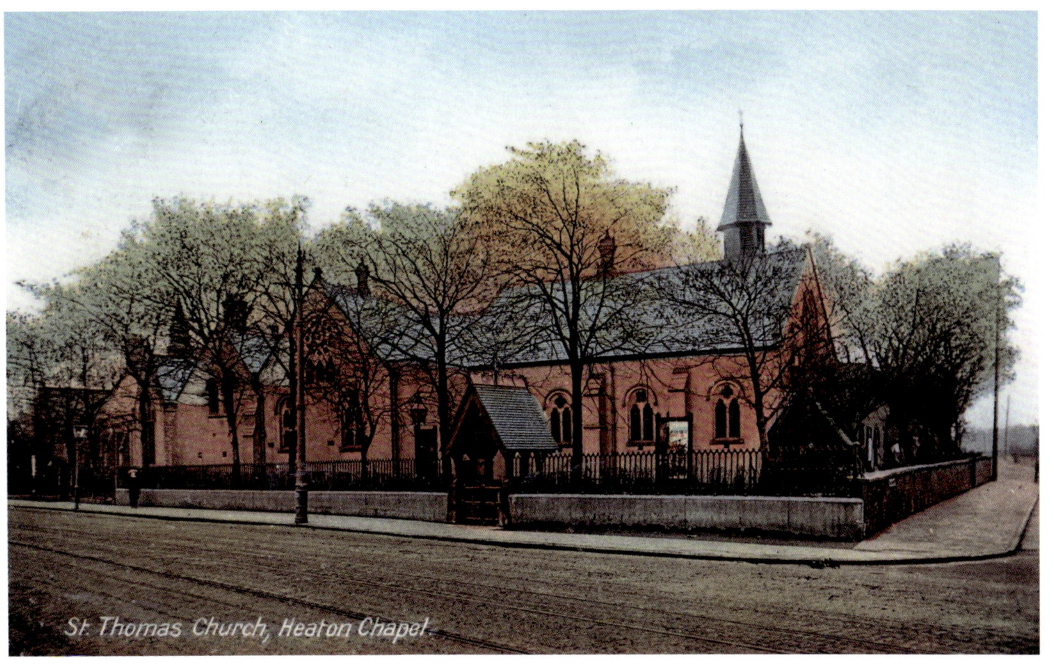

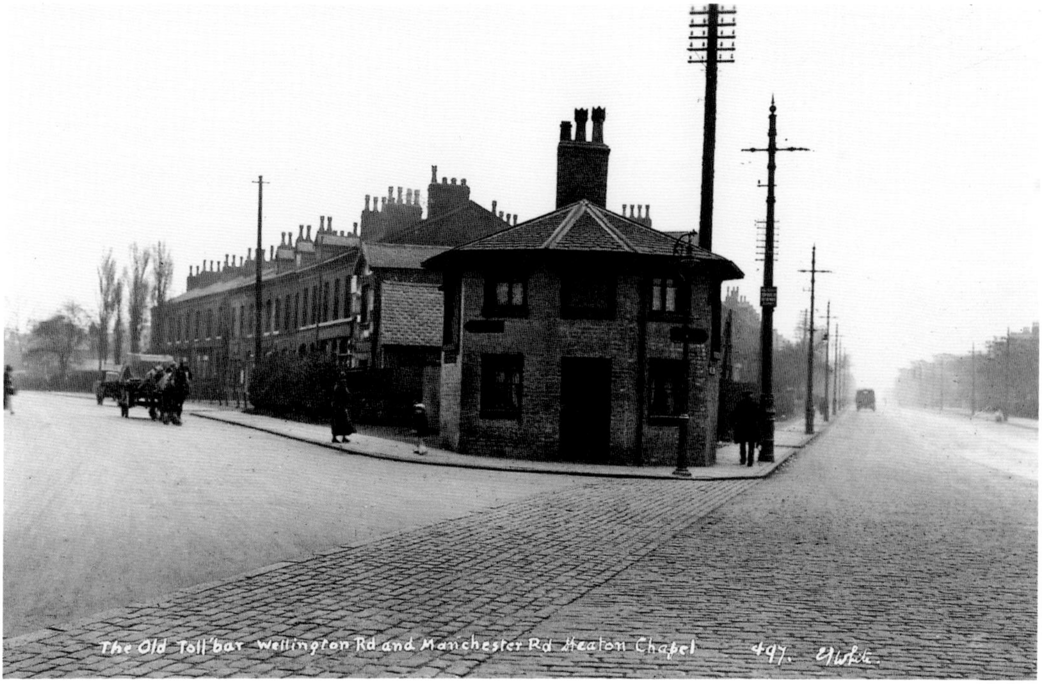

The Old Toll'bar Wellington Rd and Manchester Rd Heaton Chapel. 497. C White.

The Toll House Manchester Road, 1905 and 1920s

During the eighteenth and nineteenth centuries, Acts of Parliament set up the Turnpikes Trust whose job it was to collect tolls from travellers to fund the maintenance of the roads. Manchester Road was the original main road from Manchester to Stockport, and a toll gate was built opposite St Thomas' Church when the road was designated a turnpike in the early 1720s. The toll booth survived right up until the 1960s when it was demolished in a road traffic accident.

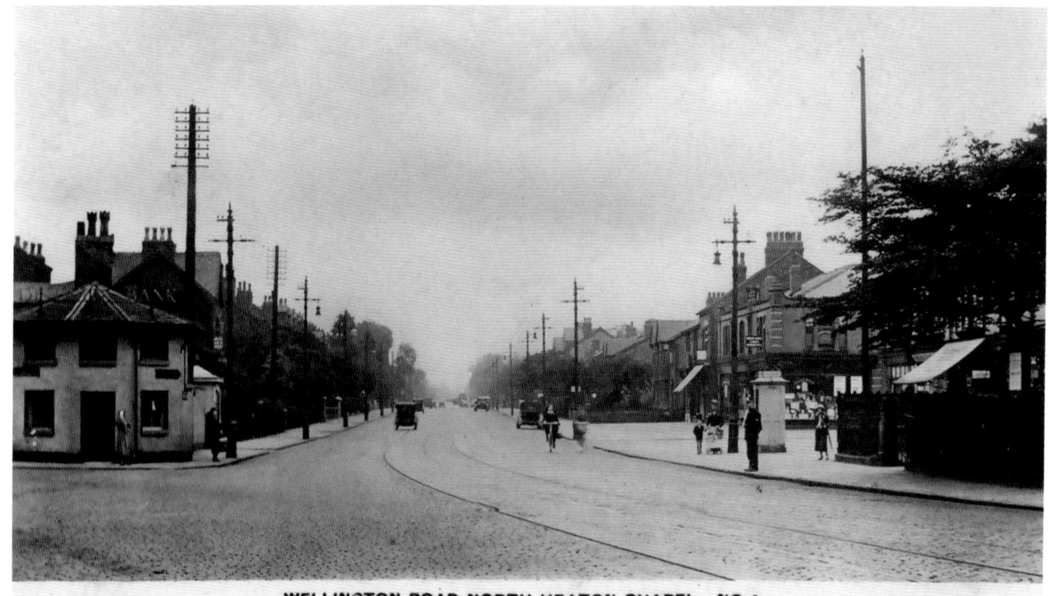

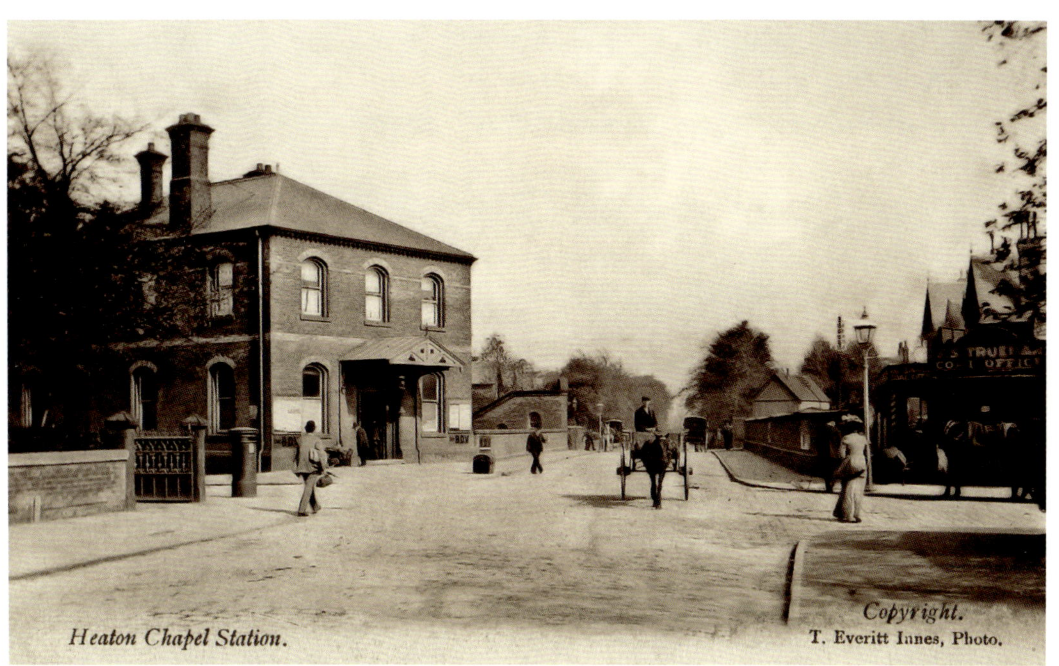

Heaton Chapel Station, 1908 and 1910

Heaton Chapel Station was constructed largely at the instigation of a local clergyman, and ex Manchester Grammar School master, Edward Jackson of St Thomas' Church, Heaton Chapel. He was determined to put the area on the map and enlisted the help of a former pupil who was the superintendent of the northern division of the LNWR. The station opened in 1852 and had an immediate impact on the surrounding area, which became a fashionable address for wealthy families, with a commuter line into Manchester firmly established.

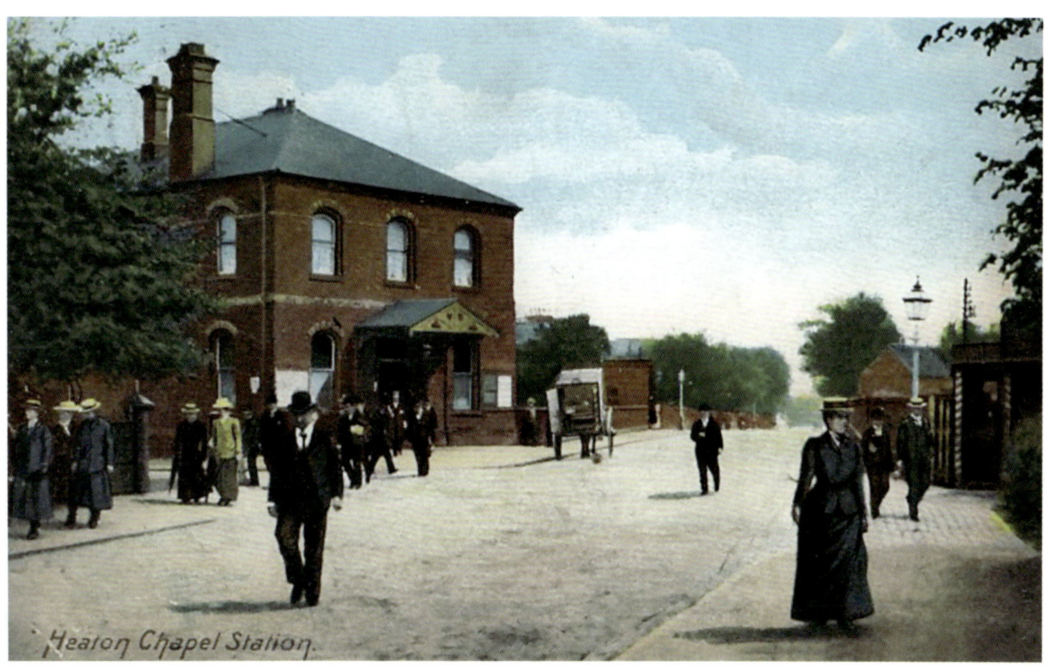

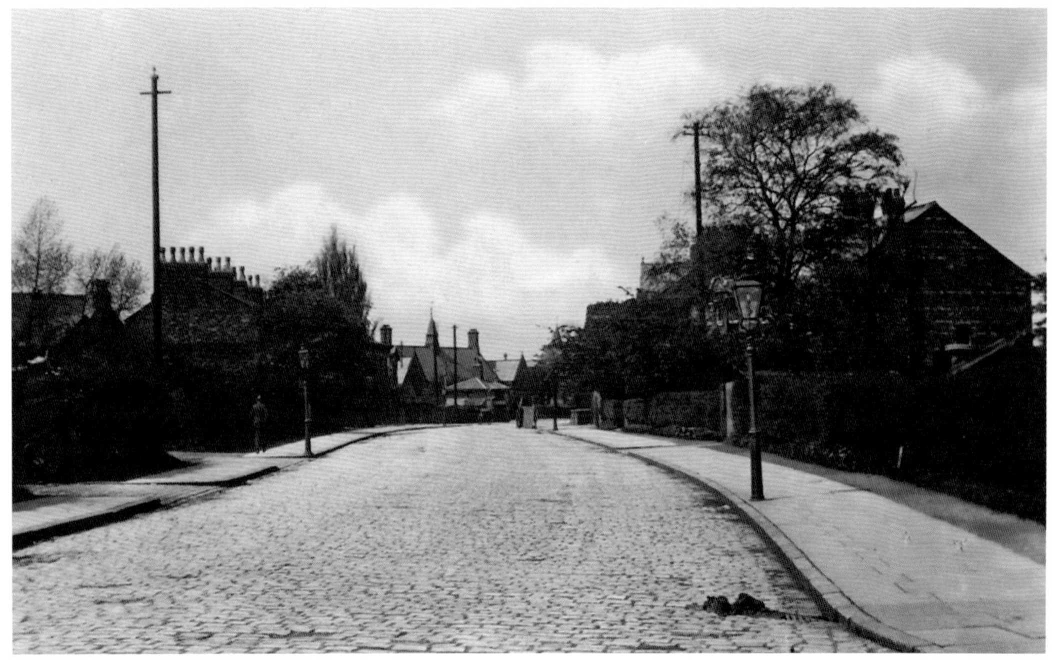

Manchester Road, 1910 and 1927

Manchester Road is thought to be of Roman origin and was an extension of the original main road from Manchester to Stockport, entering the town down Lancashire Hill. The presence of St Thomas' Church, at the junction with Heaton Moor Road, resulted in the development of the area with many shops and businesses contributing to the emergence of Heaton Chapel village. Some of the early businesses were Caldwell's haberdasher's, Brearley's ice-cream shop and a wallpaper shop.

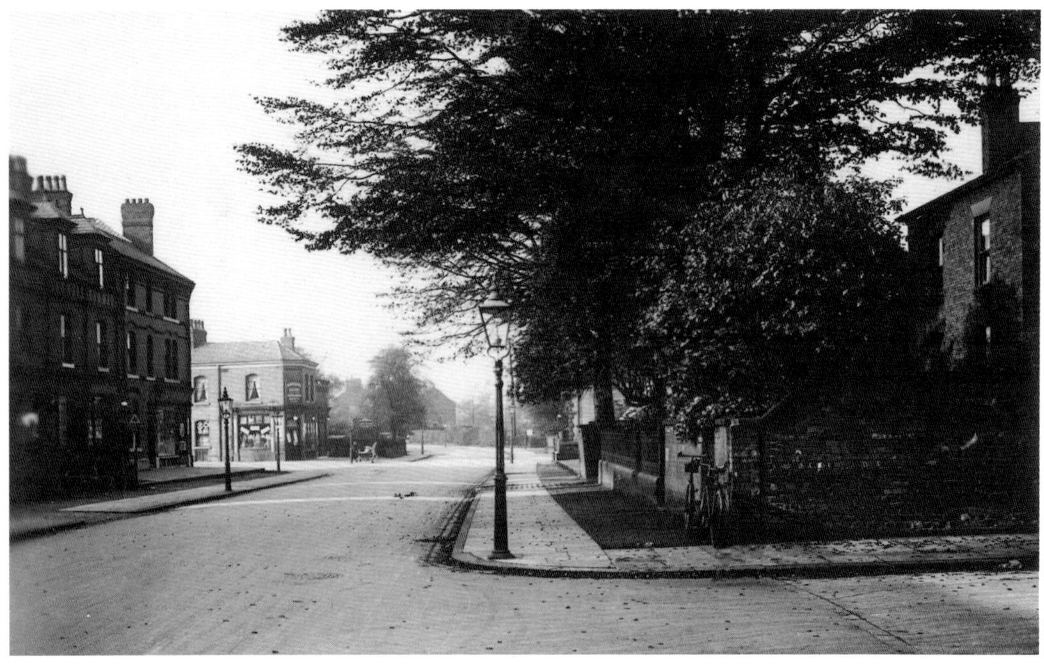

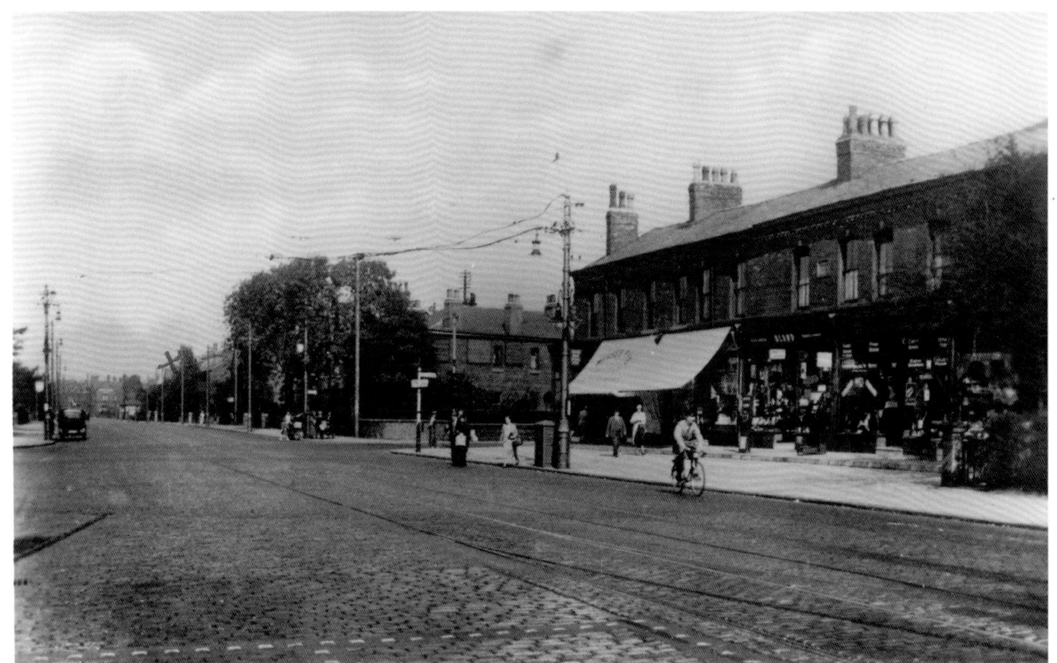

Wellington Road, 1920s and 1950s

The earlier picture of Wellington Road shows a cobbled road surface bearing tram tracks which followed this busy route from Stockport to Manchester. By the 1950s, the road surface has been tarmacked, and an early version of traffic lights to control the junction with Heaton Moor Road and School Lane can be seen on the right of the picture. Unlike today, crossing the road seems to present few problems to pedestrians.

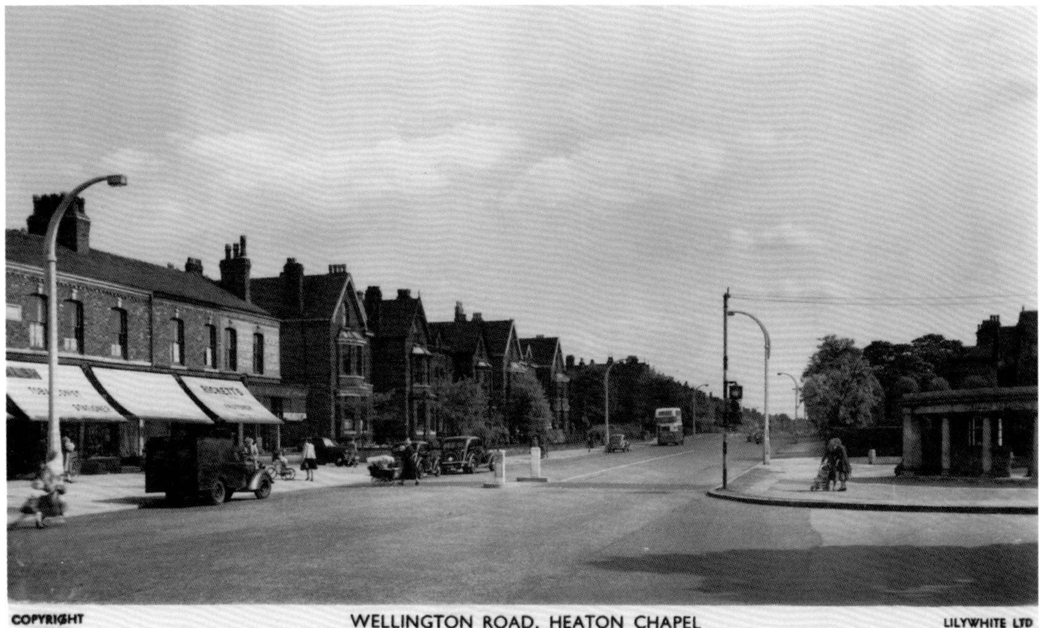

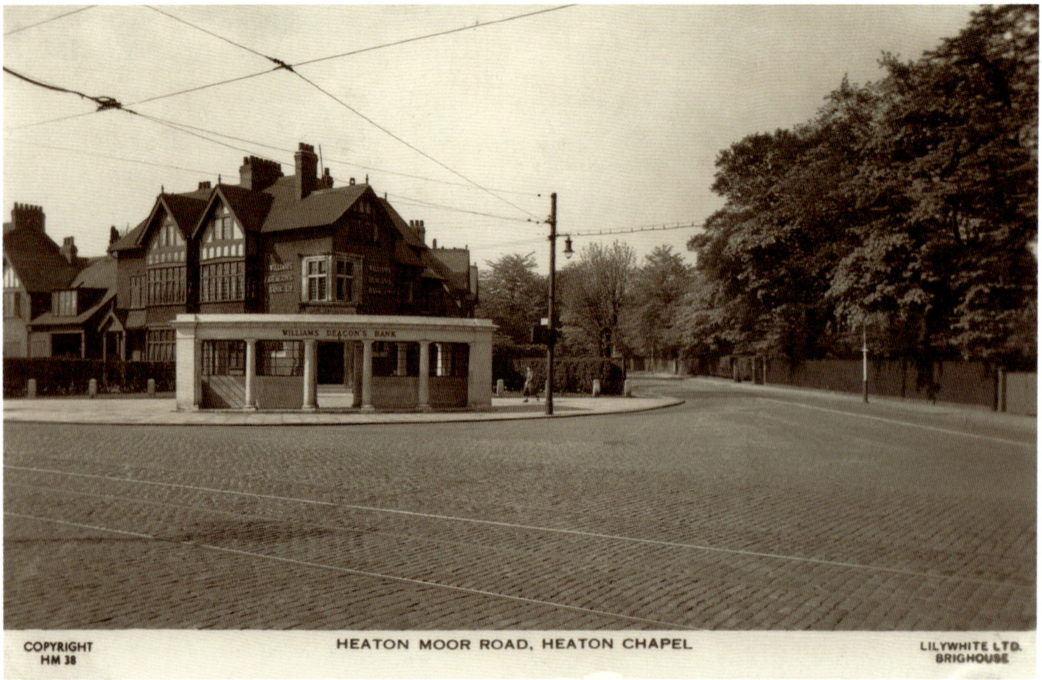

Wellington Road, 1930s and 1950s

The shelter outside Williams Deacon's Bank on the corner of Wellington Road and Heaton Moor Road was a landmark for many years. The bank was bought by the Manchester and Salford Bank in 1890 and eventually changed to Williams Deacon's and Manchester and Salford Bank. However, this was shortened back to the more common name in 1901. The Bank was eventually acquired by the Royal Bank of Scotland in 1931.

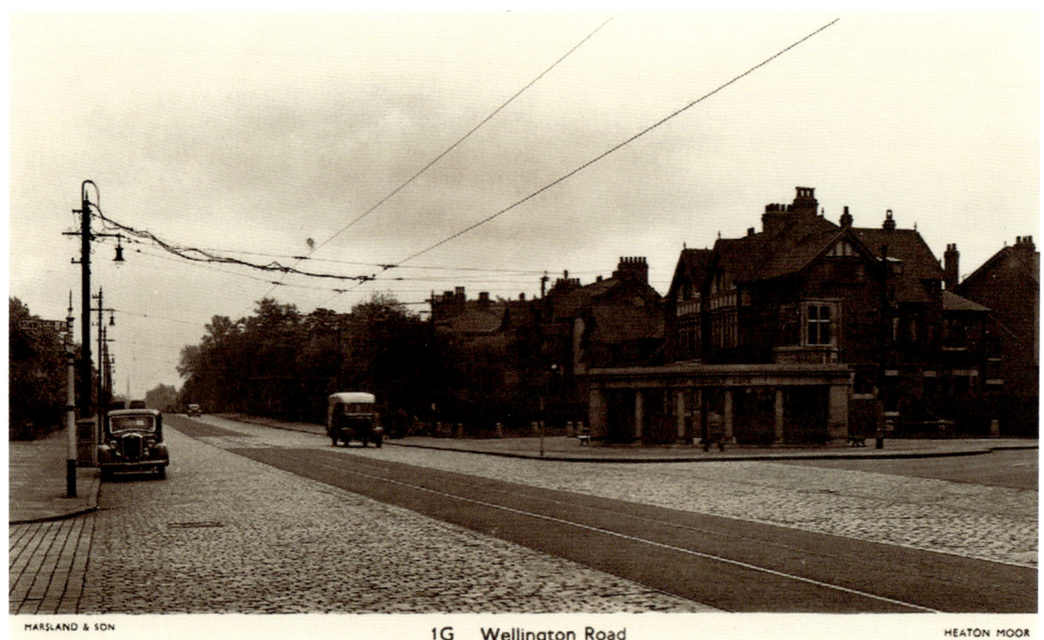

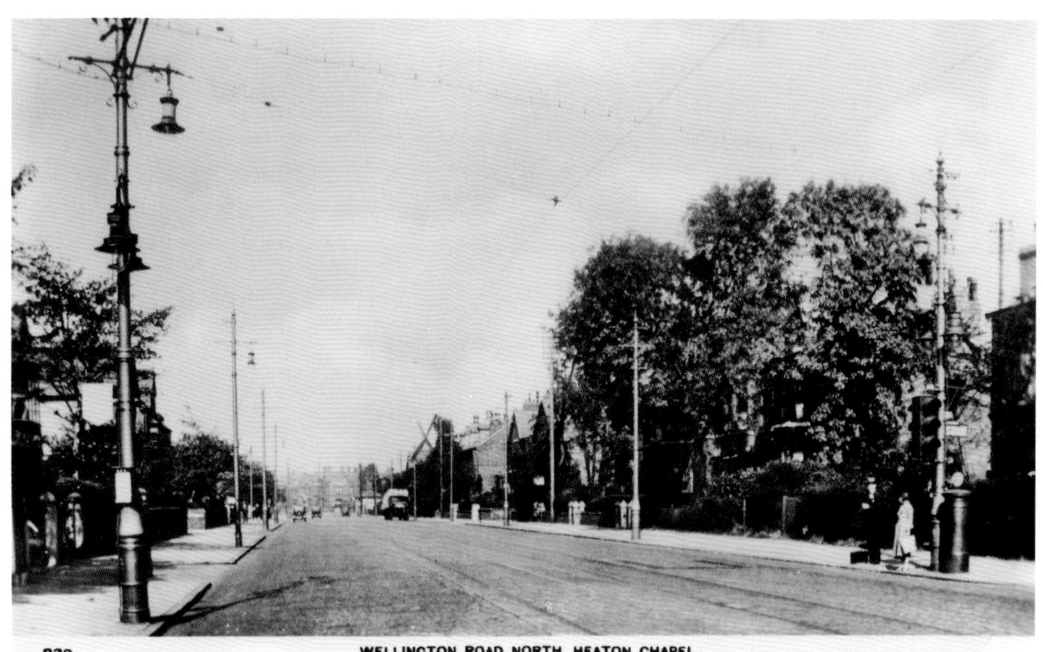

Wellington Road, 1906 and 1950s

Wellington Road was constructed after the Napoleonic wars and officially opened with great ceremony in 1826. Horse-drawn trams were used from 1889, when the service started at Torkington Road in Hazel Grove, and an electrified route into Manchester established by 1900. The trams ran successfully until just after the Second World War when they were replaced by buses which had established a regular service into Manchester by 1949. Over the last sixty years, the road has become one of the busiest in Britain with the main 192 bus route now handling over nine million passengers annually.

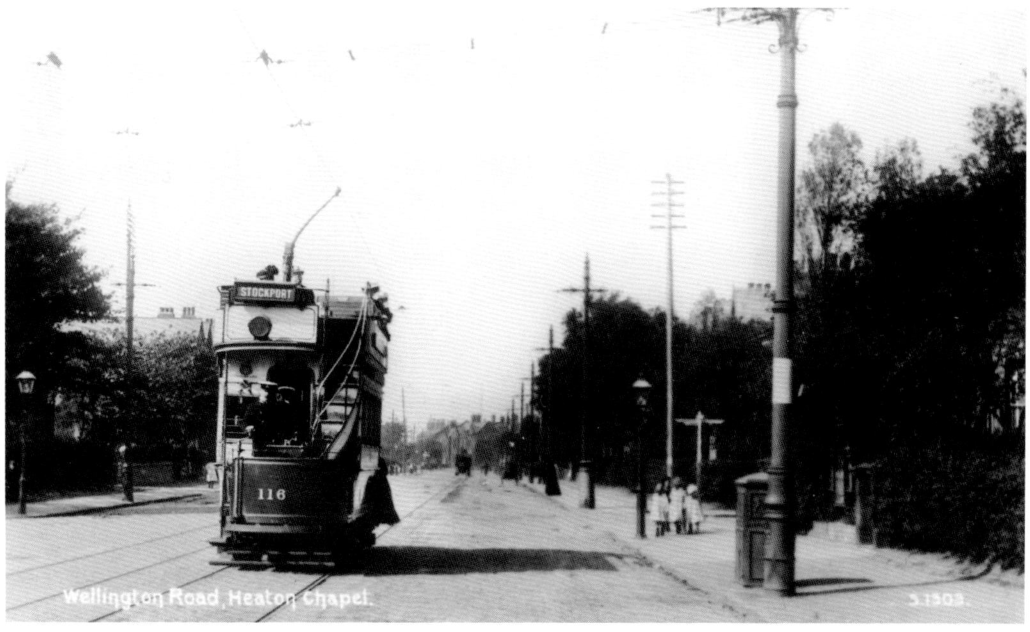

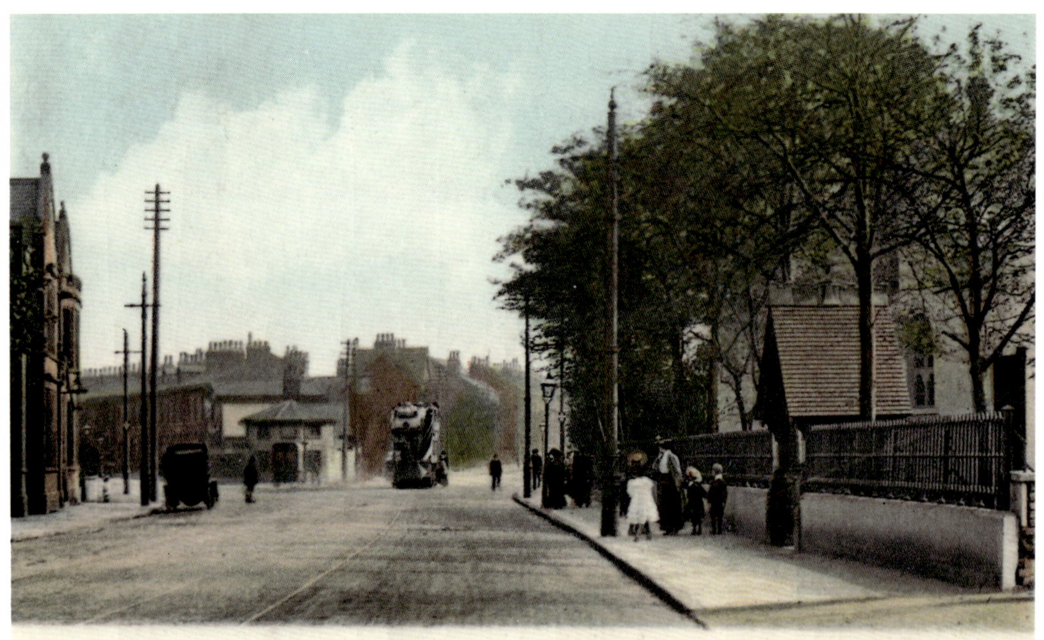

Wellington Road North, 1910 and 1930s

The building of St Thomas's Church on Manchester Road resulted in the area becoming known as Heaton Chapel. The new building was first used as a chapel of ease, a subsidiary institution acting simply as an outpost for local churches, but after seventy years in this roll, St Thomas's was assigned its own parish, making it the parish church for the entire Heatons . Across the road, the Chapel House pub took its name from the area and some church meetings were regularly held at the inn with the church registers were kept there, locked safely away in an iron chest.

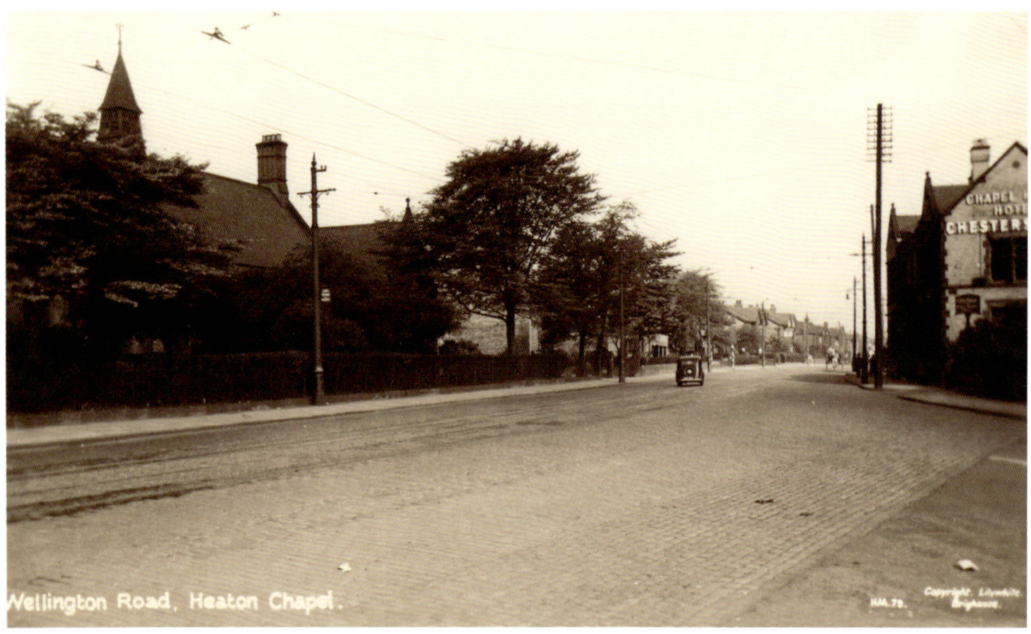

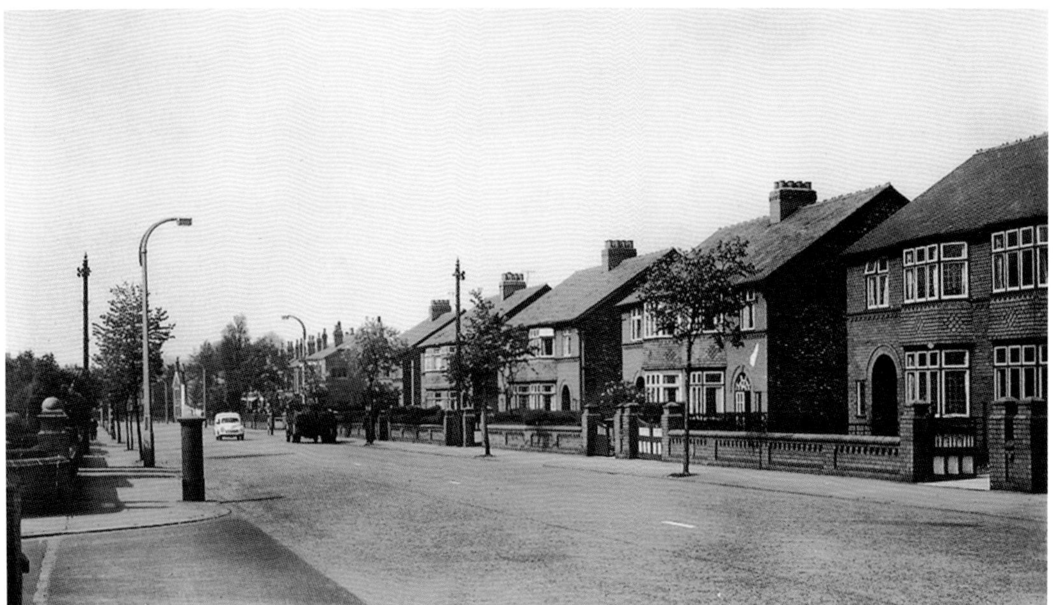

BROADSTONE ROAD, HEATON CHAPEL

Broadstone Road and Gladstone Grove, 1950s
These two roads are typical of the residential housing which developed across the Heatons during the 1930s. Streets of affordable housing appeared on rural land across Heaton Moor and Heaton Chapel, acquired by local builders such as T. Costello and W. H. Hammond. Their sales literature proclaimed the Heatons as, 'a wonderful district, combining with it all that gives health, enjoyment and happiness'. The wide tree-lined roads were often a feature of the developments, and there are still several examples of these across The Heatons.

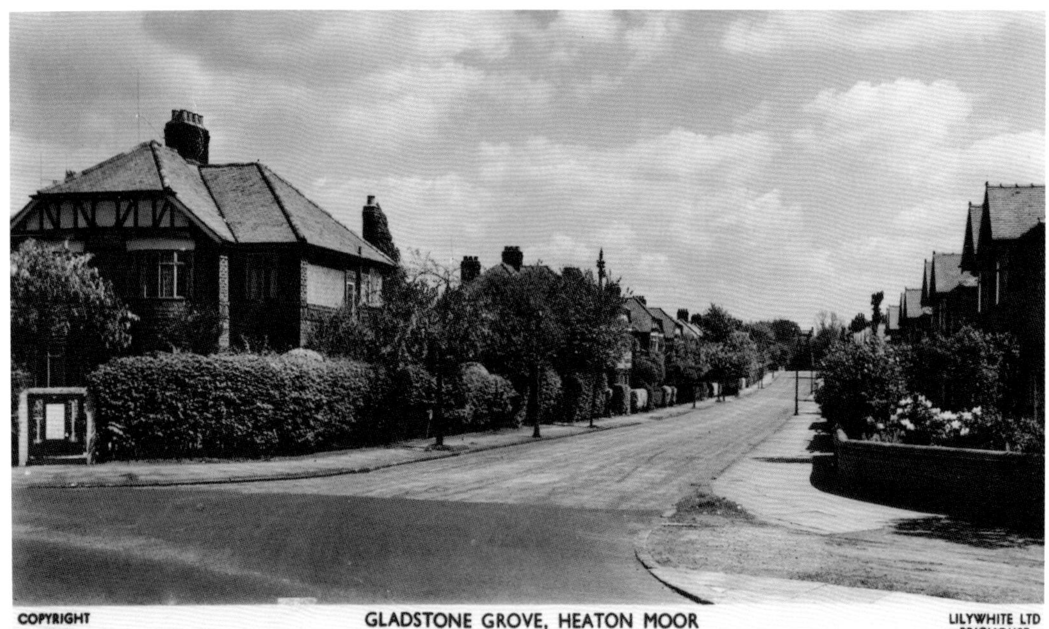

GLADSTONE GROVE, HEATON MOOR

ABOUT THE AUTHORS

Ian Littlechilds and Phil Page are professional photographers and writers who have been working together on a number of photographic projects since 2005. After running a wedding photography business for over five years, they embarked on book projects to further improve their photographic, writing and research skills. Both have lived and worked in Greater Manchester for over thirty years. This is their fifth publication for Amberley, their previous four being, *The Four Heatons – Through Time* (2013), *River Mersey from Source to Sea* (2014), *Secret Manchester* (2014) and *From Bugsworth to Manchester, History of the Limestone Trail* (2015). In addition to writing, they deliver talks on local history to community groups in Greater Manchester, regularly contribute articles to local publications and run workshops on the development of photography skills to both adults and children.

ACKNOWLEDGEMENTS

We would like to thank the following people and organisations for their help in compiling the book: David Boardman for the Belle Vue image; Fergus Wilde, Chetham's Library, for the Belle Vue image and information (www.chethams.org.uk/bellevue) and Mary Griffiths James, Stockport Heritage Society. We would also like to acknowledge the following publications, which were an invaluable source of information when researching some of the facts to go with the photographs: Jones, Elizabeth, *Old Heatonians* (Stockport Libraries 1997); Heaton Mersey Research Group, *Heaton Mersey. A Victorian Village, 1851–81* (Stockport Historical Society. 1985); Rowbotham, Phil. *Heritage Walk Series*, Editions 5, 6 and 9 (Stockport Heritage Trust).

Every effort has been made to trace the owners of photographs included in this book and to obtain permission to use copyright material.